MARIA CALLAS:
The Art Behind the Legend

MARIA CALLAS

The Art Behind the Legend

by Henry Wisneski

With Performance Annals 1947–1974

by Arthur Germond

DOUBLEDAY & COMPANY, INC.
GARDEN CITY, NEW YORK
1975

Book design by James K. Davis

Library of Congress Cataloging in Publication Data

Wisneski, Henry.
Maria Callas: the art behind the legend.

"Discography of private recordings": p. 385.
Bibliography: p. 397.
1. Callas, Maria, 1923– I. Germond, Arthur. II. Title.
ML420.C18W6 782.1'092'4 [B]
ISBN 0-385-07837-4
Library of Congress Catalog Card Number 74–18837

Printed in the United States of America
First Edition

TO
NINO COSTA
TEATRO ALLA SCALA

AUTHOR'S NOTE

The purpose of the author has been to document the stage career of Maria Callas through a combination of photographs, text, and performance annals. References to her personal life have been limited to those which have a direct bearing on her professional activities. Many of Callas's interpretations are preserved on disc and tape, but visual documentation—particularly of her performances before 1953—is becoming increasingly difficult to obtain. Most of the original negatives for action photos of her appearances in Rome, Venice, Palermo, Genoa, and Florence, for example, have been misplaced or destroyed. My aim has been to organize this book as both a survey of the extant Callas photographs and a supplement to her performances on tape and disc.

It is a pleasure to acknowledge the many debts I have contracted in the course of researching and writing this book. I wish to thank George Louis Mayer and David Young, who, from the beginning, offered incalculable professional help. I am indebted to Armando Angelo Bona for his research in Milan, Genoa, and Parma, and his numerous efforts to locate the still-elusive photographs of Callas in her three Wagnerian roles.

I also wish to make special mention of Carlos Díaz Du-Pond, who furnished detailed firsthand information concerning Callas's three seasons in

Mexico City, as well as many unique photographs from his private collection. BJR Enterprises put at my disposal their entire collection of Callas tapes and photographs. Thanks are extended to the publishers of books, magazines, and newspapers quoted, with special thanks to Harold Rosenthal, editor of *Opera* magazine, for his kindnesses. Many photographers and their assistants gave generously of their time, and I thank them. Doctor Hilde Köster of Berlin allowed me to spend several hours selecting photographs from the files of her late husband, *Bildjournalist* Heinz Köster, and I wish to express my gratitude.

Matahiko Okada of Japan made available a tape and many photographs of the Osaka "Seminar Concert" given by Callas and Giuseppe di Stefano. Alberto Grimberg, editor of the three-volume history of the Teatro Colón in Buenos Aires, obtained permission from the theater's archives allowing me to reproduce their unique photograph of Callas in the role of Turandot, and graciously loaned me the original print during a visit to New York.

A number of other people answered queries and placed research or photographic material at my disposal. Chief among them were: Doctor Luigi Bellingardi (Rome), Sir Rudolf Bing, Lawrence G. Blochman, José Burgos, Louise Caselotti, Claudia Cassidy, Dino Conti (Venice), Devereux Danna, Frank Derbas, Gary Gisondi, Peter Hoffer (Milan), Bodo Igesz, Charles Jahant, George Jellinek, Newell Jenkins, Shirley Manley, Gregg Newbern, Giuseppe Pugliese (Venice), Mrs. Brenda Houston Rogers, Cesare Siepi, Mrs. Dario Soria, Winfried Stiffel (Essen), Sir William Walton, Ralph White, Monica Wiards (Milan), and Eric Zafran.

My special thanks go to my editor Ken McCormick, art director James Davis, who designed the book, and Glenn Rounds, who gave unstintingly of his time and corrected many gaffes in the final typescript.

CONTENTS

I

Biographical Note
The Early Years

The one-year-old Cecilia Sophia Maria Kalogeropoulou and her parents, New York, 1924.

Georges and Evangelia Callas in Riverside Park, New York, 1935.

The Early Years

MARIA CALLAS was born in New York's Fifth Avenue Hospital (then called Flower Hospital) on the fourth of December, 1923.* Her parents, Georges and Evangelia Kalogeropoulos, had recently emigrated from Greece. For the first four days in the hospital, Evangelia Callas refused to look at her daughter. She had lost her son Vasily in a typhoid epidemic a few months before and had prayed for another son.

At the age of three, Callas was christened Cecilia Sophia Anna Maria Callas at the Greek Orthodox Cathedral on East Seventy-fourth Street in Manhattan. It was at this time that Georges Kalogeropoulos legally shortened the family surname to Callas for practical reasons. When Callas was five, she was nearly killed in an accident. While walking with her mother, she saw her older sister Jackie across the street. She darted into the street and was struck by a speeding car. She remained unconscious for twenty-two days.

Callas has few warm memories of her childhood. She was quiet, shy,

* Callas's actual birthdate has appeared in various published sources as the second, third, or fourth of December. Although her United States passport stated December second (she is now a Greek citizen), she prefers December fourth—the date given by her mother.

and insecure and considered herself to be clumsy and fat. Her main pleasure was music. She sang, took piano lessons, and listened to the Saturday broadcasts from the Metropolitan Opera. Her mother did her best to be a good wife to Georges Callas, but all love had died between them within a year of their marriage and they quarreled frequently. From 1929 to 1932 the effects of the Depression forced the family to move yearly to successively less expensive apartments.

During 1926 to 1933, New York audiences saw the exploitation of many child prodigies, most notably pianist Ruth Slenczynska, violinists Ruggiero Ricci and Yehudi Menuhin, soprano Marion Talley, and the three "baby ballerinas" Tamara Toumanova, Irina Baronova, and Tatiana Riabouchinska. Evangelia Callas believed that her daughter was also something of a child prodigy and she entered her in various radio competitions.

By the time Callas was thirteen, her mother was convinced that she had an exceptional voice and decided to take her to Greece where they could expect financial help from relatives. In March 1937 they sailed for Athens. Jackie had left for Athens a few months earlier. The family eventually found a modern apartment at 61 Patission, where they lived for the duration of the war.

In September 1937, Callas had an audition with Maria Trivella, a teacher at the Ethnikon Odeon, the National Conservatory. She sang the "Habanera" from *Carmen* and Trivella accepted her as a student. Callas was given a scholarship, although she was only fourteen and it was necessary for her mother to say she was sixteen—the minimum age for a scholarship at the conservatory.

A few days before her fifteenth birthday, in November 1938, Callas made her stage debut singing Santuzza in a student performance of Pietro Mascagni's *Cavalleria Rusticana*. She continued studying with Trivella until December 1939.

Elvira de Hidalgo, a celebrated coloratura soprano of the past (active from 1908 to 1930), had recently joined the teaching staff of Athens' leading conservatory, the Odeon Athenon. De Hidalgo had sung at the Metropolitan, La Scala, and Covent Garden and Evangelia Callas was anxious to have her daughter audition for her. Callas sang the strenuous aria "Ocean! Thou mighty monster" from Weber's *Oberon*. De Hidalgo, writing of the audition in an article for the Italian magazine *Oggi* twenty years later, said that Callas produced violent cascades of sound, not entirely controlled, but full of drama and emotion. De Hidalgo listened with her eyes closed and imagined what it would be like to develop such a voice. The admissions board entered Callas in the conservatory—tuition free—as De Hidalgo's student.

"I started going to [Elvira de Hidalgo's] classes from morning till night," Callas told interviewer Derek Prouse, "from ten o'clock, when she began till we went to lunch or had a sandwich there, and then on through to eight o'clock at night—it would have been inconceivable to stay at home, I shouldn't have known what to do there" (London *Sunday Times,* April 2, 1961).

De Hidalgo realized that Callas was temperamentally and vocally suited to the bel canto repertory of Donizetti and Bellini. Although her voice was basically a heavy instrument, De Hidalgo concentrated on making it light and agile, without losing any richness at the bottom. "Elvira de Hidalgo used to lend me the full scores of operas," Callas recalled in 1969, "which I could not have bought. I used to learn them off by heart, so as to give them back as soon as possible . . . I learned, for instance, *Norma* and *La Gioconda* before I could ever have sung them properly. So I could rehearse them in my mind, on the top of a bus, or walking in the street" (*Kenneth Harris Talking to Maria Callas,* 1971).

On October 28, 1940, early in World War II, the Italians invaded Greece from Albania, but the Greeks eventually drove them back and occupied about a fourth of Albania. Sometime in 1940—possibly in November—Callas made her professional stage debut, at the age of sixteen, at the National Lyric Theater of Athens. She was one of four girls who sang and danced in a barrel in Franz von Suppé's operetta *Boccaccio.* The following year, in April, the Germans attacked Greece by way of Bulgaria and Yugoslavia. By April 27 they had occupied Athens, where they were to remain, along with their Italian allies, until 1944.

The first evening of the German invasion, Callas tried to cheer her mother and sister by singing "La Paloma" and other favorite songs of her childhood, but with little success. In the ensuing months, food became difficult to find and people died of starvation in the streets.

At the age of eighteen, in Athens. Callas had already sung the soprano leads in student performances of *Cavalleria Rusticana, Aida, Un Ballo in Maschera,* and *Suor Angelica,* and probably her first professional *Tosca,* in July 1941.

With the Greek baritone Evangelios Mangliveras in Eugen d'Albert's *Tiefland,* the National Lyric Theater in Athens, April 1944. Callas received her first international publicity for her portrayal of Marta, although the coverage was restricted by the war to the German-language papers of the Axis nations.

From *Callas: Portrait of a Prima Donna.* Courtesy of George Jellinek

In the summer of 1941, Evangelia Callas took in two British officers who had escaped from the Germans. Six weeks later the Greek underground hid them in another house. Evangelia Callas wrote in her book *My Daughter—Maria Callas:*

> The day after the two British officers left Patission 61 Italian soldiers came to search the house, pounding on the door to demand admittance. Someone had denounced us to the authorities.
>
> When the Italians came, we had not time to hide any incriminating evidence such as the photograph albums and letters which would have meant our death if the Italians had found them. Maria saved us. As they pushed into the house with their revolvers drawn, she guessed what was happening, ran to the piano and began to sing. She sang *Tosca,* and never have I heard her sing better than she did that day—a girl of seventeen singing for her life.
>
> Listening to her, the Italians forgot what they had come for and sat down on the floor in a circle around the piano. Only when she stopped singing did they go away. They didn't touch anything in the house. The next day they came back, not to arrest us but to bring food for Maria . . .
>
> The Italians never did search our house, but that second time they wouldn't have found a thing.

The Germans had allowed schools and theaters to reopen by the fall of 1941. Maria Kalogeropoulou, as she was known in Athens, returned to the opera company as first soprano. Her salary was three thousand drachmas a month (about six dollars). Callas's most important roles at the National Lyric Theater were Tosca, Marta in Eugen d'Albert's verismo opera *Tiefland,* and Santuzza in *Cavalleria Rusticana.* Judging by the handful of reviews which exist from this period, her unique interpretive gifts were apparent even from the beginning. Musicologist and critic Friedrich W. Herzog wrote after the first *Tiefland* (*Deutsche Nachrichten in Griechenland,* April 23, 1944): "Maria Kalogeropoulou was a Marta of earthy naturalness. What other singers must learn, she possesses by nature: the dramatic instinct, the intensity of her acting, and the freedom of interpretation. Her voice at the top displays a penetrating metallic power and in quiet moments she knows how to reveal all of the colors of her precious youthful and innately musical soprano voice."

Callas sang Leonora in the Greek première of *Fidelio* at the amphitheater of Herodes Atticus, Athens, on August 14, 1944, when she was twenty. In the cast were, left to right: G. Moulas (Rocco), Zoe Vlachopoulou (Marzelline), the conductor Hans Hörner, Callas, Evangelios Mangliveras (Don Pizarro), Antonios Delendas (Florestan), A. Tzeneralis (Don Fernando). Kneeling: G. Kokolios (Jaquino).

Two weeks later Herzog wrote of her performance in *Cavalleria Rusticana* (*Deutsche Nachrichten,* May 9, 1944): "Maria Kalogeropoulou was a Santuzza of impulsive temperament. Her dramatic soprano voice showed itself to be both effortless and sensitive in a broad, sweeping operatic manner in which the 'tears in the voice' were also not lacking."

Callas received her greatest ovations and critical acclaim, however, for her Leonora in Beethoven's *Fidelio*. She had been perfecting her vocal technique as well as the techniques for dealing with opera house rival-

„Fidelio" in Athen

Ludwig van Beethovens „Fidelio" erstmalig in Griechenland aufgeführt

Im Theater des Herodes Attikus zu Füssen der Akropolis erklang zum ersten Mal unter griechischem Himmel Beethovens „Fidelio", das Hohelied der Gattenliebe und -treue, das sich in dem grossartigen Chorfinale zu einem Jubel steigerte, der die vielen tausend Zuhörer mit in seinen Bann riss. Generalintendant Oskar Walleck, einer der führenden deutschen Opernspielleiter, gab der Darstellung den monumentalen Aufriss und eine Stilhoheit von grossartiger Geschlossenheit. Unter der Stabführung von Dr. Hans Hörner vereinigten sich die hervorragendsten Sänger der Griechischen Staatsoper zu einer Wiedergabe, die schon in dem berühmten Quartett des ersten Aktes ihren ersten Höhepunkt fand. Unsere Bilder zeigen: Generalintendant Oskar Walleck während der Probe (oben rechts); Anton Delendas als Florestan (oben links) und die Quartettszene (unten) mit Maria Kalojeropoulou (im Vordergrund links) in der Titelpartie. Eine ausführliche Besprechung von Werk und Aufführung, die als künstlerisches Ereignis von Rang besteht, folgt. Der Beifall war stürmisch und begeistert.

Aufn.: Kemmerich (3)

The first act quartet, Beethoven's *Fidelio,* August 1944. Left to right, Callas (Leonora), G. Kokolios (Jaquino), G. Moulas (Rocco), and Zoe Vlachopoulou (Marzelline).

From the *Deutsche Nachrichten in Griechenland,* August 15, 1944

ries and cabals. She wrote in *Oggi* (January 10, 1957): "We were to stage *Fidelio* and another prima donna was doing everything to get the part and she succeeded in obtaining it; but she didn't worry herself about learning it. Since it was necessary to begin the rehearsals immediately, as next in line they asked me to substitute and naturally I accepted, because I knew the score perfectly . . . Immediately after the performances of *Fidelio,* which were given in the marvelous amphitheater of Herodes Atticus, near the Acropolis, came the 'liberation' [1944] . . ."

Several of the principal singers of the company had been openly hostile to Callas, and her enormous success in *Fidelio* did not help matters. In a 1958 broadcast interview she told Harry Fleetwood: "I suppose I got on my colleagues' nerves. They were older people. I don't blame them. And I was so young. And they couldn't understand why I was chosen for certain roles. I suppose *I* could explain that very easily. It was just that I was always ready instead of gossiping and going around trying to—you know—get parts from other people. I just studied and was ready when the good time came."

In September 1945, after a performance in Karl Millöcker's operetta *Der Bettelstudent,* Callas left for New York on the S.S. *Stockholm.* She was twenty-one years old and had six years of stage experience behind her.

II

The Performer

Tosca

CALLAS first sang the title role of Giacomo Puccini's *Tosca* at the National Lyric Theater in Athens in the summer of 1941. The leading soprano of the company was scheduled to appear but she became ill at the last minute and Callas was asked to substitute for her. Greece was an occupied country at that time and Callas successfully sang the role to an audience crowded with Italian and German soldiers. She was only seventeen and this was her first professional starring role. Twenty-four years later, at a gala performance of *Tosca* given in London before Queen Elizabeth, Callas made her unofficial farewell to the operatic stage.

Although Tosca was ideally suited to Callas's temperament and unique gifts, it was one of her least favorite roles. She performed it more than thirty times in seven countries, but the majority of her Toscas took place during the last eighteen months of her stage career. She recorded it twice for EMI—in 1953 and 1964. In 1967, during a broadcast interview, she told Edward Downes: "Well, [*Tosca*] is not that beautiful, frankly, because the first act is just a nervous girl that is always complaining. And the second act automatically goes on its own, with the

The second act entrance in *Tosca,* the Royal Opera House, London, January 21, 1964.
Dominic

'Vissi d'arte,' which I think should be cut out eventually, because it stops completely the action of the second act. In fact, I was pleased to hear that [even] Puccini didn't want it . . . You can feel it. It just stops the movement." She commented in an interview for *The New Yorker* (April 24, 1971): "Everybody wants me to sing *Tosca.* The trouble with Puccini is that you can sing his operas without a perfect bel canto technique. This has shortened many a singer's career."

The earliest Toscas with Callas known to exist in sound are from Mexico City (1950 and 1952) and Rio de Janeiro (1951). The Mexican broadcast of July 1, 1952—Callas's last appearance in Latin America—is easily the most exciting of the three performances on tape and considerably more flamboyant than her later *Toscas.* Giuseppe di Stefano, in the role of Mario Cavaradossi, was in excellent voice and his third act aria "E lucevan le stelle," which was encored, was sung with ravishing *mezza voce* tones. Callas presented a stormy, full-blooded interpretation. Her voice was extraordinarily rich and vibrant. She swept up to all of the high notes without taking a breath and the dramatic phrases were delivered with fiery authority. In Act II, when Cavaradossi is being tortured offstage, particularly memorable was the way in which she attacked and held the high C and then dropped into chest voice at the words "Non è ver! Sogghigno di demone" ("It's not true! Leering devil").

The final ovation, preserved on tape along with the performance, offers a vivid record of the affection and esteem in which the twenty-eight-year-old soprano was held by the Mexican public and her fellow musicians. She had appeared for three consecutive seasons at the Palacio de Bellas Artes in Mexico City and it was known that she probably would not return the following year. The orchestra greeted her appearance on stage with a drum roll. As the musicians began to play "Las Golondrinas" ("The Swallows"), the chorus walked on stage and joined the standing audience in serenading her. The radio announcer, in a running commentary for the listening audience, explained that Callas was kneeling on stage in tears. She attempted to bring out Giuseppe di Stefano, but he refused to come on stage, allowing her to have the triumph alone.

Between July 1952 and January 1964, Callas appeared as Tosca a total of only seven times, in Genoa and New York. In March 1965 she returned to the Metropolitan Opera after a seven-year absence. She was engaged for a Metropolitan Opera Guild benefit *Tosca* at a fee—according to *Newsweek* magazine—of $14,000. The cast included Franco Corelli and Tito Gobbi—both superstars in their own right. A second performance was scheduled for a regular subscription night. Thousands of mail orders poured in for the tickets, which were stored in a Guild office safe, and the proceeds quickly reached $84,500. Standees were allowed to buy a place for only one performance and consequently a double line encircled the opera house for over two days before the box office opened, with house officials holding a roll call every three hours around the clock.

An hour before the first performance, hundreds of celebrity seekers blocked traffic before the Broadway entrance to catch a glimpse of the famous, among whom were Jacqueline, Robert, and Edward Kennedy, Bette Davis, and Leonard Bernstein. Orchestra seats were sold openly and quickly for as much as $500 and standing room places fetched $75. Harold Schonberg wrote of her return (New York *Times,* March 20, 1965):

> When the act was well under way, several things were apparent. This was going to be one of the best-acted "Toscas" in Metropolitan Opera history. It was also apparent that Miss Callas was singing with great care, trying to make the best of her vocal resources, avoiding as cannily as possible the vocal traps of the role . . . Her conception of the role was electrical. Everything at her command was put into striking use. She was a woman in love, a tiger cat, a woman possessed by jealousy. In the second act she physically threw herself at the soldiers carrying off her Mario. Her face mirrored every fleeting expression implicit in the music during her colloquy with Scarpia. This was supreme acting, unforgettable acting.

In the opinion of Alan Rich (New York *Herald Tribune*):

> The voice I heard last night was not the voice of a woman that, in some respects, was in any sort of vocal trouble whatever. It had a creamy lightness to it which summoned up memories of her earliest recordings. She has somehow achieved this without losing her astounding ability to make the voice the servant of the drama . . . It was—simply as singing—one of the most remarkable vocal achievements in my memory . . . What she did with her voice in the

first act was an extension of the totally delightful, girlish conception she has devised. What she did with it in the second act was even more remarkable, because it stripped this piece of old-fashioned broad melodrama down to human proportions. Her "Vissi d'arte," soft and floating, became what it is supposed to be: a prayer from a frightened, confused, trapped human being. The whole act, in fact, was a stunning study in humanity.

Callas's second Tosca was with the American tenor Richard Tucker. Some opera fans, gambling on early rumors that Callas would sing a regular subscription performance, had placed advance mail orders for tickets to all the Toscas of that season. The performance on March 25, 1965, was to be Callas's last stage appearance in the United States. Three months later, on the fifth of July, she sang Tosca at the Royal Opera House in London. She was not to sing again in public for over eight years. Her return, a concert with Giuseppe di Stefano, took place in Hamburg on October 25, 1973.

Tosca, Act I, at the Palacio de Bellas Artes, Mexico City, June 28, 1952, with Giuseppe di Stefano (Cavaradossi). Luis Quintero

Tosca, Act II, Mexico City, June 1952. Cavaradossi defiantly predicts the downfall of the tyrants of Italy. Luis Quintero

"È morto! Or gli perdono" ("He's dead! And now I pardon him"). Piero Campolonghi is Scarpia. *Tosca,* Act II, Mexico City, June 1952. Luis Quintero

The Metropolitan Opera return of March 19, 1965, photographed from the wings during the long ovation which greeted Callas's Act I entrance. This performance was Callas's only United States appearance with tenor Franco Corelli.

Melançon

From Franco Zeffirelli's production of *Tosca,* Act II, the Royal Opera House, London, January 21, 1964, with Renato Cioni as Cavaradossi. Houston Rogers

La Gioconda

AFTER leaving Athens in September 1945, Callas was without a professional engagement for two years. She auditioned for the Metropolitan Opera but declined the two parts offered her (*Madama Butterfly* and *Fidelio* in English) as being unsuitable, much to the amazement of her friends. An audition with Gaetano Merola, impresario of the San Francisco Opera, yielded only the advice that she make a career in Italy and then return to the United States. Two of Callas's closest friends at that period were lawyer E. Richard Bagarozy and his wife Louise Caselotti, a professional singer and coach with whom she studied repertory almost every day for over a year. Through the Bagarozys, Callas met the young bass Nicola Rossi-Lemeni at the end of 1946. Rossi-Lemeni had a contract to sing Alvise in *La Gioconda* at the 1947 summer festival in Verona and he knew that Giovanni Zenatello, the artistic director of the festival, was auditioning sopranos for the title role.

Zenatello, a former tenor who created the role of Pinkerton in the 1904 world première of *Madama Butterfly,* was living in New York. With Louise Caselotti at the piano, Callas auditioned for him, opening with Gioconda's soliloquy "Suicidio!" Zenatello enthusiastically joined her in

As La Gioconda in the Arena of Verona, July 1952, in a production designed by Nicola Benois. Piccagliani

singing the Act II duet between Enzo and Gioconda, and at the end of the audition, Callas had the contract.

Callas, Louise Caselotti, and Rossi-Lemeni arrived in Italy on June 29, 1947. Twenty-four hours later, at a dinner held in her honor in Verona, Callas met Giovanni Battista Meneghini. In a 1957 article for *Oggi,* she recalled that she was struck immediately by his sincerity and honesty. On April 21, 1949, after a two-year courtship, they were married. During her first month in Verona, Callas rehearsed the role of Gioconda with conductor Tullio Serafin, worked on her Italian pronunciation, and went sight-seeing with Meneghini. Everything went smoothly until the dress rehearsal in the ancient outdoor arena. While walking around the artificial sea in Act II, she fell down a stone chute which in Roman times had been used as the passageway for wild animals. A wooden railing broke the fall, but her ankle was badly swollen by the third act.

British critic Harold Rosenthal was in the audience at Callas's Italian debut on August 2. In a feature article devoted to Callas (*Opera,* November 1952), Rosenthal discussed the debut of "the remarkable Gioconda . . . whose then rather metallic timbre of voice seemed to me already to have a most moving and individual quality, and whose phrasing was unusually musical." He was taken to see her during the final intermission. "She was most agreeable to her visitors," he recalled, "but appeared worried about two things: one was that she had a rather badly sprained ankle and could only just limp about the stage, the other that we might not intend to stick out the opera's extreme length, and so would miss her big aria in the last act. About the second point at any rate she need have had no fear; 'Suicidio' was most impressive—and I very much doubt if any one of that 25,000 audience left before hearing it."

Callas sang five Giocondas at a fee of 40,000 *lire* (about sixty dollars) a performance. Five years were to elapse before she sang the role again. When she returned to Verona to sing two performances in July 1952, she had become an established artist at La Scala and her fee had risen to 500,000 *lire.* In the superspectacle tradition of the Verona festival, 800 extras, 400 chorus members, and 100 dancers took part in those two performances. As an added festive touch, 200 doves were released into the air at the start of the first *Gioconda.* Although none of Callas's stage Giocondas are known to exist in sound, the Cetra recording of the role, taped but a few weeks after her 1952 Verona performances with the same conductor and tenor, is almost certainly a faithful documentation of her stage portrayal.

Amilcare Ponchielli's opera, produced at La Scala in 1876 and set in seventeenth-century Venice, typifies the full panorama of grand opera, both in looking back to the elaborate scenic effects of Meyerbeer, and in pointing the way harmonically and melodically to the *verismo* style of Mascagni and Puccini. The title role is one of the longest and most strenuous parts in Italian opera. During a discussion of bel canto repertory in a 1967 broadcast interview, Callas referred to the role as "just on the border of decent singing," although she also felt that Ponchielli still touched the bel canto tradition.

Zinka Milanov, the Metropolitan Opera's most popular exponent of the role after Rosa Ponselle, discussed the difficulties of the part in an article for *Opera News* (December 29, 1952). She told interviewer Mary Jane Matz:

> Gioconda is frequently unkind to the voice, for several reasons. First, Gioconda is not a mechanical role, but one which requires intense concentration on voice production and technique. It is an opera which tires the singer enormously. Heavy orchestration. Long, dramatic lines. The soprano almost loses her breath, singing, singing, singing. No other opera has such jumps. What could Ponchielli have thought when he wrote those jumps? Octave, octave-and-a-half, two octaves. This opera is full of them . . . It's not easy.

Callas easily meets the vocal and histrionic demands of the role in the Cetra recording—her first commercially recorded opera set. Although she often pushes her voice to its limits, her interpretation of the ballad singer Gioconda is one of the most spectacularly uninhibited performances on disc. In several dramatically crucial passages, she forces the chest voice, carrying it so high up the scale that her tone production is thrown out of balance. Six first-rate singers are essential in order for the beauty in Ponchielli's masterpiece to be fully realized. In the 1952 recording, most of the principals—other than Callas and bass Giulio Neri —are vocally so inadequate that some of the most inspired moments of the opera are nearly ruined.

Callas's voice is youthful and untroubled in the opening scene, as Gioconda tells her blind mother that she will wait in the shrine for her beloved Enzo. When Barnaba steps forward, blocking her path and reiterating his love for Gioconda, Callas employs some of her most venomous tones, as Gioconda literally tells him to take his guitar and go to hell. Later in the first act, Callas's handling of the phrase "Enzo adorato! ah, come t'amo!" ("Beloved Enzo! Ah, how I love you!") is magnificent. Both Ponselle and Milanov were famous for the way they floated an ethereal *pianissimo* high B flat on "t'amo." Callas also touches the note softly, but for seven seconds she allows the tone to swell, filling it with emotion, and then draws it down to a whisper.

In Act II, Callas is particularly thrilling in the way she infuses both anguish and rage into the lines beginning "Vedi là, nel canal morto," as Gioconda tells Enzo that Laura has left him, while she has remained faithful. Also extraordinary is her piercingly beautiful reading of the lines "Or più tremendo è il sacrifizio mio . . . io la salvo per lui" ("Now my sacrifice is even more enormous . . . I am saving her for him") in the third act, as she slowly pours out the two-octave melody with near-Wagnerian power.

In the last act, Callas's "Suicidio!" is projected with floods of molten sound and Gioconda's final words to Barnaba before she stabs herself —"Volesti il mio corpo, demon maledetto? e il corpo ti do!" ("You wanted my body, accursed demon? The body is yours!")—are chilling.

Callas's final stage appearances as Gioconda took place at La Scala in December 1952 and January 1953. Although the management almost canceled the new production because of casting difficulties, they eventually assembled a stellar ensemble which included Giuseppe di Stefano, Ebe Stignani, Carlo Tagliabue, and Italo Tajo. Seven years later, Callas returned briefly to the role to re-record it in stereo for EMI. She had two months without engagements before the recording sessions and she was in very good vocal estate. Although the 1959 *Gioconda* lacks some of the savage intensity and fearlessly attacked high notes of the Cetra set, Callas adds another dimension to the role, creating a softer, more sympathetic character, particularly in the final act. Unfortunately, three pages of Gioconda's Act IV music are cut (although available on the Cetra set), beginning with the words "Questa canzone ti rammenti." All the principals are vocally more satisfying on the EMI set than their Cetra counterparts.

La Gioconda, Act I, as seen at La Scala, Milan, December 1952. La Gioconda with her blind mother, La Cieca (Lucia Danieli), before the Doge's palace in Venice. Piccagliani

Act IV, La Scala, December 1952. Gioconda, on the island of Giudecca in the Adriatic, contemplates suicide. Piccagliani

Turandot

CALLAS began studying the title role of Giacomo Puccini's *Turandot* in September 1946. Her lawyer-turned-impresario friend E. Richard Bagarozy had formed an opera company together with Italian impresario Ottavio Scotto and conductor Sergio Failoni. The roster included Mafalda Favero, Cloe Elmo, Hilde and Anny Konetzni, Galliano Masini and Max Lorenz. The company's first performance was to have been a production of *Turandot,* presented in Chicago on January 6, 1947, with Callas, Favero, and Masini in the principal roles.

Although Bagarozy and Scotto had invested heavily in the venture, the business of producing opera proved to be financially more prohibitive than they had anticipated. Shortly before opening night, the American Guild of Musical Artists insisted on a substantial deposit to protect their chorus members, and Bagarozy and Scotto were forced to declare bankruptcy. After all the bills were paid, Bagarozy had lost $100,000. A benefit concert was given in the Chicago Opera House to finance the homeward trip of the European artists. Bagarozy's wife, Louise Caselotti, recalled in a 1973 interview that the European singers were understandably disappointed, but not particularly upset. Most of them had ex-

Callas at the time of her South American debut in *Turandot,* Teatro Colón, Buenos Aires, May 20, 1949. Courtesy of the Teatro Colón

perienced hardship during the war and the trip to the United States was a pleasant vacation. They liked their hotel accommodations and several of them auditioned successfully for the Metropolitan and the New York City Opera.

Caselotti and Callas rehearsed *Turandot* every day for over three months. During one session devoted to the Act II riddle scene, Callas spent fifty minutes on one phrase which fell awkwardly at a register break. She enjoyed learning the role, but when it entered her active repertoire in January 1948, she soon came to dislike it.

Callas's Verona debut in *La Gioconda* in the summer of 1947 was only a moderate critical success, but conductor Tullio Serafin recognized her exceptional gifts. He had conducted in all of the major theaters of the world for almost fifty years and had coached sopranos Claudia Muzio, Amelita Galli-Curci, Elisabeth Rethberg, and Rosa Ponselle. Ponselle had been his greatest protégée and between 1924 and 1934 he had conducted over 150 performances for her.

Serafin was to coach Callas in seventeen roles over a period of seven years. He saw faults in her singing at first and tried to eradicate them, but he also knew how to develop the unique qualities of her voice and incorporate them into the repertoire for which she was temperamentally suited. Serafin emphasized elegance of phrasing and clean vocal attacks. He taught her to prepare a phrase in her mind, so that the audience would see it in her face before she actually sang it.

In an article for the Italian magazine *Discoteca* (September 1961), Serafin wrote of Callas:

> I was not acquainted with her, nor had I chosen her for the *Gioconda* which I was to conduct in the Arena of Verona in the summer of 1947. The former tenor Zenatello, acting as an agent in New York, had sent her to me. She came to Verona and sang two or three arias and I realized immediately what Maria Callas could do—what, in fact, she did do later. *La Gioconda* went very well and soon after I asked her to sing in *Tristan* which I was to conduct in Venice.

During a broadcast interview with Edward Downes in 1967, Callas recalled the 1947 *Tristan* audition with Serafin:

> He remembered me from Arena di Verona and he called me to

perform Isolde—very quickly, December, and I knew this, November . . . I had just looked at the first act by curiosity and at the last minute he asked for an audition with me. And I wouldn't dare say I didn't know the opera, for I would have lost the audition . . . So I just bluffed. I said, "Yes of course I know Isolde," and I sight-read the second act. I don't know how. God must have helped me . . . And he turned around and said, "Excellent work. I must say you know the role well." And then I confessed. "Look, Maestro," I said, "I must say I bluffed. I didn't, I sight-read the second act." Well, he was surprised and he appreciated me even more then.

But then I had to study. So I sang Isolde, then I sang Turandot also. I was engaged for the contract. Then as soon as I could have gotten out of these roles, well, I got out. In fact, I dedicated myself to the bel canto roles to do good for the voice, and I dropped all these other roles.

Serafin was the first great maestro with whom Callas worked. He was strict with his singers, insisting that they avoid drinking or staying out after 11 P.M. Shortly after his death in 1968, Callas told interviewer Jan Maguire (*Saturday Review,* March 30, 1968):

> During rehearsal he was after every detail, but in performance he left you on your own. "When I am in the pit I am there to serve you because I have to save my performance," he would say. We would look down and feel we had a friend there, in the pit. He was helping you all the way. He would mouth all the words. If you were not well he would speed up the tempo, and if you were in top form he would slow it down to let you breathe, to give you room. He was breathing with you, loving it with you. It was elastic, growing, living.

In 1961, when asked how she studied a new role, Callas told interviewer Derek Prouse (London *Sunday Times,* March 19, 1961): "Serafin once told me a marvelous thing. He said: 'You want to find out how the opera should be acted? You only have to listen to the music and you'll find everything there for you.' I seized on that immediately. I felt I knew exactly what he meant, and that is perhaps my biggest secret! I act according to the music—to a pause, to a chord, to a crescendo."

Callas sang in *Turandot* for the first time at Venice's Teatro La Fenice on January 29, 1948, and Louise Caselotti was in the audience. Callas told her after the performance: "The only acting you do in *Turandot* is walk up and down stairs." In 1958, while reminiscing about her

A rare photograph of Callas, at the age of twenty-five, in her first stage appearance as Turandot, Teatro La Fenice, Venice, January 29, 1948. The microphones at the footlights indicate that the performance was probably broadcast, but none of her performances at the Fenice are known to be preserved.

Giacomelli. Collection of Carlos Díaz Du-Pond

early career, Callas told interviewer Harry Fleetwood: "By and by I started getting going and I sang *Turandot* all over Italy, hoping to God that I wouldn't wreck my voice. Because, you know, it's not really very good for the voice . . . It's ruined quite a few voices. Well, you see, it's a rather nasty part, and it keeps on singing in a nervous way. And it taxes your vocal cords." After appearing as Turandot twenty-four times in seven cities, she dropped the role from her active repertoire.

In the spring of 1949, Callas appeared in Buenos Aires, singing in *Turandot, Aida,* and *Norma* under the direction of Serafin. The critic for *La Nación* wrote of her Argentine debut on May 20: "In the role of Turandot, the soprano Maria Callas showed all her vocal gifts as well as a magnetic presence, overcoming in top form the great difficulties inherent in the role; however, she did not make us forget other memorable interpretations offered in this theater, and her voice, particularly in the loud, high passages, sounded a little metallic."

Although a complete stage performance of *Turandot* with Callas is not known to exist in sound, a brief selection from a Buenos Aires broadcast, with tenor Mario del Monaco, is in circulation among collectors of Callas tapes. This tantalizing fragment (less than three minutes in duration) begins with Calaf's Act III line "Io son Calaf, figlio di Timur" (I am Calaf, son of Timur") and continues through Turandot's final line, "Il suo nome è Amor!" ("His name is Love"). It is possible to draw only general conclusions about her approach to the role from the excerpt on tape (the earliest known example of her singing in performance), but the awesome power of her voice at that time is readily apparent. Her delivery of the climactic final lines is almost violent in its intensity. The words "So il tuo nome!" ("I know your name"), set to repeated A's above middle C, are taken in a chest voice carried extraordinarily high and her steely high notes easily cut through the heavy orchestration.

In July 1957, between performances of Bellini's *La Sonnambula* in Cologne and Edinburgh, Callas committed the role of Turandot to disc for EMI. The recording, conducted by Serafin, may be a close approximation of her stage characterization, but her voice had become warmer and more expressive in the eight years which separated her final stage Turandot and the recording. Her EMI Turandot is well sung, with imaginative enunciation of the text, but her voice lacks some of the thrust and security at the top which are indispensable for a totally satisfying portrayal of this role.

Aida

CALLAS first sang the title role of Giuseppe Verdi's *Aida* in Turin in September 1948, according to the singer herself, and not in Rovigo, as has been stated in several publications. The role remained in her active repertoire for five years. Of the eleven cities in which she sang Aida, her most enthusiastically received performances of the role were in Mexico City in 1950 and 1951. Antonio Caraza Campos, general director of the Opera Nacional, had dreamed for years of presenting a *soprano absoluta* at the Palacio de Bellas Artes. Italian bass Cesare Siepi had appeared with Callas in *Norma, Aida, La Forza del Destino,* and a 1950 radio concert. He recommended her to Caraza Campos, praising her range, vocal color, and dramatic intensity. Caraza Campos immediately engaged her for the 1950 Mexico season through the artists' management Agenzia Lirica Concertistica Internazionale.

After the *Aida* general rehearsal, Caraza Campos told Callas about the nineteenth-century Mexican soprano Angela Peralta who was famous in local operatic history for taking a full-voice high E flat at the end of the *Aida* Triumphal Scene. He showed her Peralta's score with the note written in and asked her if she could duplicate the feat in her forthcom-

Callas relaxing in her dressing room at the Palacio de Bellas Artes, Mexico City, before the Triumphal Scene in *Aida,* May 30, 1950. Du-Pond

ing *Aidas.* She said that vocally she could, but she would never tamper with the score. He quickly enumerated the operas in which unwritten high notes had become tradition. He urged the conductor to persuade her and she eventually agreed after receiving permission from co-stars Giulietta Simionato and Robert Weede. On May 30, 1950, Callas became the first singer of this century known to have taken a high E flat in *Aida.* The interpolated note, sustained for six seconds, gave the

Aida admits her love for Radames and implores Amneris to take pity on her. Callas at the Teatro San Carlo, Naples, April 27, 1950. Troncone

impression of equaling the combined volume of the chorus and orchestra.

The *Aidas* for the following season were scheduled with Callas and tenor Mario del Monaco. The public had come to expect the E flat, but the management knew that Del Monaco's consent would be necessary. Callas said, in recalling the performance years later: "There was also the rather notorious incident of the high E flat in Mexico City, which,

I found out later, was recorded. My conductor there argued me into singing that note at the end of the Triumphal Scene in *Aida,* but when our tenor heard about it he told everybody that *he* had a high E flat too . . . Well, we both sang the note, but mine was in my natural voice and his was in falsetto, so it was me everybody heard" (*The New Yorker,* April 24, 1971).

Del Monaco told the members of the company that he would sing the note again at the next performance, only this time he would wait until Callas was almost out of breath and *then* sing the note, so that his high E flat would continue after she had stopped singing. Once again Del Monaco was not heard past the footlights. The audience broke into spontaneous applause as soon as Callas sang her note, drowning out both singers.

During the three brief Mexico City seasons, Callas sang eight roles, three of them for the first time, including Gilda in *Rigoletto,* a role which she never repeated anywhere else. She gave the audiences everything she had to offer vocally and dramatically and she quickly established herself as the favorite of the press and public. Several of her 1951 and 1952 appearances were televised. For her third season, the marquee of the Palacio de Bellas Artes proclaimed: INBA PRESENTA OPERA NACIONAL A.C. CON MARIA MENEGHINI CALLAS, LA SOPRANO ABSOLUTA DEL SIGLO ("... the *soprano absoluta* of the century").

All eight of her Mexico City roles were broadcast and carefully preserved on large acetate transcription discs and paper-base magnetic tape. This recorded legacy from Mexico City now constitutes the most important documentation of her early career.

The Nile Scene, with Callas, Kurt Baum (Radames), and American baritone Robert Weede (Amonasro), Palacio de Bellas Artes, Mexico City, May 30, 1950.
Luis Quintero

Norma

CALLAS first sang the title role in Vincenzo Bellini's *Norma* in Florence on November 30, 1948. The role of the Druid priestess—more than any other interpretation—is the one most closely associated with her name. She appeared as Norma ninety times in eight countries and recorded it twice (in 1954 and 1960). Tapes of her Norma include performances from Mexico City (1950), London (1952), Trieste (1953), Rome (a Radio Italiana studio production, 1955), Milan (1955), and Paris (1965).

In an interview for the New York *Herald Tribune* (October 28, 1956), given before her Metropolitan Opera debut as the Bellini heroine, she told Jay Harrison: "With an opera like Bellini's *Norma* . . . I work as though I had never sung it before. It is the most difficult role in my repertory; the more you do it, the less you want to." In 1961, at a period when her stage appearances had become increasingly infrequent, she mentioned Norma in an interview held in Monte Carlo with Derek Prouse: ". . . Maybe she's something like my own character: the grumbling woman who is very proud to show her real feelings and proves at the end exactly what she is. She is a woman who cannot be nasty or

At the time of her Mexican debut as Norma, May 1950. Luis Quintero unjust in a situation for which she herself is fundamentally to blame" (London *Sunday Times,* March 27, 1961).

Callas first studied the role in Athens before she was twenty. In 1948, almost a decade later, Tullio Serafin was engaged to conduct *Norma* in Florence and he invited her to undertake the title role for the first time. She successfully auditioned for him in Rome and he gave her valuable advice for the study of Bellini's recitatives. He told her to find the rhythm and proportions of the recitatives by singing them over to herself as if she were talking.

Norma is almost unanimously considered to be the most difficult soprano role in operatic literature. The ideal interpreter must have enormous stamina, great breath control to sustain the long, arching melodies, a wide range and complete mastery of bel canto ornamentation. Norma is one of the longest parts in opera and the soprano must be able to pace herself so that she has enough voice for the powerful utterances of the last act. The part does not require a great deal of movement on stage and the protagonist must express the full gamut of emotions—fear, jealousy, passion, friendship, rage, despair, maternal love, exaltation, selflessness, and piety—almost entirely through vocal acting.

Although Callas's earliest preserved Normas, dating from 1950 and 1952, were remarkable achievements, some of the most dramatic lines were rather roughly delivered and the basically cool timbre of her voice at that time was not ideally suited to the more lyrical passages. By the time she opened the 1955–56 Scala season in *Norma,* her voice had become a warmer instrument capable of a wealth of tonal gradations. Each word and phrase had its own color, yet the entire portrayal was of one piece. Most important, her voice was healthy and responsive to all of her interpretive demands.

In the spring of 1965, when Callas made her final appearances as Norma at the Paris Opéra, her characterization was profoundly moving, but it was necessary for her to husband her vocal resources. Being too exhausted to leave the stage to change into her last act costume during the penultimate performance, Callas had the red and gold cloak for the final act placed over the costume which she was wearing. Five nights later, against medical advice, she began the final *Norma* of the series, but she was unable to finish the performance and the fourth act was canceled.

In February and March of 1950, Callas appeared at the Rome Opera as Norma and Isolde. She was the first soprano since Lilli Lehmann (1848–1929) to sing both roles. "If I have to judge between Isolde and Norma," she told interviewer Edward Downes in 1967, "I'm afraid Isolde is nothing in comparison to Norma." Walter Legge, director of Great Britain's Electric & Musical Industries Ltd. (EMI), was in the audience for her first Norma in Rome. He hurried back to his hotel during the first intermission to urge his wife, soprano Elisabeth Schwarzkopf, to return with him to the theater. She had been listening to the performance on the radio and needed little encouragement. He had been looking for a major soprano for EMI's projected series of Italian operatic recordings. Although Callas was under contract to Cetra-Soria records at that time, Walter Legge eventually signed her to an exclusive contract on July 21, 1952.

Callas chose the role of Norma for her Mexico City debut on May 23, 1950. The opening recitative, beginning "Sediziose voci, voci di guerra" ("Seditious voices, voices of war"), received a powerful, explosive delivery, with glottal attacks and cutting top notes. "Casta Diva" was sung calmly and with an attractive tone, but her reading did not approach the beauty of subsequent performances. In the cabaletta, "Ah! bello a me ritorna," she took the long phrases in one breath and executed the florid passages with considerable brilliance. Although the Norma-Adalgisa duets were well sung, neither Callas nor Giulietta Simionato were at their best for the opening night performance, which was broadcast.

In the Act III *scena* in which Norma contemplates killing her children, Callas sang the lines beginning "Teneri figli . . . essi pur dianzi delizia mia" ("Tender children, until now the joy of my life") with a light but cold sound. Her treatment of the text became highly emotional at the words "Ah! no . . . son i miei figli" ("Ah no! They are my children") and she sobbed. This emotional device is not to be found in any of her subsequent performances on tape. In the final act, when Norma tells Pollione that both he and Adalgisa shall die, Callas hurled out her lines with almost savage force and at one point—on the word "indegno" ("contemptible one")—her voice broke from the vehemence of her delivery.

In 1951, Callas's portrayal of Norma was heard in Sicily and Brazil. In January 1952, she sang the role for the first time at La Scala. Newell Jenkins reported on the seventh performance of the series (*Musical America,* March 1952):

> She electrified the audience by her very presence even before singing a note. Once she began to sing, each phrase came out effortlessly, and the listeners knew from the first tone of a phrase that she felt instinctively as well as consciously just where and how that phrase would end. She never rushed and she never dragged. Her tones came out round and full, with a legato like that of a stringed instrument. Her agility was breathtaking. Hers is not a light voice, but she negotiated the most difficult coloratura without batting an eye, and her downward glissandi made cold shivers run up and down the hearer's spine. There was occasionally a slight tendency to shrillness and hardness on the high notes, although her pitch was faultless.

Callas selected *Norma* for her London debut on November 8, 1952, at the Royal Opera House at Covent Garden. The cast included Ebe Stignani as Adalgisa, Mirto Picchi as Pollione, and Joan Sutherland, in her third assignment at the theater, as Clotilde. Vittorio Gui conducted four of the five performances. Callas quickly became a favorite of the British audiences. Her London appearances were virtually an unbroken series of triumphs and she sang at Covent Garden for more years than in any other theater (1952–1965).

In 1969, Callas told interviewer Kenneth Harris: "I have had a love affair with London. It was in Covent Garden, 1952, that I sang *Norma.* Until then *Norma* had not been heard in London since Rosa Ponselle had sung it there in 1930. She was the greatest singer of her time; and the British are not easy to please; after all, immortal names are written on Covent Garden's walls. I was given a great reception. I was hailed as 'the' new Norma. It was a tremendous compliment."

Andrew Porter wrote of her debut (*Musical Times,* January 1953):

> Maria Meneghini Callas is the Norma of our day, as Ponselle and Grisi were of theirs . . . Who will forget the dream-like phrases of

"Casta Diva"; the simple phrase "O rimembranza" which opens the first duet with Adalgisa, the pathos of "Ah, perchè, perchè, la mia costanza"; the fire of the phrases flung at Pollione; the "Son io" or, simply, the grace of her *gruppetti?* To be sure, there were one or two moments when the tone became less beautiful, a shade nasal. But these could hardly detract from a superb assumption.

Norma was chosen for the opening night of La Scala's 1955–56 season. The new production was directed by Margherita Wallmann and designed by Salvatore Fiume. Antonino Votto conducted and the cast included Giulietta Simionato and Mario del Monaco. The December 7 *prima* is unquestionably the finest total performance of all the *Normas* with Callas which exist on tape or disc. Del Monaco's rich voice rang out with extraordinary power in the climaxes. In the softer passages, he phrased his lines with a sensitivity seldom to be found in his commercial recordings. Both he and Simionato gave the impression of being totally involved in the drama. Callas was at her absolute best, both vocally and histrionically. In the final act, during her singing of "Deh! non volerli vittime del mio fatale errore" ("Do not let them be victims of my fatal mistake"), the Scala musicians began to play as if they were inspired. They "sang" with their instruments, matching the intensity of Callas's performance on stage.

On October 29, 1956, Callas made her long-overdue debut at the Metropolitan in the Bellini opera, in company with Mario del Monaco, Fedora Barbieri, and Cesare Siepi. She was to sing for the first time in the city in which she was born and the enormous publicity surrounding the event made her understandably tense and nervous. The performance had also been sold out for months at benefit prices. At the dress rehearsal she found the old production and other costumes to be so shabby that her own costumes appeared to be slick and inappropriate. Two days before her debut she read a destructively critical magazine article which made her lose confidence in her ability to carry off the opening night. Sixteen years later, Sir Rudolf Bing referred to her opening night as "undoubtedly the most exciting of all such in my time at the Metropolitan," but Callas was not in good voice for her debut. The performance was one of the very few times in her career that she was plagued by pitch problems. The reviews were favorable but not enthusiastic and the critics adopted a "wait-and-see" attitude.

Some three months later, in February, Callas returned to Covent Garden for two guest appearances as Norma. She was in exceptionally fine voice and at the end of each of the two performances she received a standing ovation from the capacity audience. At the second performance, after the "Mira, o Norma" duet with Ebe Stignani (in one of the last performances of her career), such pandemonium reigned that the conductor, John Pritchard, had no alternative but to grant the first encore in decades at the Royal Opera House. Rudolf Bing cabled to congratulate Callas on her London triumph and she wrote back that she was sorry she had been unable to give him personally in her first season what other theaters had had.

Although Callas moved to Paris in the early 1960s, she did not appear in opera at the Théâtre National until May 1964. She chose *Norma* for her debut. The new production was designed by Franco Zeffirelli, with costumes by Marcel Escoffier. Zeffirelli created a lavish and detailed set reminiscent of the elaborate Opéra productions depicted in mid-nineteenth-century prints. One basic set—suggesting a clearing in a French wood—was employed for the entire opera and the foliage was varied for each act to indicate a change of seasons.

Judging by reviews, Callas's Paris Normas were vocally uneven and no two were alike. At one performance she cracked on a high note. The house fell into an uproar, half the audience booing, half cheering. She took an extraordinary risk and raised her hand and motioned the conductor to begin again. The second time the note was perfectly placed and she received a thunderous ovation.

Harold Rosenthal reported on the fifth Paris *Norma* (*Opera,* August 1964):

> . . . Even now with her flawed vocal technique, Callas can get more out of this Bellini role than anyone else, and the weight and vocal colour she gives to individual words and phrases is still an object lesson to all . . . I found it difficult to relax during most of the first two acts . . . though by the time she had reached the Norma-Adalgisa-Pollione trio she had struck form, and as she rounded on Pollione with the words "Tremi tu? e per chi?" flashing her scornful eyes at him and pointing at him accusingly, the drama flared to life, and we were almost back in 1952 . . . Then in the last scene the miracle happened—in the dramatic recitative before the

"Guerra, guerra" chorus, there was a slight vocal mishap which seemed to act as a spur, for from that moment until the end of the evening (some twenty-five or so minutes) she produced a stream of tone, firmly-based, such as I had not heard from her since those first Covent Garden *Normas*. She raged, she pleaded, she was in complete command of the stage, and had an electrifying effect on her companions. The audience went mad, and rightly so, for once again the Callas magic had worked.

The "Casta Diva," Mexico City, May 23, 1950. Luis Quintero

Callas and the Junoesque mezzo-soprano Elena Nicolai rehearse the Norma-Adalgisa duets with Maestro Antonino Votto in the Teatro La Fenice, Venice, before the performance of January 13, 1950.

Giacomelli. Collection of Carlos Díaz Du-Pond

Act IV, Teatro Bellini, Catania. Norma, despite the urging of the crowd and Oroveso (Boris Christoff), cannot bring herself to kill Pollione (Gino Penno).

Giovanni Consoli

One of the loveliest of the early photographs of Callas, "Casta Diva," Teatro Bellini, Catania, Sicily, November 3, 1951. Giovanni Consoli

Callas in Margherita Wallmann's production of *Norma,* La Scala, Milan, December 1955.
Piccagliani

The second act of Franco Zeffirelli's sensuously elegant production of *Norma,* Paris Opéra, May 1964. Fiorenza Cossotto is Adalgisa. Bernand

Act IV, Paris Opéra, May 1964. Bernand

I Puritani

BETWEEN 1949 and 1955, Callas sang sixteen performances of *I Puritani* in six cities. Along with Norma and Violetta, Elvira was to become one of the three roles which she considered to be the most challenging and satisfying in her repertoire. Perhaps no other Callas portrayal has received the unanimous, unqualified critical acclaim accorded her characterization of the Bellini heroine.

I Puritani, Vincenzo Bellini's last opera, was premièred in 1835 at the Théâtre-Italien in Paris. It was written at the suggestion of Gioacchino Rossini, who had recently been appointed director of the theater. Although the opera nearly equaled *Norma* in popularity for a few decades, it had disappeared from most houses by the turn of the century. The difficulty of casting the extremely high tenor role was partially responsible for the decline in the number of stagings.

Callas first sang the role of Elvira at the Teatro La Fenice in Venice on January 19, 1949. The opera had received only a handful of Italian productions in this century—most notably with sopranos Mercedes Capsir, Margherita Carosio, and Lina Pagliughi. The role of Elvira was generally considered to be the domain of *lirico-spintos* and high colora-

Callas, in a 1952 studio photograph, wearing her elaborate wedding dress for the third scene of Act I, *I Puritani,* and holding the veil which Elvira playfully gives to the mysterious guest. Semo

tura sopranos. It was inconceivable that Italy's finest new Isolde, Brünnhilde, Turandot, and Aida could also spin out the fragile melodies and handle the vocal scrollwork of *I Puritani.* Nevertheless, Callas sang three performances of the work in between a series of appearances in *Die Walküre.* This feat of virtuosity became the talk of musical Italy.

Callas had not planned to sing Elvira in Venice. Her familiarity with the opera was limited to a couple of arias which she had studied with Elvira de Hidalgo in Athens. Tullio Serafin, whose experience conducting *I Puritani* included a memorable production at the first Florence May Festival in 1933, with Mercedes Capsir, Giacomo Lauri-Volpi, and Ezio Pinza, described in a 1961 article for *Discoteca* the circumstances concerning the choice of Callas for the part:

> Margherita Carosio was suddenly taken ill and we didn't know where to find a light soprano to substitute for her. We were all staying in the same hotel and while we were discussing it, my daughter said, "Papa, Callas can sing *Puritani.*" In fact, she had heard her singing an aria from it in her room while warming up. She had never sung this opera, but she learned it so quickly that she debuted in it after only eight days, and made it one of the most remarkable works in her repertory. Her musicality is extraordinary, almost frightening.

Almost two years elapsed after the Venice performances before Callas sang the role again. She wanted to keep it in her active repertoire, but the work was not an established box-office favorite and she had to urge opera house directors to mount it for her. In 1950, when Rudolf Bing first attempted to engage her for the Metropolitan, her agent in Milan included *I Puritani* in the list of operas in which she would like to appear. Bing successfully resisted Callas's request for *I Puritani* and—sixteen years later—a similar one from Joan Sutherland.

In an article for *Opera* (April 1973), Carlos Díaz Du-Pond, assistant to Antonio Caraza Campos, the general director of the Opera Nacional in Mexico, recalled Callas's first rehearsal in Mexico. As soon as she and Giulietta Simionato finished singing the duets from *Norma,* Du-Pond telephoned Caraza Campos. He reported that Callas was the finest dramatic coloratura he had ever heard. Caraza Campos arrived with a score of *I Puritani* and told Du-Pond to ask her in Italian to sing the arias, so that he could hear her high E flat. Callas told Du-Pond, "Tell Mr. Caraza Campos that if he wants to listen to my E flat he must sign me for next year in *I Puritani.*" Caraza Campos and the audiences at the Palacio de Bellas Artes heard her high E flat on several occasions during her first Mexican season, and he promised to open the 1952 season with a production of *I Puritani* for Callas.

In November 1951, the Sicilian city of Catania, Bellini's birthplace, presented a series of performances commemorating the one-hundred-fiftieth anniversary of his birth. The festival included a broadcast performance of Verdi's *Requiem* with Renata Tebaldi and Ebe Stignani, a new production of Bellini's *Il Pirata* with Lucy Kelston and Giangiacomo Guelfi, and a staging of Bellini's *La Sonnambula* with Margherita Carosio and Cesare Valletti. Callas appeared in a broadcast revival and three other performances of *Norma* with Giulietta Simionato and four performances of *I Puritani* with Boris Christoff. Francesco Pastura, a biographer of Bellini, wrote in the *Giornale dell'Isola:*

> Maria Callas has repeated the feat, not unusual in former times, but today almost astonishing, of interpreting two Bellini operas which require two different sopranos. Thanks to the enormous range of her voice and the precious technical devices which allow her to sing with absolute ease of emission, the exceptional soprano demonstrated last evening, in the difficult part of Elvira, the marvelous vocal resources at her disposal.

Nine weeks later she sang in two performances of the opera at the Teatro Comunale in Florence. The impressive cast, under the direction of Serafin, included American tenor Eugene Conley, who had sung the role of Arturo with success at his La Scala debut in 1949, Carlo Tagliabue as Riccardo, and Grace Hoffman in the role of Enrichetta. Musicologist Newell Jenkins reported in *Musical America* (March 1952):

> This opera must be superlatively sung in order to be bearable, but the performance was a sensation. One can only deal in superlatives in describing Miss Callas's singing—her velvet tone, her exciting phrasing, her heart-rending emotion, her hair-raising coloratura, her stage presence, her majesty of bearing, her fine acting. At the end of each act a phenomenon occurred such as I have not witnessed in any Italian opera house or concert hall since the return of Tosca-

nini to La Scala after the war. The audience shouted, stamped, and rushed forward to clamor for Miss Callas in curtain call after curtain call. The orchestra, inured to singers of all types and nationalities, stood in the pit applauding as vociferously as the audience.

Her first Rome performance followed on May 2, 1952, scheduled between Florentine appearances in Rossini's fiendishly difficult *Armida.* Callas's Arturo on this occasion was the veteran tenor Giacomo Lauri-Volpi, who was to praise her generously in his 1955 book *Voci parallele.* Lauri-Volpi first sang Arturo in 1919 in Viterbo, Italy, four years before Callas was born. Giorgio Vigolo, music critic for *Il Mondo,* wrote:

> Lauri-Volpi has demonstrated that he still has twenty more years of high notes. As for Maria Callas, one can only speak of a personal triumph. Without the slightest sign of fatigue from dividing her time between Florence and Rome, there in the enchantments of Armida, and here in the passions of Elvira, she demonstrated not only the agility, extension, and "four voices" which are contained in her throat, but also a rich and vibrant interpretation, the likes of which we have never heard from her.

Four weeks later, Callas began her third Mexican season with *I Puritani.* The opening night, May 29, which was broadcast, is her only stage appearance as Elvira known to exist in sound. She was in good voice, but the rest of the performance was generally poor. The conductor was lethargic and overly indulgent and the male singers ranged from adequate to appalling. Baritone Piero Campolonghi, who was to have a brilliant success five nights later in *La Traviata,* only approximated much of his part. Giuseppe di Stefano sang with beautiful tone and ringing top notes, but musically his performance was one of his least distinguished endeavors in Mexico. The main value of the preserved Mexican performance is that it shows Callas's recorded version, taped ten months later under the direction of Serafin, to be a faithful documentation of her performing edition for the stage.

She was in exceptionally fine voice for the recording sessions. She employed a dark, penetrating tone for the role, except in the florid passages where her voice took on a soft, limpid quality. Most of the repeated sections were omitted, in keeping with the conviction of both

Callas and Serafin that musical repetitions are monotonous and standard cuts are necessary in order to make opera palatable for contemporary audiences. Callas did not add to the *fioriture* of her part, but she did interpolate several high D's and a high E flat. Near the end of the Act I ensemble, "Oh vieni al tempio," she sang the bass melody transposed up two octaves, placing the vocal line around high C. An unusual but practical change took place in the tenor aria "Credea si, misera." Callas sang eight measures of the second stanza (sixteen measures in Mexico City) as a solo, thereby augmenting her part with one of the most inspired melodies in the opera and also giving Di Stefano an opportunity to rest before singing the concluding series of high notes.

Callas's voice was captured at its most hauntingly beautiful in "Qui la voce." Noteworthy was the way she punctuated the phrases with the slightest suggestion of a sob or gasp, yet without impairing the flow of Bellini's *cantilena.* Although her delivery of the celebrated aria is generally more intense than that found in recorded interpretations by other sopranos, her approach is faithful to Bellini's written indication—"con tutta la disperazione del dolore" ("with all the despair of sorrow").

Immediately after taping the opera for EMI, Callas was scheduled to leave for London to sing in Verdi's *Requiem* for the first time. The April 1, 1953, performance was announced for Royal Festival Hall, with soloists Fedora Barbieri, Gianni Poggi, and Giulio Neri, under the direction of Sir Malcolm Sargent. Because of an influenza epidemic in Milan, she was unable to enter England, and the soprano solo was sung by Sara Menkes. Callas was never to sing the *Requiem.* She was scheduled for two performances in Dallas for November 1969, but her appearances never materialized.

After Callas opened the 1955 season in Chicago with *I Puritani,* the opera left her repertoire. It had not been heard in the United States for over thirty years. When Callas appeared on stage, she was greeted by an ovation that stopped the show. "It was fantastic," Claudia Cassidy wrote, "to see Callas make Elvira a totally different creature from her Lucia. Where Lucia was a normal girl gone mad for love, Elvira is a fey, unstable creature who is off and on again like Finnegan. The glint in her eyes, the dark hair, the lovely hands—you can't take your eyes off her. And her singing is magnificent."

Stewart Manville reported in *Opera* (January 1956):

> It was most gratifying to watch her madness evolve in Scene three. First came the simple question, "Where is Arturo?" then a realization that something was amiss, followed by the moment of unbearable disappointment leading to her loss of contact with reality, all worked out with the creative detail of a great actress. One remembers still how she took the wreath of white roses from her hair and her anguish when, as if by accident, it dropped to the floor. Unforgettable too was the grand sweep of her mad scene in Act III, the sort of impersonation one rarely experiences even in the spoken theatre.

Act I, scene 3. Elvira and Arturo (Giuseppe di Stefano) reiterate their love, Palacio de Bellas Artes production, Mexico City, May 29, 1952. Luis Quintero

Act II. Elvira, who has lost her reason upon being deserted by her fiancé, urges her father (Roberto Silva) to be happy on her wedding day. Mexico City, May 1952.
Luis Quintero

With conductor Gabriele Santini, Paolo Silveri (extreme left), and Giacomo Lauri-Volpi (second from right) at the Teatro dell'Opera, Rome, May 1952.

Nabucco

VERDI'S *Nabucco,* which was premièred in 1842 when the composer was twenty-eight, has received few productions in this century. Although the opera towers above all the other early Verdi operas as a work of genius (with the exception of *Macbeth*), the formidable difficulties of the soprano part have discouraged most sopranos from learning the role of Abigaille or from keeping it in their repertories. (Elena Suliotis is the most notable exception, and four years of *Nabuccos* between 1965 and 1969 nearly ruined her basically fine voice. In a 1966 interview for *Opera News,* she stated that "Abigaille has to shout.") The part requires a powerful voice ranging from high C to low B flat, capable of cutting through large ensembles and heavy orchestration. The soprano must also possess a secure coloratura technique.

In February 1949, Callas debuted in Naples at the Teatro San Carlo (built in 1737) in Puccini's *Turandot.* Her three performances earned her an invitation to open the 1949–50 season in *Nabucco.* Fortunately for opera historians, Callas's first *Nabucco* was preserved in a small archive of primitive recordings dating from 1949–1952. The performances include such rarities as Renata Tebaldi in Spontini's *Fernando*

Callas in a costume for the Teatro San Carlo production of *Nabucco,* December 1949.
Troncone

Cortez, Rossini's *L'Assedio di Corinto,* and Gounod's *Faust* (sung in Italian); Mafalda Favero in Leoncavallo's *Zaza;* and Beniamino Gigli in Mascagni's *L'Amico Fritz*—all unrecorded commercially but now preserved on limited-edition pressings.

Callas's 1949 Abigaille easily qualifies as her gutsiest, most spectacularly fearless performance we have available to us. The role of Abigaille (a vindictive warrior-maiden determined both to rule Babylon and to destroy her enemies) requires unrestrained singing in order to be totally effective, but extramusical influences also added to the intensity of Callas's performance. She had recently turned twenty-six and was on the threshold of a major career. Fully aware of her capabilities, she was competing for opening-night honors with the popular baritone Gino Bechi who was singing the title role. A major success in one of Verdi's most notoriously difficult roles also carried with it the guarantee of further engagements.

Abigaille's opening lines to her unfaithful lover were delivered in cold, contemptuous tones and "Di mia vendetta il fulmine su voi sospeso è già" ("The thunderbolt of my revenge is already suspended over you") was hurled out with chilling vehemence. Raw chest tones and glottal attacks on the high notes were used freely in the opening scene to heighten the dramatic effect, and the high C's were attacked securely and effortlessly sustained. (During the middle 1950s, high C's became more difficult for Callas to control than high D's or E flats.) The repeated lines "Colei che il solo mio ben contende, sacra a vendetta forse cadrà" ("That girl who contests my only love, perhaps will fall victim to revenge") in the Act I finale poured out with ferocious intensity.

Although Abigaille's one tender aria, "Anch'io dischiuso un giorno ebbi alla gioca il core" ("I too once opened my heart to happiness"), was beautifully phrased, it was sung with a cold, metallic tone that aroused little sympathy for the character. In the 1958 recording of the aria and cabaletta, Callas, singing to a microphone rather than in a large auditorium, invested the music with warmth and a myriad of vocal colors. Unfortunately, the cabaletta "Salgo già del trono aurato" ("I now ascend the golden throne") does not approach the *slancio* and sweep of the Naples performance, and the final high C has a pronounced beat in the tone. When Callas included "Anch'io dischiuso . . ." on her 1963

Callas in two costumes for the Teatro San Carlo, Naples, production of *Nabucco,* December 1949. Troncone

European concert programs, her precarious vocal health forced her to abbreviate the final cadenza, thereby avoiding the high B and sustained high C.

Callas's most brilliant singing in the Naples performance occurred during Abigaille's confrontation with the deranged and pathetic Nabucco, whom she has imprisoned. Singing with a voice of Wagnerian proportions, Callas negotiated the runs, trills, and two-octave arpeggios with astonishing ease. Her steely, almost whining tone was ideal for the passages in which Abigaille taunts Nabucco. Callas ended the scene with a full-voice, sustained high E flat. For the death scene, in which the repentant Abigaille begs forgiveness, Callas employed a colorless, sickly sound which she was to use extensively in later years for the last act of her *La Traviata* performances. After three *Nabuccos,* Callas dropped the opera from her repertoire and returned to the roles of Norma and Aida, which she found more congenial.

Il Trovatore

CALLAS sang the role of Leonora in Giuseppi Verdi's *Il Trovatore* for the first time in Mexico City on June 20, 1950. During the next seven years she performed it twenty times in seven cities and recorded it for EMI. Broadcast tapes of her Leonora exist from Mexico City, Naples, and Milan. Between her first Mexican performance and the 1957 recording, Callas's Leonora underwent a gradual refinement, both in tone quality and interpretation. In 1950, her portrayal was passionate and full-blooded. By 1957, her characterization had become more lyrical, elegant, and aristocratic. The most striking differences in her preserved performances are in the treatment of the cadenzas in the arias "Tacea la notte" and "D'amor sull'ali rosee." Her phrasing and inflections of the text remained basically unchanged, but she employed different endings for the arias at almost every series of performances.

Callas's co-stars in her first *Trovatore* in Mexico were Giulietta Simionato, Leonard Warren, and Kurt Baum. She began "Tacea la notte" with a veiled tone, but in the "con espansione" section her voice took on a free, soaring quality, appropriate to the mounting ardor implied in the text. She abbreviated the music at the close of the piece

Before her first *Trovatore,* Mexico City, June 1950. A year later, the wedding dress for the third act of *Il Trovatore* was also to serve as Callas's Act V costume in the Florence and Milan productions of Verdi's *I Vespri Siciliani.* Semo

but sang the written high D flat and followed it with an interpolated high C and high E flat. The cabaletta, "Di tale amor," was sung in a vibrant, powerful manner, the octave scale up to high C and down again being particularly brilliant. She ended the aria with an untraditional and electrifying high E flat.

The Act I trio, with Callas, Baum, and Warren, although sung with great intensity and abandon, showed little subtlety. Callas and Baum ended the trio with an interpolated high D flat, held for seven measures, neither singer apparently being anxious to release the note first. "D'amor sull'ali rosee" was taken at a deliberate tempo and presented as an eloquent prayer. The trills were cleanly articulated and performed as an integral part of the musical line. The high notes were attacked with great intensity, unlike the equally effective approach of Leontyne Price in which the high notes are sung *pianissimo* and floated with a shimmering, disembodied sound. Callas ended with Verdi's rarely performed high D flat.

In the "Miserere," introduced by a tolling bell and a mournful ecclesiastical chant, Callas conveyed Leonora's feeling of terror and desperation through a wealth of telling vocal effects. In the Act IV *scena* in which Leonora pleads with Di Luna to spare Manrico, Callas and Warren reached dramatic heights seldom approached in this familiar music. Leonora's aside, "M'avrai ma fredda, esanime spoglia!" ("You will have me, but as a cold, lifeless corpse!") must have been particularly horrific for the people following the performance over the radio. At that moment, Callas walked directly in front of the microphone and hurled out the words, employing her most evil-sounding chest tones. Her singing in the final scene was very moving, but much of it was covered by Kurt Baum's *fortissimo* declamation. The June 20 *Trovatore* was the only time that Callas appeared with Leonard Warren in a complete performance. Warren began the *Trovatore* of four nights later, but he became indisposed during the performance and the Act IV *scena* was omitted.

The *Trovatore* of June 27 (with Ivan Petroff substituting for Warren) was Callas's last appearance in Mexico for the 1950 season and her voice showed signs of fatigue. Her singing in "Tacea la notte" was virtually identical with her first performance, except for the final high E flat which she almost lost. In the cabaletta, "Di tale amor," instead of attempting another high E flat, she opted for Verdi's original ending of a sustained trill followed by an A flat. In the Act I trio finale, Callas and Baum delivered their lines with all the vehemence of a heated public debate. In the first *Trovatore,* both singers ended with an unwritten high D flat, held for seven measures. This time the note was held for nine measures!

Before singing her first Leonora, Callas had asked Tullio Serafin to coach her in the role, but he told her that it was not one of his operas. When he made one of his rare appearances conducting three performances of the score early in 1951 in Naples (he never conducted *Trovatore* in Milan, Verona, London, or New York), Callas was engaged for Leonora and he worked with her on the part. The cast for the January 27 *prima* included Giacomo Lauri-Volpi as Manrico, Cloe Elmo as Azucena, and Paolo Silveri as Count di Luna. Although Callas was in beautiful voice, the performance, which was broadcast, was generally wretched. The orchestra often played like a street band. All of Cloe Elmo's high notes came out as G's and Lauri-Volpi often only approximated the correct rhythm and pitch. The audience vociferously expressed its displeasure after his "Di quella pira." He canceled his third appearance and addressed an open letter to the Naples press, protesting what he considered to be an indifference to vocal art.

Callas's Naples performance was similar to her first *Trovatore* of seven months earlier, except for the Act I aria and cabaletta. In Mexico she shortened the ending of "Tacea la notte" and added high notes. In Naples she performed the aria as written, up to and including the high D flat, but she substituted a variant cadenza and transposed the final A flat up an octave. The climactic A flat was a curious interpolation which could have encouraged applause in the middle of the *scena.* At the conclusion of the cabaletta, "Di tale amor," she chose neither of the two endings performed in Mexico. She omitted Verdi's trill and interpolated a high B flat, followed by the A flat in the score.

Two years later, on February 23, 1953, Callas sang her first *Trovatore* in Milan. It was her third new production at La Scala within eleven weeks. The *prima* had been scheduled for February 19, but an influenza epidemic affected the *Trovatore* cast and *La Gioconda* was substituted at the last minute. The principals for the series, under the baton of Antonino Votto, included Gino Penno as Manrico, Ebe Stignani as Azucena, and Carlo Tagliabue as Di Luna. The first performance, which was broadcast, was good but not exceptional. Votto kept the performance bouncing along with brisk, tightly controlled tempos, but the singers had little breathing space in which to make musical points or to shade key phrases. Peter Dragadze reported in *Opera* (April 1953):

> This *Trovatore* was worth waiting for, and had the success that it truly merited. The success was not due though to the usually dominating figure of Manrico, but to the almost unforgettable singing of Leonora and Azucena taken by Maria Callas and Ebe Stignani. Maria Callas again passed a difficult test and showed once more her remarkable artistic intelligence, her exceptional gifts as a singer, and the fact that she possesses a vocal technique second to none. Her handling of the dramatic content of her part was a masterpiece of artistry.

Verdi considered Azucena to be the leading female character in the opera and Stignani's glorious vocalism, beginning with "Condotta, ell'era in ceppi al suo destin tremendo" ("They led her in chains to her execution"), vividly realized the full dramatic possibilities of the role. Although she had been singing at La Scala for over a quarter of a century, her voice was still capable of soaring up to the high A's and B flats of the part without apparent effort. The heart-rending anguish of "Il figlio mio avea bruciato" ("I had slain my own son") elicted a spontaneous ovation from the audience.

Callas's singing was somewhat reserved. The "Tacea la notte" was an impeccable example of Verdian singing, but Votto's stiff tempo did not allow for any *rubato* or nuances. She sang Verdi's ending up to the cadenza, but instead of going directly to the high D flat, she inserted a few preparatory notes, and concluded with the variant cadenza which she first sang in Naples. In "D'amor sull'ali rosee," she did not sing the phrase with the high D flat, but substituted the lower, more traditional alternate music. She ended with a prolonged trill on G above the staff, followed by an A flat—a version of the final measures different from her previous performances.

In the summer of 1953, Callas returned to London for her second engagement at Covent Garden, where she was scheduled to appear in *Aida, Norma,* and *Il Trovatore.* Although part of her *Aida* exists in sound from that season, the highly praised *Trovatore,* with James Johnston in the title role and Giulietta Simionato as Azucena, is apparently lost. Cecil Smith wrote of Callas's performance (*Opera,* August 1953):

> Without resorting to old-fashioned Delsartian plastique she was more fortunate in carriage and gesture than I feel she was, on the whole, in *Norma;* and in some way I cannot define she embodied both Leonora's passionate humanness and the formality with which the score and libretto universalise her emotions.
>
> Her voice—or, rather her use of it—was a source of unending amazement. For once we heard the trills fully executed, the scales and arpeggios tonally full-bodied but rhythmically bouncing and alert, the portamentos and long-breathed phrases fully supported and exquisitely inflected. The spectacular ovation after "D'amor sull'ali rosee" in the last act was still less than the soprano deserved . . .

December 1953 brought Callas's first *Medeas* at La Scala, with Leonard Bernstein in the pit, and three performances as Leonora at the Rome Opera. Unfortunately, the Rome *Trovatores* followed a brilliant production of *Don Giovanni* staged and conducted by Herbert von Karajan, with Mario Petri, Elisabeth Schwarzkopf, Nicolai Gedda, and Sesto Bruscantini. The critics found the *Trovatore* performances to be roughly conducted and indifferently sung in comparison with the meticulously rehearsed Mozart opera. Verdi scholar William Weaver reported in *Opera News* (February 15, 1954) that the performance was "dominated by the incredibly tasteless singing of Lauri-Volpi . . . His Leonora was Maria Callas, who sang a little coldly at first, but was as impeccable as her partner was hammy. In the last act her 'D'amor sull'ali rosee' was the brightest spot in a dire evening . . . Maestro Santini, ordinarily a sound, firm conductor, allowed himself to be carried away by the tenor's insistence. The tempi grew so uncertain that in the concerted numbers singers were as much as two bars off."

At the second performance, Fedora Barbieri, cast as Azucena, fainted onstage just before "Stride la vampa" and was replaced by Miriam

Pirazzini. After the third *Trovatore,* Callas returned to La Scala for additional appearances in *Medea* and Caterina Mancini took over the part of Leonora.

Callas's final stage appearances as Leonora took place in Chicago in November 1955. The stellar cast for the first performance included Jussi Björling, Ebe Stignani, and Ettore Bastianini. The two *Trovatores* were her only appearances with the great Swedish tenor. Although one of the performances is rumored to exist—taped by two Chicagoans who carried a tape recorder hooked up to a battery into the auditorium—it has not yet been made available to collectors of Callas tapes. Roger Dettmer reported that the "Chicagoans yelled themselves hoarse." Claudia Cassidy described the applause as "roof-shattering" and called Callas's fourth act "a wonder of the western world."

Rudolf Bing had been trying since 1950—without success—to sign Callas for the Metropolitan. He wrote in his autobiography, *5000 Nights at the Opera:*

> To sign that contract in 1955, we had to take the mountain to Mahomet: Francis Robinson and I flew to Chicago, where the managers of the Lyric Opera, Carol Fox and Lawrence Kelly, were not pleased to see us. (They feared, correctly, that once Callas signed in New York, Chicago would hear her no more.) We heard Miss Callas sing in *Trovatore,* with Björling as Manrico, and I remember saying that during "Ah si, ben mio" in the third act it was Callas's quiet listening rather than Björling's voice that made the dramatic impact . . . Then we went backstage, where I offered my very best version of the kiss-the-hand routine I had learned as a child, and the picture got into all the papers—and, finally, the Metropolitan signed Maria Callas to a contract.

In August 1956, Callas committed her interpretation of Leonora to disc for EMI. The cast, led by Herbert von Karajan, included Giuseppe di Stefano, Fedora Barbieri, and Rolando Panerai. Her handling of the Act I "Di tale amor" differed considerably from her earlier preserved stage performances. Instead of singing the music dramatically, she delivered it with bel canto delicacy. At the words "Ah! sì, per esso morrò" ("Yes, I would die for him"), set to an *appoggiatura* figure which is repeated seven times, Callas trilled on every other note, matching the embellishments played by the orchestra. "D'amor sull'ali rosee" received an unusually introspective, dream-like interpretation. Her singing in the "Miserere" was also dramatically understated and she did not use the powerful chest voice and dark vocal quality which characterized her first performances in Mexico.

The most interesting feature of the EMI recording is the inclusion of the rarely sung cabaletta "Tu vedrai che amore in terra." The major technical difficulties come in three measures near the end of the aria, where the soprano must execute—in a fast tempo—an octave chromatic scale up to five repeated A's, followed by a two-octave scale from high C down to low C. In recent years, only Montserrat Caballé and Martina Arroyo have performed it in major opera houses. It is a pity that Callas never sang it on stage, because it is one of the most magnificent pieces of vocalism in her recorded portrayal.

Act I, scene 2: Callas's first performance of *Il Trovatore,* with Kurt Baum as Manrico (at left) and Leonard Warren as Count di Luna, Palacio de Bellas Artes, Mexico City, June 20, 1950. Luis Quintero

Di Luna (Paolo Silveri) demands that the Troubadour (Giacomo Lauri-Volpi) reveal his identity, Teatro San Carlo, Naples, January 27, 1951. This was Callas's first *Trovatore* in Italy. Troncone

Act III, scene 2: Manrico (Lauri-Volpi) attempts to quiet Leonora's fears, Teatro San Carlo, Naples, January 1951. Troncone

Callas, in her Act IV costume, with Cloe Elmo, as Azucena, and Tullio Serafin (at right), by the bust of Verdi in the Teatro San Carlo, Naples, January 1951.
Troncone

Il Turco in Italia

In the spring of 1950, the Associazione Anfiparnaso, a group of eleven men in Rome which included Luchino Visconti, began planning a two-week season of intimate operas. They commissioned four new Italian operas, including Luigi Dallapiccola's *Job,* and scheduled two rarely performed works of the past, Gioacchino Rossini's *Il Turco in Italia* (1814) and Orazio Vecchi's *L'Amfiparnaso,* first performed in 1594. The 1,300-seat Teatro Eliseo on the via Nazionale was chosen, and several of Italy's finest young singers were invited to participate. Radio Italiana was given permission to broadcast the performances and was responsible for furnishing the orchestra and chorus.

Although Callas had sung only heavy dramatic roles in Rome up to that time, two radio concerts in 1949 and 1950 containing coloratura showpieces indicated that she had the florid technique necessary for Rossini's *Turco* and she was offered the part of Donna Fiorilla. Callas wrote in a 1957 article for *Oggi:*

> After my return from Mexico I had three weeks of rest. Immediately after, I accepted the offer from Maestro Cuccia to take part in

A repentant Fiorilla in the last act of Franco Zeffirelli's production of *Il Turco in Italia* for La Scala, Milan, April 1955. Piccagliani

a comic opera by Rossini, *Il Turco in Italia:* a proposition which particularly appealed to me . . . because it allowed me to stray from the subject—by this time frequent—of great tragedies in music and to breathe the fresh air of a very funny Neapolitan adventure.

While I was preparing myself under the direction of Maestro Gavazzeni in Rome to interpret this difficult opera, I had the opportunity to know better Luchino Visconti, who had previously complimented me. I remember my surprise at seeing a man of his distinction sit in attentively at almost all of the rehearsals, which lasted a minimum of three or four hours—and we rehearsed two times a day.

In *Il Turco in Italia,* Fiorilla, the young wife of Don Geronio, preaches in favor of infidelity. She becomes involved in a flirtation with a sultan who happens to visit Naples, only to return to her husband when the sultan departs with another woman. Although the music bubbles along and the many ensembles are brilliantly constructed, the score lacks the kind of memorable tunes which help to keep an opera in the repertory.

Callas lightened her voice almost to the quality of a soubrette for the florid role. Only during the mock anguish of Fiorilla's confrontation with her husband, "Voi crudel mi fate oltraggio" ("Cruel one, you wrong me"), did her voice pour out with the normal volume and intensity. *Opera*'s Rome correspondent reported: "Maria Callas was the surprise of the evening in that she sang a soprano leggiera role with the utmost ease in what one imagines was the style adopted by sopranos at the time this work was composed, making it extremely difficult to believe that she can be the perfect interpreter of both Turandot and Isolde. In Act I she astounded everyone in the theatre by emitting a perfectly pitched high and soft E flat at the end of an extremely attractive and vocally difficult aria . . ." (T. de Beneducci, February 1951).

Callas committed her interpretation to disc in September 1954 and La Scala staged the opera for her seven and a half months later in a new Zeffirelli production. Peter Hoffer wrote: "The month's undoubted triumph has been Rossini's *Il Turco in Italia,* not given at La Scala for 130 years or more . . . It was given superb production—Franco Zeffirelli both designed and produced, with a charm and lightness rarely seen on any stage, let alone in an opera house . . . Maria Callas was brilliant—looking delightful, singing and acting magnificently with the finesse and subtlety and technical and artistic ability that usually one only dreams of . . . A memorable and all too rare evening" (*Music and Musicians,* June 1955).

Fiorilla and Zaida (Jolanda Gardino), rivals for the affection of the Turk, trade insults in the Act I finale of *Il Turco,* La Scala, Milan, April 1955. Piccagliani

La Traviata

CALLAS sang her first performance of Giuseppe Verdi's *La Traviata* in Florence on January 14, 1951, under the direction of Tullio Serafin. Although the role of Violetta was to become one of her most celebrated interpretations, performed more than sixty times in seventeen cities, she declined offers to sing the role for over a year before she attempted it because she considered herself to be unsuitable for the part. She stated that she was a dramatic soprano and she felt that Violetta should be sung by a lighter voice.

In May 1949, Callas and Serafin went by ship to Buenos Aires for seven weeks of performances at the Teatro Colón. She did not have any immediate plans to sing in *La Traviata,* but they worked on the opera during the trip to Argentina. In a 1960 interview, Serafin told George Jellinek that Callas's first *Traviata* in Florence was a great accomplishment that surprised many people.

Callas's conception of the role underwent a remarkable refinement during the eight years in which *La Traviata* remained in her active repertoire. She experimented with phrasing, vocal coloration, dynamic levels, and optional high notes and cadenzas in an attempt to offer a

La Traviata, Act I, "Oh amore," Royal Opera House, London, June 20, 1958.

Roger Wood

portrayal of Verdi's heroine which was both believable and faithful to the composer's score. Her first *Traviatas* in Florence and Cagliari are not known to exist in sound, but her Mexico City appearance of July 17, 1951, was broadcast and preserved on acetate discs. The performance, with Cesare Valletti as Alfredo and Giuseppi Taddei as Germont, was vocally glorious, if not particularly subtle. Callas's voice was enormous and dark. In *forte* passages, her upper register took on a somewhat metallic quality. The "Sempre libera" was sung with almost violent abandon and astonishing agility. She lingered on the high notes and swept up to the final high E flat without taking a breath. Her over-all performance reflected an emotional, unrestrained approach to the role which she was to modify within the year. Valletti's singing in the duets and aria "De' miei bollenti spiriti" was impassioned and his voice had a richness and vibrancy that bore little resemblance to the light, lyric quality which he was to employ during most of his later career.

In September 1951, Renata Tebaldi sang *La Traviata* with considerable success in São Paulo, Brazil, and Callas attended the performance. A week later the opera was repeated with Callas as Violetta. The highly publicized animosity between the two sopranos began during this brief season in Brazil. According to a local critic and a member of the cast, Callas made a few unappreciated negative comments to Tebaldi about her performance. When the two singers appeared in Rio de Janeiro later in the month, a series of misunderstandings and verbal exchanges brought their onetime casual friendship to an end.

The following month, in Italy, Callas appeared as Violetta (substituting for Tebaldi) at the Teatro Gaetano Donizetti, Bergamo. The performances were under the direction of Carlo Maria Giulini, who was conducting his first staged opera. Their next *Traviata* together would be at La Scala in the controversial Visconti production of 1955. On December 29, 1951, between the sixth and seventh performances of Verdi's *I Vespri Siciliani* at La Scala, Callas made the only appearance of her career in Parma. The gala performance of *La Traviata* was presented in commemoration of the fiftieth anniversary of the composer's death. Parma's notoriously critical opera public accorded her an ovation rare in the history of the Teatro Regio. Agostino Landini wrote in the *Gazzetta di Parma* that she was "an interpreter of Violetta the likes of which we have never heard before." He reported that Callas "was continually cheered and acclaimed—even during the performance and not just between the acts—with a fervor which has not been heard in this theater in many years."

In the summer of 1952, Callas returned to Mexico City for her third and final season at the Palacio de Bellas Artes, where she appeared in eleven performances of five operas. In contrast to the vocally uneven but thrilling *Traviata* of the previous year, her singing in the June 3 broadcast indicated a greater control over her vocal resources and the metallic quality of her high notes was less evident. Her approach was still that of a dramatic soprano singing Violetta, with Callas emphasizing the heroic rather than the fragile, vulnerable aspects of the role.

In Act I, the lines beginning "È strano" were forcefully delivered. The "Ah, fors'è lui" was sung *forte,* in a preoccupied, almost impersonal manner. The "Sempre libera" received a full-voice reading, with gleaming top notes and powerful chest tones. Particularly memorable was her desperate, incredibly intense delivery of the second act text beginning "Non sapete quale affetto," in which Violetta tells Germont of her fatal illness and her love for Alfredo.

Giuseppe di Stefano was appropriately ardent as Alfredo and his impassioned outburst in Act III, beginning "Questa donna conoscete?" was one of the high points of the evening. Callas ended the third act with a high E flat—an unusual interpolation which exists in sound only in her *Traviata* from Mexico City.

Baritone Piero Campolonghi appeared with Callas in all of her 1952 Mexico City performances. His voice was consistently rich and beautiful in all of the preserved performances of the season, but his eloquent reading of "Di Provenza il mar" in the June 3 *Traviata* reached a level of dramatic involvement unsurpassed in any of his other interpretations.

During the second act curtain calls, the radio announcer said that enthusiasm was "coming out of the pores of the audience." Callas agreed to a brief radio interview upon leaving the stage. She and the announcer spoke in Italian and he repeated her comments in Spanish. She praised the Mexican audiences and said that she would like to be perfect for them. She asked him to tell the Mexican public that she did not know how to show her true appreciation for their affection and that she would never forget them.

Eight weeks later she appeared in four performances of *Traviata* in the Arena of Verona. Peter Dragadze reported in *Opera* (October 1952):

> The greatest thrill of the season was *La Traviata,* excitingly conducted by Molinari-Pradelli and with Maria Callas as the protagonist . . . Hearing Callas sing Violetta was an unforgettable experience. Her acting technique is of the simplest and she appears to make no effort to dramatise the situation physically, as the colour of her voice clearly depicts every emotion and sensation she is experiencing. The difficult *È strano* was sung with such amazing ease and lack of effort, that one had the impression that she could go on singing indefinitely without losing the strength and perfect line of her voice.

On January 8, 1953, Callas returned to Venice's Teatro La Fenice after a three-year absence. The occasion was a gala performance of *La Traviata* celebrating the one hundredth anniversary of the opera's world première at the theater. The following week, Callas appeared in three *Traviatas* in Rome. Gabriele Santini conducted and the cast included tenor Francesco Albanese and baritone Ugo Savarese. Her interpretation of Violetta had received almost unanimous praise for two years, but to some members of the Rome opera public, her dramatic approach to the role was inappropriate. Cynthia Jolly wrote in *Opera* (April 1953):

> *Traviata* drew a storm of disapproval from the local press which found in Maria Callas an unsuitable Violetta: the public, undaunted, went to see her in large numbers and quarrelled over her loudly in the foyers. Even the ushers took sides: one would be enchanted by her sheer expertise and the other shocked by her lack of feeling in the part and *la voce troppo forte.* Even the most unprejudiced were startled by the unusual things she put in and the customary things she left out or modified. An exciting, questionable performance, in fact, from a magnificent and highly capricious singer.

> The first act succeeded admirably if untraditionally, when one remembers the bird-like coloratura Violetta is used to receiving. This, clear-cut and sturdy, belongs to the Callas of *Armida:* and never have I heard the descending couples of semiquavers (when she hears Alfredo outside) so beautifully handled. She seems to have acquired a new beauty of tone in the high register (though her very top notes are still acid) and the whole voice is becoming better blended. In the second act, however, more than dramatic brilliance and vocal relaxation is required, and here she failed to find true tenderness or to penetrate the pain of the renunciation.

Several months later, the conductor and three principals of the Rome production recorded the opera for Cetra. Although none of Callas's Rome Opera appearances are known to exist in sound from this period, her Cetra recording is probably a close approximation of the January 1953 performances.

The Roman critics who found Callas's voice to be too powerful for the role in 1953 would certainly have been appalled if they had heard the torrents of sound which she had unleashed in Mexico City. Her singing in the recording is more relaxed and her tone lighter in quality than in the Mexico broadcasts. All of her music is beautifully phrased, but emotionally she seems strangely uninvolved. Both Albanese and Savarese are acceptable at best. The Cetra recording is the only extant performance in which Callas inserts a variant cadenza in Act I, after the words "croce e delizia, delizia al cor."

In 1955, EMI signed Giuseppi di Stefano, Tito Gobbi, and Tullio Serafin for a recording of *Traviata.* Callas's conception of Violetta had changed considerably in the two years after the Cetra recording and understandably she wanted to re-record the opera under the direction of the man with whom she had first prepared the role. It was one of the great disappointments of her career when she learned that the part had been promised to Antonietta Stella. Between 1965 and 1968, it was reported in various magazines that EMI was planning to record *Traviata* in Paris with Callas and conductor Georges Prêtre, but the project was never realized.

Callas's first Scala *Traviata* took place in May 1955, with co-stars Giuseppe di Stefano and Ettore Bastianini, under the baton of Carlo Maria Giulini. Director Luchino Visconti transferred the period to about 1890. He and Callas spent many hours perfecting nuances of movement, gesture, and facial expression. Peter Hoffer reported in *Music and Musicians* (August 1955) that "the whole was so full of subtleties and minor inventions that it became a joy to watch." In the first act, Callas presented a restless, high-strung courtesan. When Violetta suddenly becomes weak and urges her guests to go into the ballroom, Visconti had the chorus chatter and laugh as they strolled offstage, underscoring the guests' lack of concern for the health of their hostess. Sitting quietly before a fireplace, Callas projected the intimate thoughts of the "Ah, fors'è lui" in a straightforward manner, as if Violetta were thinking out loud. At the beginning of the "Sempre libera," Visconti instructed Callas to sit on a table and throw off her slippers—an innovation which displeased several critics. A more felicitous touch came when Alfredo's voice was heard offstage and she cradled her face in her hands for the words "Oh, amore."

In the second act, Callas dropped to her knees and embraced Alfredo as she sang the impassioned outburst "Amami, Alfredo." The final act was remarkable for the way in which she conveyed the despair of a woman dying and abandoned. In sharp contrast to the morbid atmosphere on stage, Visconti had raucous laughter punctuate the music of the offstage carnival chorus. Only his staging of Violetta's death evoked almost unanimous criticism. Instead of collapsing, Violetta died upright, supported by Alfredo and Germont, her eyes open, and with her hat and coat on, ready to leave the house.

Musically, the May 28 *prima* was very fine. Di Stefano was in exceptionally good voice and his singing was so intense in the Act III section beginning "Ogni suo aver tal femmina" that the audience spontaneously broke into applause. This was to be his only performance of *Traviata* at La Scala with Callas. He left the production after they had a dispute over solo curtain calls. Giacinto Prandelli sang the remaining performances of the 1955 series.

Callas wrote in a 1959 article for *Life:* "I see the role, and therefore the voice, as fragile, weak and delicate. It is a trapeze part filled with sick *pianissimo*." In the earlier preserved performances, the final act was generally sung with a full, round tone, but in the Scala production she experimented with a weak, colorless sound, almost as if she were talking on the pitch. In a 1961 interview with Derek Prouse (London *Sunday Times,* March 19, 1961), she discussed her use of *pianissimo* singing:

> I had strived for years to create a sickly quality in the voice for Violetta; after all, she *is* a sick woman. It's all a question of breath, and you need a very clear throat to sustain this tired way of talking, or singing, in this case. And what did they say? "Callas is tired. The voice is tired." But that was precisely the impression I was trying to create. How could Violetta be in her condition and sing in big, round tones? It would be ridiculous.
>
> And in the last act they even said: "Callas is having trouble with her breath." Thank Heaven I eventually attained what I was trying to do and got the proof that it had been appreciated.

Callas's use of a disembodied sound for most of the last act enabled her to throw key phrases into relief with a sudden change in tone quality. Her vocal acting in the phrase sung to Alfredo, "Ma se tornando non m'hai salvato, a niuno in terra salvarmi è dato" ("But if your return has not saved me, then nobody on earth can ever do it"), was extraordinarily powerful. She began the line slowly, with a hollow, almost nasal sound and ended it with her darkest, most somber tones.

The Covent Garden *Traviata* of June 20, 1958, is Callas's last and in many respects her finest Violetta preserved in sound. After the first few minutes of Act I, it was obvious that she and Cesare Valletti were totally absorbed in their parts. Every word was meaningful and in the logical context of the drama. Valletti's singing in "Un dì felice" was vocally exemplary and dramatically a touching declaration of love. In the section in which Violetta tells Alfredo that he should forget her, Callas no longer sang the music in the preoccupied manner of her earlier performances. Her rebuff was gentle and warm. "Ah, fors'è lui" was sung softly and introspectively. The concluding cadenza was sung without flourish and Callas ended the aria quietly, taking Verdi's original low ending. Her brilliant execution of the "Sempre libera" belied the fact that she had been placing very heavy demands on her voice for almost twenty years. The high C's and D flats were easily reached and she ended the act with a perfectly placed high E flat.

The Act II Germont-Violetta scene was a complete entity, with Callas closely observing all of Verdi's nuances and dynamic shadings as indicated in the score. Baritone Mario Zanasi's singing was more noteworthy for his observance of textual values than for the display of his vocal resources. His voice was attractive, but somewhat light in quality. In Act IV, Callas employed a warm, attractive tone, suggesting Violetta's failing health by coloring individual words, instead of singing entire phrases with a weak sound.

Critic Harold Rosenthal attended the first, third, and fifth of Callas's five Covent Garden *Traviatas* and discussed her interpretation in detail (*Opera,* August 1958):

> In the first act Callas showed us a brittle, highly strung Violetta, unable to be at rest; the charming hostess who talks to as many of her guests as she can, who does not want to spoil the party when she feels ill, and who can only joke at first over Alfredo's declaration of love. For this Violetta, love does not come in the duet, but in the middle of the "Sempre libera" when she hears Alfredo's "Amor, amor e palpito." As Callas uttered the simple word "Oh!" and then "Oh, amore!" we knew the truth, just as earlier in the scene when she looked at herself in the mirror and sighed "Oh, qual pallor!" we knew that this Violetta realized she was a dying woman. And what other Violetta has been able to use the coloratura in "Un dì felice" so naturally to suggest, as Callas does, the nonchalant carefree life of the courtesan?
>
> The second act Violetta had become softened, and was wholly and utterly devoted to her Alfredo. The long central scene with Germont was outstanding, and here Callas was supreme. From the moment she drew herself proudly to her full height at the words "Donna son' io, signore, ed in mia casa," through the changing emotions of the conversation with Germont . . . , to the resigned "È vero! è vero!" as Germont pointed out that she would one day grow old and Alfredo would tire of her, and on to the great moment of renunciation—"Ah! Dite alla giovine": this was operatic singing and acting at its greatest. The beginning of "Dite alla giovine" was a moment of sheer magic, with the voice curiously suspended in mid-air; and the final request to Germont to embrace her as a daughter was profoundly moving.
>
> In the writing of the letter and the short scene with Alfredo, Callas achieved a great intensity. At the first two performances

under review the "Amami, Alfredo," passage was rather subdued; at the final performance she rode the orchestra, opened up her voice and achieved the maximum degree of intensity, which aroused the audience to a spontaneous outburst of applause.

In act 3 . . . Callas successfully depicted the conflicting emotions of Violetta in the party scene. Again it was the odd word and phrase that assumed a new significance, as for example the heartfelt "Ah! Taci" to Alfredo before the denunciation—and at the same time the nervous hands touched her face and patted her hair. Then in the great ensemble, "Alfredo, Alfredo, di questo core" was sung as if Violetta's heart was truly breaking.

Callas's last act was superb. Dramatically one felt how Violetta suffered, one saw the effort with which the dying woman dragged herself from bed to dressing table, from dressing table to chair. "Oh, come son mutata" brought a lump to the throat as she eagerly scanned the tell-tale glass for some glimmer of hope. The reading of the letter was quiet and intimate, and then came a moving "Addio del passato." When Alfredo was announced, Violetta hurriedly tried to tidy her hair and look her best, and then came the reunion, with Violetta's hands (and how Callas had made the most of her beautiful long fingers throughout the evening) clasping at the longed-for happiness, and hardly believing that Alfredo really was a flesh and blood figure. "Ah! Gran Dio! Morir sì giovine" was sung with terrific intensity—and at the final performance Callas took the whole phrase in one breath without a break.

The drama moved to its close, and gently Violetta gave Alfredo the locket. The death scene was almost horrific, the last "È strano!" was uttered in an unearthly voice, and as Violetta rose to greet what she thought was a new life, a glaze came over her eyes, and she literally became a standing corpse. This was at the first night, but the death scene varied from performance to performance.

In the fall of 1958, Callas sang the two final *Traviatas* of her career in a new Zeffirelli production in Dallas, Texas. In 1969, she and Visconti signed a contract with the Paris Opéra for a new production of *Traviata,* but when they asked for twenty to thirty days of rehearsals for the orchestra and chorus, the Opéra's administration said they could not comply with the request and the production was canceled.

Callas in her second act costume for *La Traviata,* Mexico City, July 1951. Semo

The early Violetta, Palacio de Bellas Artes, Mexico City: Act I, with Giuseppe di Stefano as Alfredo, June 3, 1952. Luis Quintero

Callas's alternate costume for the second act; with Piero Campolonghi as Germont, Mexico City, June 1952. Jorge Gutiérrez

Alfredo (Giuseppe di Stefano) refuses to heed Violetta's warnings, Act III, Mexico City, June 1952. Luis Quintero

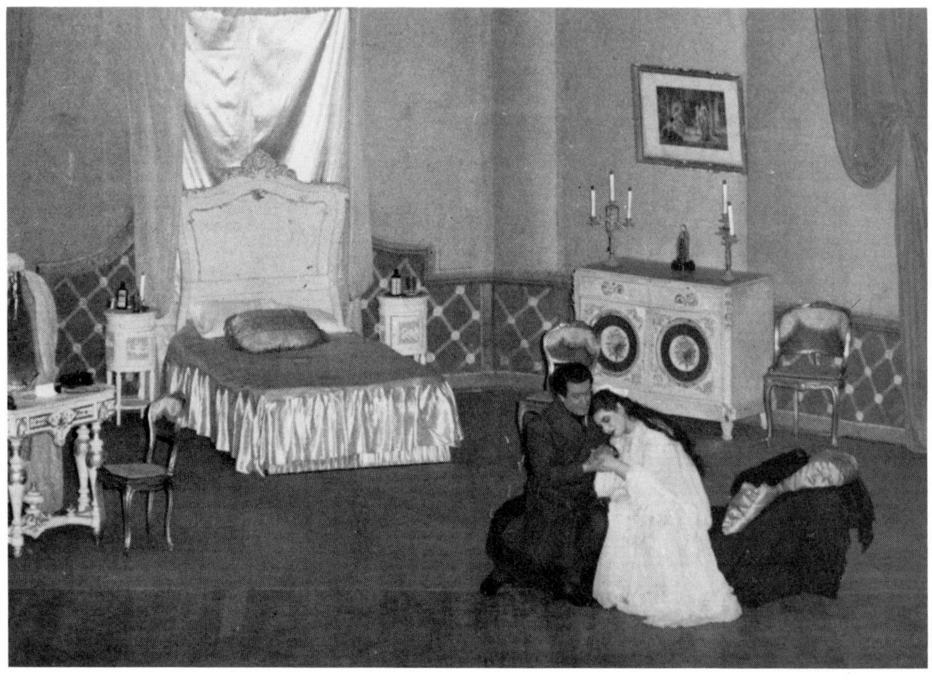

Callas and Di Stefano during the fourth act duet "Parigi, o cara," Mexico City, June 1952. Luis Quintero

Callas as Violetta in March 1958, during a rehearsal with Spanish tenor Alfredo Kraus, Teatro Nacional de San Carlos, Lisbon.

Luis Mendes. Collection of Michael Grasso

Violetta agrees to renounce Alfredo. Callas and Ettore Bastianini, as Germont, in Act II of Luchino Visconti's production, La Scala, Milan, May 28, 1955.
Piccagliani

The note of farewell to Alfredo, La Scala, May 1955. Piccagliani

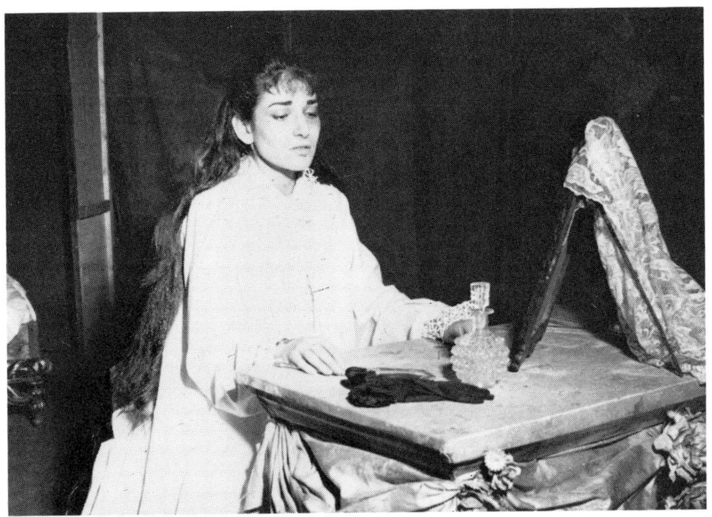

Act IV. "Addio del passato," La Scala, May 1955.
Piccagliani

Violetta's death, Royal Opera House, Covent Garden, June 1958, with Cesare Valletti as Alfredo.
Roger Wood

I Vespri Siciliani

HISTORICALLY, the event known as the Sicilian Vespers is the massacre of the French by Sicilians at Palermo on March 30, 1282. Giuseppe Verdi's *Les Vêpres Siciliennes,* based on that event, was commissioned by the Paris Opéra and premièred during the Great Exhibition of 1855. Grand operas written for mid-nineteenth-century Parisian audiences were usually in five acts with a lengthy ballet. Although Verdi successfully met the formal requirements of the Opéra and lavished great care on the orchestration and ensembles, much of the solo and duet music is undistinguished. The opera has received infrequent revivals in this century and usually in Italian translation as *I Vespri Siciliani.*

In 1951, the Florence May Festival presented four performances of *I Vespri Siciliani* as part of the fiftieth anniversary commemoration of the composer's death. The cast included Callas in her first appearances as Elena, Boris Christoff as Procida, Enzo Mascherini as Monforte, and Giorgio Bardi-Kokolios as Arrigo. The performances were led by Austrian conductor Erich Kleiber, who was making his Italian operatic debut. Although cuts were made in the score, the opening night performance did not end until nearly 2 A.M. Verdi's thirty-minute Act IV ballet

Callas as the Duchess Elena in *I Vespri Siciliani,* Florence May Festival, 1951.
Locchi

was performed virtually complete, with soloists that included Violette Verdy and Jacqueline Moreau.

Critic Harold Rosenthal attended one of the early stage rehearsals and recalled his impressions of Callas's entrance in a feature article for *Opera* (November 1952): ". . . The French have been boasting for some time of the privileges which belong by rights to an army of occupation, when a female figure—the Sicilian Duchess Elena—is seen slowly crossing the square. Doubtless the music and the production helped to spotlight Elena but, though she had not yet sung and was not even wearing her costume, one was straight away impressed by the natural dignity of her carriage, the air of quiet, innate authority which went with her very movement."

The May 26 *prima* was broadcast and exists in sound. Callas's opening scene was a brilliant piece of vocal acting. When the drunken French soldiers insist that Elena sing for them, Callas did not make a vocal showpiece of the cavatina and cabaletta in which Elena, under the pretext of singing a ballad, urges her countrymen to rebel. The cavatina "Deh! tu calma, o Dio possente" was sung with deceptive sweetness and little emotion. The cabaletta, beginning "Corragio, su corragio," was delivered with veiled, insinuating tones. It did not equal the electrifying vocal outpouring of Anita Cerquetti in her famous Radio Italiana broadcast of *Vespri* in 1954, but Callas's furtive approach was dramatically more appropriate. Unfortunately, the Florence production included only one stanza of Elena's cabaletta and the concluding florid music in the *scena* was deleted.

A vocal highlight of the evening was Boris Christoff's singing of the bass aria "O tu Palermo." His rich voice rolled out with extraordinary power and feeling. The handling of the Act II love duet by Callas and Bardi-Kokolios, beginning "Presso alla tomba," was outstanding. The tenor observed all of Verdi's dynamic markings, singing his high phrases *pianissimo*. Callas gave the impression of projecting one long uninterrupted musical thought, and sang with an exquisite thread of shimmering sound.

Her Act IV solo, "Arrigo! ah parli a un core," was sung with a penetrating sweetness, tinged with sadness, as Elena tells Arrigo that her declaration of love makes her imminent death more bearable. Kleiber's introductory measures were taken *andante,* but Callas, realizing that an open, impassioned reading would result if the music were taken at this tempo and the repeated words "io t'amo" were sung *forte* as indicated in the score, began singing at a considerably slower tempo. After a brief musical tug-of-war, Kleiber adjusted his accompaniment. Callas's sustained approach to the music allowed her to infuse each word with emotion.

When she recorded the aria for EMI almost thirteen years later (released in 1972 on "Callas by request"), the music was taken at the same tempo. The commercial performance is easily one of her most intimate and deeply felt on record. The high B and C are unattractive, but the middle and low notes are extraordinarily vibrant and warm. In the Florence performance, Callas sang the closing cadenza of two octaves and a fifth (the widest required *tessitura* in nineteenth-century operatic literature) in one breath, lingering on the high C and barely reaching the low F sharp in chest. In the 1964 recording, the high C was quickly abandoned, but the lowest tones were full and secure. Although it became increasingly difficult for Callas to sustain her high notes after 1958, a comparison of the low notes in these two versions illustrates a downward shifting of her voice, with fuller and richer lower tones than she had earlier in her career, rather than simply a shortened upper range.

Callas's singing of the Act V bolero "Mercè, dilette amiche" was unconventional, but faithful to the score. The technical difficulties of the aria include two trills—each sustained for three measures—and two florid passages ranging from high C sharp to A below middle C. In sixty years of recordings of the bolero by Joan Sutherland, Anna Moffo, Anita Cerquetti, Rina Gigli, Miliza Korjus, Rosa Raisa, Claudia Muzio, Rosa Ponselle, Luisa Tetrazzini, and Lillian Blauvelt, only Callas and Ponselle sang both the trills and runs as written. Though the piece is traditionally performed as a sparkling bravura aria, Callas chose a deliberate tempo, more appropriate to the dramatic situation since the text includes a reference to political revenge and the heroine is in the home of the man who murdered her brother. The phrases usually sung staccato were sung legato, as written, and Callas ended the aria with an unwritten high E. The note nearly cracked when she sang it, but she immediately gained control and sustained it. Except for a couple of changes in dynamic levels and a perfectly placed high E, her 1954 recording of the aria for EMI closely follows her Florence interpretation.

Lord Harewood wrote of Callas's performance in *Opera* (August 1951):

> She was, I believe, not at all well at the time of the first performance but all the same there was an assurance and a tragic bravura about her singing which was frequently thrilling. She has an astonishing technique, to which she owes her quite unusual versatility . . . At this performance, her voice showed a tendency to lose quality in *forte* passages (apart from a ringing top E at the end of the "Bolero"), but her soft singing in the duets of Act II and IV was exquisite, and the long and crystal clear chromatic scale with which she ended her Act IV solo made a most brilliant effect.

In April 1950, Callas sang three performances of *Aida* at La Scala, substituting for the indisposed Renata Tebaldi. She had hoped to be engaged as a regular member of the theater but did not receive a contract. A year later, after her success in the Florence *Vespri,* Antonio Ghiringhelli, superintendent of La Scala, offered her a contract for thirty performances during the forthcoming season. Her fee was to be 300,000 *lire* (about $500) per appearance and she was given the honor of opening the season in *Vespri.* The opera had not been heard at La Scala since 1908. Mascherini and Christoff were retained from the Florence staging and Eugene Conley was signed for the role of Arrigo.

After seven Scala appearances as Elena, the role left Callas's repertory. None of the seven performances are known to exist in sound, but reviews indicate that her debut was a success. The critic for the *Corriere del Teatro* reported that her "warm, burnished, agile voice with its prodigious extension had dominated the difficulties of the music with admirable brilliance." Franco Abbiati, writing in the *Corriere della Sera,* also praised her "prodigious extension and some tones of a phosphorescent beauty, especially in the low and middle registers."

In 1973, Callas returned to *Vespri,* but in the new role of stage director. The opera was selected for the April 10 reopening of Turin's rebuilt Teatro Regio, which had been destroyed by fire in 1936. The production was plagued by problems and the press was highly critical of Callas's

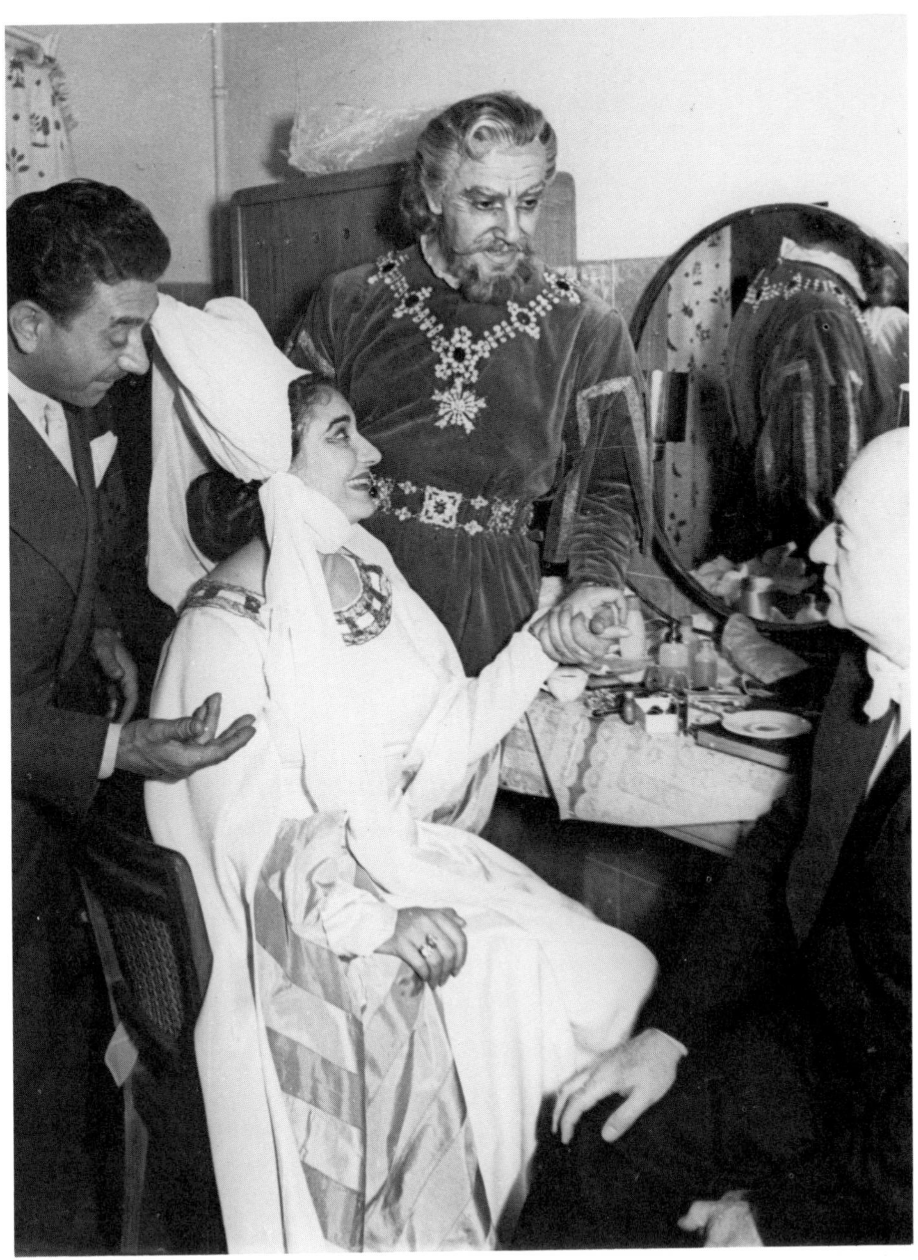

Callas relaxes in her dressing room at the Teatro Comunale, Florence, with Boris Christoff and conductor Erich Kleiber (right), before the *prima* of *Vespri,* May 26, 1951. Locchi

first directorial venture. When it was announced that Giuseppe di Stefano would co-direct, conductor Gianandrea Gavazzeni asked to be released from his contract. He stated in an interview that the theater's artistic director should have consulted him first and as a matter of principle he would not conduct.

The eighty-eight-year-old conductor Vittorio Gui agreed to step in for Gavazzeni. When a reporter asked him, "Aren't you perhaps afraid of Callas the tiger?" he replied, "Better a tiger than an ass." Gui ignored solicitous warnings from friends that he should turn over some of the routine rehearsals to an assistant, and he became ill before the opening night. Fulvio Vernizzi, artistic director of the Teatro Regio, was entrusted with the performance.

Because of problems with the lighting system on opening night, tenor Gianni Raimondi sang in near darkness for twenty minutes. Callas and Di Stefano had requested a boat for the French revelers in the Act II barcarolle scene, but the management informed them that none was available. In a November 1972 interview for Milan's *Corriere della Sera,* Callas expressed her views on directing. She stated that she had accepted the Turin engagement because she was tired of seeing melodrama massacred. She explained that today's singer has been buried alive beneath fussy staging details that do a disservice to the composer.

Callas worked quietly with the principals and chorus, urging them to limit their gestures to movements which evolve naturally from the dictates of the score, but critics found the result to be static and rigid. Only the dancing of Natalia Makarova in the Act IV ballet received unanimous praise.

Callas leaving the stage after her triumphant Scala debut in *I Vespri Siciliani,* with, left to right, Boris Christoff (Procida), conductor Victor de Sabata, and Enzo Mascherini (Monforte). Milan, December 7, 1951. Piccagliani

Singing the "Bolero" in Act V of Herbert Graf's production of *Vespri* at La Scala, Milan, December 7, 1951.
Piccagliani

Callas, Erich Kleiber, and Boris Christoff, as Creonte, during the dress rehearsal of *Orfeo ed Euridice,* Teatro della Pergola, Florence, June 1951.

Bocchi. Collection of Armando A. Bona

Danish tenor Tyge Tygeson, as Orfeo, and Callas during the world stage première of Haydn's *Orfeo ed Euridice,* June 9, 1951.

Bocchi. Collection of Armando A. Bona

Orfeo ed Euridice

CALLAS'S stage career of forty-six operas in twenty-six years included one world première—Franz Joseph Haydn's *Orfeo ed Euridice,* written in 1791. Haydn composed the work in London where it was to have had its first performance at the King's Theatre, but it never reached the première. Sir John Gallini, who was to stage it, had his royal patent withdrawn by George III on the first day of rehearsals.

Orfeo waited 160 years for its first performance, which took place at the intimate Teatro della Pergola in Florence on June 9, 1951. Euridice's elegant and florid music, ranging from high C to low A, was ideally suited to Callas's vocal capabilities. The young Danish tenor Tyge Tygeson was cast as Orfeo. He was an excellent musician and his voice had a lovely timbre, but his basically light tone was occasionally covered by the orchestra. The celebrated Bulgarian bass Boris Christoff was engaged for the role of Creonte. In the opinion of Giuseppe Pugliese (*Opera,* August 1951), Christoff "was a magnificent and imposing Creonte and his splendid and colorful voice told well in this role." The most difficult bravura aria in the score, "Al tuo seno fortunato," was performed by soprano Juliana Farkas in the brief part of the spirit. (When

Joan Sutherland sang the role of Euridice in Vienna and New York sixteen years later, she was unwilling to leave the best number in the opera to a supporting singer and appropriated the aria for herself.)

The Florentines devised an attractive production. The members of the chorus were seated in tiers behind a scrim that simulated a proscenium at the sides and top of the stage. When they had to sing, spotlights were turned on from the back of the stage and they materialized, suggesting the ornamental borders of muses on eighteenth-century music covers.

Newell Jenkins reported on the *prima* in *Musical America* (August 1951):

> Dramatically untold harm was done by the inadequate staging of Guido Salvini. Mr. Salvini arrived late for rehearsals, and when he finally began them he seemed to have little idea what the opera was about . . . Three days before the scheduled opening Mr. Salvini realized that a ballet was required, and what finally passed as the ballet defies description. On opening night a ripple of laughter greeted the Bacchantes as they cavorted happily around the dead Orfeo . . .
>
> The Euridice of Maria Meneghini Callas had more to do with the *Sicilian Vespers,* heard several nights earlier, than the classic style of Haydn. Her voice was rich and beautiful, but was often uneven and sometimes tired. Certainly the role was too heavy for her; but she sang the death aria in the second act with rare insight and fine phrasing.

Howard Taubman wrote of Callas's second and last performance as Euridice (New York *Times,* June 11, 1951): "The New York girl, of Greek parentage, who has done well in Verdi's *Sicilian Vespers* here, proved that she could manage the classic florid style with assurance. She has full control of voice in soft singing and she did coloratura passages with delicacy and accuracy." Although Radio Italiana announced a broadcast of *Orfeo* from the Teatro della Pergola, transcription discs or tapes of the performance are not known to exist.

Callas was not to sing in the première of another opera. Although it has been stated in several publications that she appeared in the world première of Manolis Kalomiris' *'O Protomastoras* (*The Master Builder*) in Athens in March 1943, the production presented on July 29, 1944, was actually a revival of a 1916 folk-opera. She was invited to create important roles in several contemporary operas, but she declined the offers.

Samuel Barber had hoped that Callas would create the title role in *Vanessa* at the Metropolitan Opera in 1958, but the première eventually went to Eleanor Steber. Callas discussed her views on modern opera and her objections to the part of Vanessa (an aging beauty who has waited twenty years for her lover's return) during a 1959 televised conversation with Sir Thomas Beecham, Victor Borge, and Edward R. Murrow:

> I do not like modern music because it's all complicated. Anything that's complicated today bothers me. You see, people go to the opera to be relaxed, to have a bath of beauty . . . I sing the old music where—as Sir Thomas Beecham said—"the melody is good." He said, "with tunes." In fact, that's the way it starts. The public has to have a tune to hold on to. Now, if the public cannot keep a tune in its head after it's heard an opera it means the opera is a flop . . .
>
> I could not feel the part [of Vanessa]. The part did not agree at all with my personality. I would have preferred—not the part of Vanessa—but the part of the other girl [Erika] . . . The part of Vanessa had nothing to do with my spiritual world.

During the Metropolitan Opera's Paris visit in 1966, Rudolf Bing invited Callas to create either of the two soprano leads for the projected March 1967 world première of Marvin David Levy's *Mourning Becomes Electra,* but Callas repeated her objections to singing in modern opera and refused. The roles of Christine and Lavinia Mannon were ultimately created by Marie Collier and Evelyn Lear, respectively.

Die Entführung aus dem Serail

CALLAS'S only appearances in a Mozart opera took place at La Scala in April 1952. Her four performances as Constanza in *Die Entführung aus dem Serail* (*The Abduction from the Seraglio*) were a critical and popular success, but she did not add another Mozart role to her repertoire. In the spring of 1955, Rudolf Bing offered her an opening-night *Lucia di Lammermoor* for the Metropolitan Opera's 1956–57 season, to be followed by a Queen of the Night in *The Magic Flute,* but he wrote in his autobiography that Callas refused to sing the Mozart opera in English.

During an informal question-and-answer session at the Juilliand School in New York, February 3, 1971, Callas stated that there was no doubt that Mozart was a great genius, but she had her reservations about his operas. She added that she preferred the period from Rossini to early Verdi. Nine months later, during one of her master classes at Juilliard, she told a soprano: "Mozart is often done on the tips of the toes, with too much fragility. It should be sung with the same frankness you sing *Trovatore* with—but in a Mozart style."

Although Mozart's *Entführung* was premièred in 1782, the 1952 production (sung in Italian) was its first mounting at La Scala. The cast,

Callas, photographed from the wings, on the small bridge in the third act of Mozart's *Die Entführung aus dem Serail,* La Scala, Milan, April 1952.

Piccagliani

led by Jonel Perlea, included Salvatore Baccaloni, opera's most famous *basso buffo* of that time, and tenor Giacinto Prandelli. The production was directed by Ettore Giannini and the costumes were by noted Argentine painter and designer Léonor Fini.

The role of Constanza makes enormous demands upon the soprano's range, agility, and security of intonation. The *tessitura* of her first aria, "Ach ich liebte," is very high and the singer is required to touch over twenty high C's and eleven high D's. The bravura piece "Martern aller Arten"—in essence a concert aria for solo voice and quartet of solo instruments—exploits both extremes of the voice. At one point the soprano must pass from high C to low B, and then leap back an octave-and-a-sixth to G.

Callas's Constanza is not known to exist in sound, but two of her broadcasts from that period are preserved on tape—a Radio Italiana concert from six weeks earlier, with a dazzling full-voice reading of the "Bell Song" from Delibes' *Lakmé,* and an extraordinary performance in Rossini's *Armida* from the same month as *Entführung*. They both clearly indicate the color, range, and flexibility of her voice. Her singing was characterized by a penetrating but not particularly warm tone, effortless, cutting high notes up to E natural, and a florid technique equal to that of any soprano documented on disc.

Constanza was the third and final role of Callas's first season at La Scala. Franco Abbiati, writing for Milan's *Corriere della Sera,* found Callas to be "a confident interpreter who was outstandingly agile and vibrant in the difficult part of Constanza." Mario Quaglia reported in the *Corriere del Teatro* (April 15, 1952) that "she dominated the stage in a memorable interpretation of Constanza: a tremendously difficult roll because of the *tessitura* and perilous acrobatism of the running passages, which she attacked and conquered with a vocal virtuosity that earned her unanimous admiration and clamorous ovations."

Peter Dragadze wrote in *Opera* (July 1952):

> The Milan public, which on the whole is not very Mozart-minded, was very enthusiastic and clamorously applauded the work at the end of each act. The production itself, which was not really of the first order, was mainly a success due to the excellent ensemble of artists, the most attractive scenery and notable playing of the or-

As Constanza in Act II of Mozart's *Die Entführung aus dem Serail,* La Scala production, April 1952. Piccagliani

A post-performance snapshot of La Scala's first *Entführung* cast, April 2, 1952. Left to right: Giacinto Prandelli (Belmonte), conductor Jonel Perlea, Callas (Constanza), stage director Ettore Giannini, Tatiana Menotti (Bionda), Nerio Bernardi (Selim), set designer Gianni Ratto, Salvatore Baccaloni (Osmin), and Petre Munteanu (Pedrillo), kneeling.

> chestra . . . Maria Callas scored yet another triumph in the part of Constanza, which even though it was completely different from the heavier *spinto* parts she has been singing at the Scala lately was rendered with delicacy and feeling, reaching a climax in the difficult aria during the second act.

Two versions of Callas's "Martern aller Arten" (both sung in Italian) exist on tape. In December 1954, Radio Italiana of Milan presented a series of concerts at the theater of the Casino in San Remo. Callas and the celebrated tenor Beniamino Gigli shared the December 27 program. "Martern aller Arten" was sung with elegance and impeccable Mozartean style. The rapid scale passages were sung lightly and each note was cleanly articulated.

—*Die Entführung aus dem Serail*—

In November 1957, Callas flew to Dallas for a benefit concert. The lengthy program included her second and last concert performance of the *Entführung* aria. During the orchestra rehearsal, which was taped in its entirety, she sang the piece with the same fluency and brillance demonstrated in the San Remo concert, but her interpretation was now more dramatic. Only the sustained high C near the end lacked the security evident in her earlier version. Callas was famous for being unsparing with herself in rehearsals and the preserved rehearsal is a remarkable documentation of her willingness to sing an entire program with her normal intensity—frequently repeating taxing phrases at full voice—so that the correct balance between voice and orchestra would be achieved.

Armida

IN the spring of 1952, Callas sang three performances of Gioacchino Rossini's opera *Armida* at the Florence May Festival. For power and beauty of voice, technical brilliance, intensity and range (from low G to high E), the April 26 broadcast of *Armida* is the most phenomenal of the approximately eighty Callas opera performances—including commercial recordings—known to exist in sound. (In the feature article of the Carnegie Hall program for May 1973, soprano Renata Scotto incorrectly stated, "When Callas did [Armida] she made many changes, many cuts to suit her voice." Callas performed the opera as written, except for the high E flats and E's, which were interpolated.) Callas enjoyed singing challenging new roles for receptive audiences and she was a particular favorite of the Florentine opera public. She had sung in her first performances of *Norma, La Traviata,* and *I Vespri Siciliani* in Florence, as well as the world stage première of Haydn's *Orfeo ed Euridice*.

Armida, dating from 1817, belongs to a group of musical antiques—the *opere serie*—that reached both their culmination and demise during Rossini's lifetime. Plots were usually based on mythological or historical subjects and it was not unusual for women to portray male characters.

As the enchantress Armida, Florence, April 1952. Locchi

Act II of Alberto Savinio's production of Rossini's *Armida,* Teatro Comunale, April 1952.
Carlo A. Schiavi

The *opere serie* of Rossini, most notably *Semiramide, Armida, Otello,* and *La Donna del Lago,* consist of a series of intricate arias, duets, and ensembles of great elegance and beauty, created to display the vocal accomplishments of the singers. In the duets, identical music was often assigned successively to both singers, encouraging an "anything you can sing, I can sing better" atmosphere on stage. By 1860, with the advent of Donizetti's dramatically more viable operas, Meyerbeer's spectacles, and

the more vigorous and direct appeal of Verdi's early works, the *opere serie* had almost disappeared from the opera stages.

Six rarely heard Rossini works were revived for the 1952 Florence May Festival and the noted choreographer Léonide Massine was hired to choreograph the ballet for *Armida*—the only Italian opera for which Rossini originally provided ballet music. Massine systematically had his ballets filmed during his career and his archives are now housed in the Dance Collection of the New York Public Library at Lincoln Center. Two cans of film are tantalizingly labeled "Armida 1952," but the twenty-eight-year-old Callas does not appear in the footage. Although the dramatic action requires that Armida remain on stage during the ballet, it was not necessary for Callas to be present during a filmed ballet rehearsal.

In reviewing the *prima,* Newell Jenkins wrote of the title role (*Musical America,* May 1952): "Where are such roulades, such trills, runs, leaps, such speed and fireworks demanded of the singer? One can readily believe that no one today save Miss Callas, undisputedly the finest woman singer on the Italian stage, could possibly negotiate the incredibly difficult part and make it sound like music."

Vocal highlights of the evening included the finale of the first scene, in which Callas executed a dazzling series of runs from the chest register up to high C, followed by an enormous high E. In the love duet "Vacilla a quegli accenti"—one of Rossini's most sensuous duets—Callas lightened her voice and employed her most seductive tones. She was admirably partnered by Francesco Albanese, one of four principal tenors in the performance. Albanese sang all the florid passages easily and with a rich, ringing voice.

In addition to negotiating the written difficulties of Armida's aria "D'amore al dolce impero," which include runs down to low G in chest and a chromatic scale from middle C to high B flat and down again, Callas interpolated high D's in her embellishments. During Armida's twelve-minute final scene, Callas pushed her voice to its limits, spanning almost three octaves. Armida's revilement of Rinaldo because of his infidelity, "E l'alma tua nutrita fu ognor di crudeltà" ("And your soul was always nourished by cruelty"), was delivered with torrents of sound, as Callas hurtled through some of the most florid music in operatic literature. Armida's final promise of vengeance was sung with knife-thrust attacks for key words, acidulous high notes and open chest tones.

Andrew Porter wrote in *Opera* (July 1952):

> It is possible to feel that the phrases beneath the florid passages are far too much overlaid with ornament; but it was impossible to regret it when Maria Callas was singing them. This American-born Greek

> soprano . . . deserves fully the considerable reputation she has won, for she must be one of the most exciting singers on the stage today. Her presence is imperious, her coloratura not piping and pretty, but powerful and dramatic. It must be noted that a nasty edge crept into the tone from time to time; but when she sailed up a two-octave chromatic scale and cascaded down again (in "D'amore al dolce impero," the aria from the second act) the effect was electrifying. Her brilliance continually startled and delighted, throughout the opera. But whenever tenderness and sensuous charm were required, she was less moving. This seems to be her present limitation; it may well disappear quite soon.

The opera did not receive another major production until the generally excellent revival in Venice (April 1970) with Cristina Deutekom and Pietro Bottazzo. On December 27, 1954, Callas included the aria "D'amore al dolce impero" on a concert program shared with Beniamino Gigli and broadcast from the theater of the Casino in San Remo. The aria was sung with even greater authority and tonal nuance than in the Florence broadcast, but the interpolated high D's were omitted. In the summer of 1960, she recorded the aria for EMI, but the selection has not been issued to date.

Lucia di Lammermoor

CALLAS sang her first performance of Gaetano Donizetti's *Lucia di Lammermoor* on June 10, 1952, at the Palacio de Bellas Artes in Mexico City. During the next eight years, she was to appear in over forty performances of the opera in thirteen cities and five countries and record it twice for EMI. At least seven of her Lucias were broadcast and exist in sound: Mexico City (1952); Milan (1954); Berlin (1955); Naples, Vienna, and New York (1956); and Rome (a Radio Italiana studio performance, 1957).

During a 1967 broadcast interview with Edward Downes, Callas recalled her first Lucia:

> Very sure, the first Mexico performance. Absolutely sure, beautiful top notes and all that, but it was not yet the role. Of course it was lovely. I remind you that Lucia was the same soprano that used to sing *Norma* and *Pirata* and *Sonnambula.* So you see, it is not a light role. It is a *drammatico-coloratura.* In fact, Lucia is a very low role and light sopranos have to put the third act high, because it's terribly *centrale,* as they say.

In the Mexico *Lucia,* Callas sang the Act I "Regnava nel silenzio"

Lucia di Lammermoor, Act I, scene 2, Teatro San Carlo, Naples, March 22, 1956. Callas with Anna Maria Borrelli (Alisa). Troncone and "Quando rapito in estasi" with an enormous voice and rich tone. She chose standard embellishments which took her up to high D's. During the first act duet in which Edgardo and Lucia state that only death will divide their hearts, Giuseppe di Stefano, cast as Edgardo, suffered a memory lapse which divided their voices, and Callas sang the final seven measures as a solo. Her singing was particularly poignant in the Act II section beginning "Soffriva nel pianto" ("I suffered in tears"). The "Sextet" was only adequately performed. Almost all the singers, with the exception of Callas, were slightly at odds with the accompaniment and each other.

The "Mad Scene" was well sung, but the broadcast microphone was placed directly above the prompter and the first half of the scene nearly became a duet for the radio audience. Callas's variations with the flute at the end of "Ardon gl'incensi" were traditional and identical with those used by Toti dal Monte (La Scala's only Lucia in the 1920s). They included an arpeggio up to high C, octave scales followed by staccato high B flats, downward runs from high C, a vocalise on the "Verrano a te" melody from Act I, and a sustained trill followed by a high E flat. After the "Mad Scene" she received a twenty-minute ovation and sixteen curtain calls—a record for the Palacio de Bellas Artes. The radio announcer explained that he had to shout to be heard over the demonstration in the auditorium. He also reported that Callas was being applauded by the musicians in the pit and by the chorus backstage.

Callas's first *Lucias* in Italy took place at the Teatro Comunale in Florence at the beginning of 1953. Immediately following her engagement, EMI committed her dramatic characterization to disc. The other principals, under the baton of Tullio Serafin, included Di Stefano and Tito Gobbi. The recording was the first in a series of complete operas uniting these three singers. The recorded version by Callas and Di Stefano is generally similar to that of the Mexican broadcast from eight months earlier, but Callas's voice is slightly lighter in quality in the recording and there is a greater authority in the projection of the text. Di Stefano's recorded interpretation is less impetuous and there are fewer interpolated high notes.

Milanese audiences first heard Callas's Lucia in January 1954. The new Scala production was directed and conducted by Herbert von Karajan, with Di Stefano as Edgardo and Rolando Panerai as Enrico. The sets, consisting largely of impressionistic backcloths in a fixed framework, were by Gianni Ratto. Callas was the first dramatic soprano to essay the role at La Scala in the twentieth century. The previous interpreters included the light-voice sopranos Toti dal Monte, Lina Pagliughi, and Margherita Carosio.

Peter Dragadze wrote in *Opera* (March 1954):

> After *Medea* the greatest success of this season so far has been *Lucia* with Maria Callas in the name part. Callas again had a great personal triumph, holding the public in suspense with the breathtaking clarity and agility of her coloratura, which contrasted with the almost contralto quality of her voice in the recitatives and first act arias. Her mad scene produced an emotional thrill that few other living singers are capable of, and the unusual combination of a dramatic voice, with a soprano *leggiero* "top," gave a completely new aspect to this role.

During the curtain calls after the second act—even before the "Mad Scene"—flowers rained down on the stage. "She picked them up one by one," Cynthia Jolly reported in *Opera News,* "in a graceful allusion to the coming Mad Scene, in which she outdid many a stage Ophelia." At the beginning of the "Mad Scene" she appeared at the top of the staircase with her hair disheveled. She had a glazed stare and seemed to be both mentally and physically exhausted. She did not hold a dagger. She discussed the omission of the traditional dagger in an interview with Kenneth Harris (*Observer Review,* February 8, 1970): "I dislike violence, and I find it artistically inefficient. Where it is necessary to include the shedding of blood, the suggestion of the action is more moving than the exhibition of it. I always eliminated the knife when singing Lucia: I thought it was a useless and old-fashioned business, that the action could get in the way of the art, and realism interfere with the truth."

In the fall of 1955, La Scala gave two performances of *Lucia* in Berlin. The principals and conductor of the original 1954 series were reassembled for the Berlin Festival performances. The Berlin broadcast of September 29 is easily the most inspired total performance of the Callas *Lucias* preserved on tape. She was at her best and her interpretation was a nearly perfect fusion of music and drama. Her heart-rending delivery of the Act II lines beginning "Soffriva nel pianto" was especially moving.

Di Stefano was in phenomenal voice and his handling of the text and general artistry rivaled Callas's finest singing. Rolando Panerai's tone was a little dry and harsh, but it was appropriate to the insensitive character of Enrico. Perhaps the greatest star of the evening was Karajan. He revealed Donizetti's score to be a masterpiece of operatic orchestration and the orchestral playing was profoundly beautiful throughout the entire performance. The Berlin public greeted the conclusion of each scene with thunderous ovations and the stamping of feet. The powerfully sung "Sextet" was encored and Karajan opened the traditional cut in the Act II finale. The Scala *Lucia* is apparently the only production in which Callas sang this music.

In March 1959, Callas re-recorded *Lucia* in stereo for EMI. Her interpretation had become softer and more elegant since her first recording of the role in 1953, but both she and Ferruccio Tagliavini, as Edgardo, were taxed by the highest passages. Her final Lucias took place in Dallas, Texas, the following November. The entire production, borrowed from Covent Garden, was designed and staged by Franco Zeffirelli. George Leslie wrote in *Musical America:* "Miss Callas made Lucia not the usual display for the coloratura soprano but a rare study of human emotions. Although not at her vocal best, she created a memorable character and was rewarded by a standing ovation on November 8."

Callas's first Lucia, Palacio de Bellas Artes, Mexico City, June 10, 1952. The principals, including Giuseppe di Stefano at center, wait for the applause to subside after the "Sextet." Luis Quintero

Callas singing the "Mad Scene" for the first time on stage, Mexico City, June 10, 1952. Luis Quintero

The later Lucia, Teatro San Carlo, Naples, March 22, 1956: Edgardo (Gianni Raimondi) tells Lucia of his imminent departure for France.

Troncone

Enrico (Rolando Panerai) asserts that he will be disgraced and ruined unless Lucia agrees to the marriage which he has arranged. Naples, March 1956.

Troncone

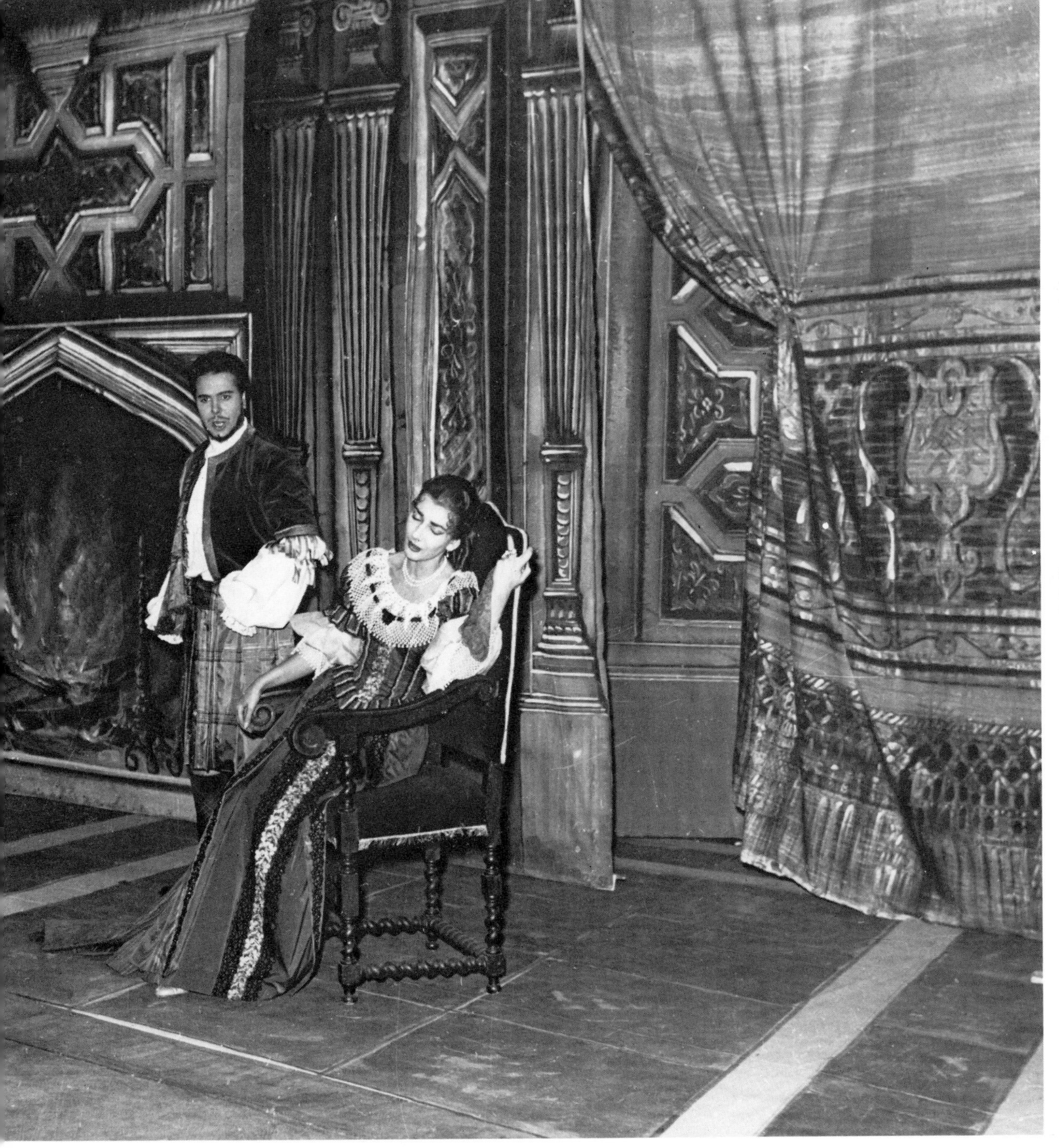

Lucia signs the marriage document. Naples, March 1956. Troncone

Edgardo demands the return of his ring and reviles Lucia for her apparent unfaithfulness. Naples, March 1956. Troncone

The "Mad Scene," La Scala, Milan, January 1954. Piccagliani

Rigoletto

AT the end of Callas's 1951 summer season in Mexico City, Antonio Caraza Campos, director of the Opera Nacional, asked her to learn Gilda and Lucia, both new roles, for the following season. She agreed, but upon returning a year later, she asked him to drop the Gildas from her schedule of appearances. She had added two taxing new roles to her repertory in the previous ten weeks (*The Abduction from the Seraglio* at La Scala and *Armida* at the Teatro Comunale in Florence), and she was exhausted from her heavy schedule, which also included *Norma, La Traviata, I Puritani,* and her first *Lucias*. Caraza Campos told her that she had signed a contract to sing the new roles at the highest fee ever paid to an artist in Mexico City, and that it was impossible to change the schedule.

The *Rigolettos* were under-rehearsed and only Callas's intuitive musicianship and the Mexican public's unrestrained enthusiasm for Giuseppe di Stefano's voice kept the first performance from becoming a critical and musical disaster. The entire cast, with the exception of Callas, indulged in unwritten "coronas" (lingering on high notes), often through the entrances of another singer. The prompter cued her throughout the performance, but possibly not since Robert Merrill sang his first Figaro at the Metropolitan and Ezio Pinza and Salvatore Baccaloni playfully fed him the wrong cues has a major singer had to work as hard in a new role in order to enter at the right time.

Vocally Callas was ideal for the Gilda set down by Verdi in his score. Although the role of Gilda has traditionally been sung in this century by high lyric and coloratura sopranos—most notably by Melba, Tetrazzini, Galli-Curci, Dal Monte, Pons, and Sayão—much of the score requires a flexible voice with strong middle and low notes, rather than soft high notes. (Toscanini considered the dramatic-soprano voice of Zinka Milanov to be the appropriate weight for Gilda.)

Callas employed a clear, youthful sound for her opening scene with baritone Piero Campolonghi. She emphasized the tragic elements of the opera and a feeling of sadness pervaded her singing. During a 1972 master class at the Juilliard School in New York City, Callas told a young soprano who was working on the "Caro nome," "Give it more freedom. You have to be a girl who is passionately in love. True, Gilda is still a virgin, but one should not be too cutesy, because of what happens to her later. Don't forget, she sacrifices her life for love."

In the rapid Act II vocal exchanges with the baritone, Callas's rhythmic precision and meticulous attention to every accent in the score gave an added feeling of tension and urgency to the role. When the Duke suddenly appeared in the garden, Callas vocally conveyed the impression of genuine terror. Upon recognizing him as the man with whom she had fallen in love, her voice became warmer and "Uscite" ("Leave me") was uttered without conviction. In the "Caro nome," each trill was cleanly articulated and approached as written—from the note above—instead of in the traditional fashion of trilling on the principal note. Callas ended the aria with a secure high E. (Three years later, when she recorded the opera with Tullio Serafin, she omitted the unwritten high note, but included the rarely sung low B in the middle of the aria.)

The performance reached the middle of the last act without any serious mishaps, but beginning with the storm scene, it turned into musical chaos. The Maddalena and Sparafucile fell behind the orchestral accompaniment and Callas had a choice of three different beats on which to sing her lines. After falling behind the accompaniment herself, she left the other singers behind and kept up with the tempo set by the conductor.

Di Stefano's ebullient performance, marred only by flatting on the high notes, earned him most of the ovations of the evening. Solomon Kahan wrote (*Musical America,* September 1952): "As an anti-climax [of the season] came a pedestrian performance of *Rigoletto,* for Mr. Campolonghi, the jester, was neither vocally nor histrionically up to Verdi's demands. Mr. Di Stefano's Duke, far from outstanding, and Miss Callas's Gilda, not an ideal role for her, did not improve the situation." After two performances of *Rigoletto* in five days, Callas dropped the opera from her repertoire. Her subsequent recording with Tito Gobbi and Di Stefano found her more confident of the part, but the recording failed to approach the spontaneity and variety of vocal colors of her first stage performance.

The first of Callas's two stage appearances as Gilda in *Rigoletto.* Act II, the end of "Caro nome." Palacio de Bellas Artes, Mexico City, June 17, 1952.

Luis Quintero

Act III: Gilda tells Rigoletto (Piero Campolonghi) of the young man who followed her home from church and her subsequent abduction in the plaintive aria "Tutte le feste." At her first performance, Callas, suffering one of the few memory lapses of her career, began the aria with the words to the second stanza.

Luis Quintero

The "Quartet," Act IV, *Rigoletto,* Mexico City, June 1952. Callas, confronted with the problem of appearing believable in male attire, chose to remain enveloped in a voluminous cloak.

Luis Quintero

Macbeth

GIUSEPPE VERDI'S *Macbeth* was selected for the opening night of La Scala's 1952–53 season. It had not been heard in Milan since Alexander Sved and Gina Cigna sang the two principal parts in 1938. The cast of the revival, conducted by Victor de Sabata, included Callas in the only stage appearances of her career as Lady Macbeth, Enzo Mascherini in the title role, Gino Penno as Macduff, and Italo Tajo in the bass role of Banquo. Carl Ebert directed and Nicola Benois created the imposing, naturalistic sets which took up the complete length and width of the stage and included a twenty-foot-high drawbridge in the first act. The Act III ballet which Verdi composed in 1865 for the Paris première was choreographed as a classical *pas de deux* for the king and queen of the witches.

The boxes inside the theater were decorated with clusters of carnations for the December 7 *prima,* and an enterprising haberdasher's firm bestowed on each male box-subscriber a gift-packaged piece of fabric sufficient for an elegant dress shirt. Gisella Seldon-Goth reported in *Musical Courier* that Macbeth was the first opera to be televised in Italy. The performance was also broadcast and now exists in sound.

Callas as Lady Macbeth, Act I, La Scala, Milan, December 1952. Piccagliani

Although several reviews stated that Callas was not in her best voice, tapes of the broadcast fail to reveal any vocal mishaps or problems. She encountered scattered booing during the evening. "Paid booers," was her explanation quoted in *Newsweek*, "paid by enemies of mine. They just made fans for me and created my triumph."

Callas's Lady Macbeth was a remarkable achievement. Although there have been more than twenty major sopranos and mezzo-sopranos who have sung the role after Callas with varying degrees of success—most notably Christa Ludwig, Birgit Nilsson, Leonie Rysanek, Anja Silja, Gwyneth Jones, Pauline Tinsley, Leyla Gencer, and Inge Borkh—few have had the vocal weight, agility, range, and acting ability to meet all of the demands of the part. The formidable difficulties of the role include two-octave runs, full-voice coloratura passages, trills in all registers, powerful chest tones down to low B, and a *pianissimo* high D flat.

A letter from Verdi to Salvatore Cammarano, who was producing *Macbeth* in Naples, contains the composer's much-quoted description of the quality of voice he wanted for Lady Macbeth:

> . . . I want Lady Macbeth to be ugly and evil . . . Lady Macbeth's voice should be hard, stifled and dark . . . Tell them that the most important numbers in the opera are the duet between Macbeth and Lady Macbeth and the sleepwalking scene. If these two numbers fail, then the entire opera will fail. And these two numbers definitely must not be sung. They must be acted and declaimed, with hollow, masked voices. Otherwise it will make no effect.

Callas's conception of the role was essentially the same. She wrote in an article for *Life* (April 20, 1959): "For Lady Macbeth the voice should be heavy, thick and strong. The role, and therefore the voice, should have an atmosphere of darkness." She portrayed Lady Macbeth as a cold, ambitious, and evil woman who was also capable of showing compassion for her husband after he became deranged.

When Lady Macbeth first appears, she is reading the letter from her husband in which he tells of the witches' prophesies. Callas declaimed the letter slowly, as if Lady Macbeth were trying to understand the full import of the message. The aria "Vieni! t'affretta! accendere ti vo' quel freddo core!" ("Come! Hasten! That I may inflame your cold heart!") was taken at a deliberate tempo and sung with a dark, cutting tone devoid of any warmth. The ensuing cabaletta, "Or tutte sorgete," in which Lady Macbeth invokes the spirits of hell to aid in her contemplated murder of the king, was attacked with fierce determination.

"Duncano sarà qui? . . . qui? . . . Qui la notte!" ("Duncan will be here? . . . here? . . . Here this night!") was at first delivered in a preoccupied manner and then exultantly, as Lady Macbeth realizes that power lies in her grasp, since King Duncan will sleep beneath her roof. In the duet following the murder of Duncan, Lady Macbeth tells her husband to return the knife to the king's chamber and smear the faces of the drugged guards with blood as he passes, so that it will appear that they are the murderers. At first, Callas's tones were scornful and cajoling, but as Macbeth continued to express his fears, she conveyed Lady Macbeth's impatience with sounds that became increasingly acidulous.

A highlight of the performance was her lusty, heavily accented rendition of the drinking song, "Si colmi il calice," in the banquet scene. One of Carl Ebert's most effective touches came in this scene. Six flaming chandeliers and innumerable torches threw their flickering lights on the scene, thereby intensifying the impact of the apparition of Banquo's ghost. Callas employed an appropriately harsh, dark sound for most of her solo lines, but in the powerful ensembles where the beauty of the melody takes precedence over the text, her voice poured out with a clear, attractive tone.

The performance reached its climax with Lady Macbeth's sleepwalking scene, which is in essence a mad scene. The *scena* was not presented as a complete vocal piece, but rather expressed as a series of unrelated states of mind, with each phrase having its own vocal color. "Una macchia è qui tuttora" ("A stain is still there") was uttered as if in revulsion or disgust. The lines beginning "Un guerrier così codardo?" ("A warrior and thus afraid?") were sung with the same taunting vocal inflections which she employed in the first act duet with Macbeth. For the repetition of the words "Chi poteva in quel vegliardo tanto sangue immaginar?" ("Who could have imagined there was so much blood in that old man?"), Callas suggested Lady Macbeth's terror with rhythmic accentuation of each syllable. The line beginning "Di Fiffe il sire" ("The Thane of Fife") was sung with a thin, disembodied tone. "Di sangue umano sa qui sempre" ("Forever stained with human blood") was half-spoken with a husky, almost eerie quality, as if Lady Macbeth were terrified that someone might hear her.

In the lyrical section beginning "A letto, a letto," in which Lady Macbeth believes she is urging her husband to bed after the murder, Callas's voice took on a pleading, more sympathetic quality. The scene ended with Callas successfully touching the difficult high D flat with the merest thread of sound, as specified in the score. She received a thunderous ovation and seven solo curtain calls.

If Callas's portrayal of Lady Macbeth did not exist in sound, it would be difficult to determine from the reviews just what her performance was like on opening night. Peter Hoffer reported in *Music and Musicians* that "Callas was not in her best voice and at one point was even whistled at." In the opinion of Mario Quaglia (*Corriere del Teatro*), "Maria Meneghini Callas bestowed on the satanic character of Lady Macbeth the rare gift of a crystal-clear voice of astonishing range." Signe Scanzoni wrote in *Opera News*, ". . . We saw Maria Meneghini-Callas as a Lady Macbeth whose vocal cords apparently must have been granted some extra strength which gives this voice an almost-inhuman quality. Without the slightest attempt to act the part, Callas won success and disapproval in the true Italian manner." According to Peter Dragadze (*Opera*), "Callas gave her part the depth and feeling that only she now can give to such a dramatic role, with a truly heart-rending climax to the sleepwalking scene . . ."

After only five performances at La Scala, the role left Callas's active repertoire. She was scheduled to make her San Francisco Opera debut in *Lucia* on September 27, 1957, followed by her first United States *Macbeth* on the fifteenth of October. On the first of September she cabled director Kurt Herbert Adler and told him that she was ill and might not be able to debut as scheduled. She consulted two doctors and they told her that she was not strong enough to sing or even travel. Two weeks before her first performance, she notified Adler that it would be impossible for her to appear at the scheduled time, but she would be able to fulfill the second half of her contract in October. Two days later, Antonietta Stella also canceled her contract because of illness. Callas was never to sing with the San Francisco Opera. Adler stated that Callas was fired and he filed a complaint with the American Guild of Musical

Artists. He managed to save his season by engaging Leonie Rysanek for Lady Macbeth and Leyla Gencer for the role of Lucia. Rysanek, in addition to singing her scheduled performances of *Turandot* and *Ariadne auf Naxos,* also substituted for Stella in *Aida* and *Un Ballo in Maschera,* singing the latter opera in German.

For her third consecutive season at the Metropolitan, in 1959, Callas was to appear in *Tosca, Macbeth,* and *La Traviata.* The *Macbeth,* with Leonard Warren in the title role, was to be her first new production in New York. She agreed to the choice of opera but objected to alternating the light role of Violetta with the heavy part of Lady Macbeth. Callas refused to accept the sequence of the roles and Bing canceled her contract. Twelve years later, Bing wrote in his autobiography: "I have always felt that the basic dissatisfaction was the tour, where she would have to sing in many cities off the international publicity circuit, under conditions she knew would be undesirable."

On February 3, 1971, during a question-and-answer session at the Juilliard School, Callas expressed regret that record companies had not recorded her in a complete *Macbeth* or *Il Pirata.* The arias "Vieni! t'affretta!," "La luce langue," and "Una macchia" (the sleepwalking scene), recorded by EMI in September 1958, constitute the only commercially available documentation of her Lady Macbeth.

Lady Macbeth welcomes her guests with a drinking song. *Macbeth,* Act II, scene 3. La Scala, Milan, December 1952. Piccagliani

As Medea, Royal Opera House, London, June 1959. David Sim

Medea

CALLAS first sang the title role of Luigi Cherubini's *Medea* at the Teatro Comunale in Florence on May 7, 1953. The opera remained in her active repertoire for nine years and she sang the part of the Colchian princess more than thirty times in seven cities. In September 1957, she recorded it at La Scala, under the direction of Tullio Serafin, for Mercury Records. Tapes exist of performances given in Milan (1953 and 1961), Dallas (1958), and London (1959). Although tapes with the attribution "Florence 1953" are in circulation, probably all of them are derived from a tape in poor sound of the 1953 Scala broadcast.

Cherubini's *Médée,* closely based on Euripides' tragedy, was premièred in Paris in 1797. Although it met with a lukewarm reception and was not revived in Paris, it quickly became a favorite, in translation, of German audiences. It contained spoken dialogue in its original form. In 1855, Franz Lachner set the spoken recitatives to music in the style of Cherubini for a performance at Frankfurt-am-Main. Since then it has invariably been given in German in Lachner's purely sung version or in an Italian translation of the Lachner edition.

Medea is a heroic role requiring incredible vocal stamina and control. The soprano must sustain a high *tessitura* for long stretches and then suddenly swoop down for low phrases in chest voice. Great interpreters of Medea have always been rare. In recent years only Eileen Farrell, Magda Olivero, and Leonie Rysanek have had notable successes in the part.

A few months before her final appearances as Medea, Callas discussed her approach to the role with Derek Prouse (London *Sunday Times,* March 19, 1961): "This opera is not *bel canto* but recitative and theatre—straight acting, speaking with the music. The strength of Cherubini's opera is not the arias but the *recitativi* . . . and if we had done it in the classical style we could never have brought it to life: there would have been no fire to it. The way I saw Medea was the way I feel it: fiery, apparently calm but very intense. The happy time with Jason is past; now she is devoured by misery and fury."

A large festival audience was present for Callas's first *Medea* at the Teatro Comunale. Gisella Seldon-Goth reported (*Musical Courier,* June 1953): "Her powerful voice and intense dedication to the exacting role gave tragic grandeur to the figure of Medea. In her final scene, while sacrificing her sons to a relentless thirst for revenge, she found accents of true poignancy."

The three Florence *Medeas,* led by Vittorio Gui, coincided with the emergence of Callas as an international star. Her interpretation, hailed by the late Herbert Weinstock as "one of the great operatic characterizations of this century" (*The World of Opera,* 1962), was the first in a series of neglected or totally forgotten operas which she turned into box-office successes through the sheer magnetism of her stage presence and her interpretive gifts. Early in 1949 in Venice, she caused a sensation by singing the bel canto role of Elvira in *I Puritani* during a series of performances as Brünnhilde in *Die Walküre.* Her Florence *Medeas*—presented between two series of *Lucias* in Catania and Rome—proved again that she was truly a vocal phenomenon who could pass successfully from high florid roles to heavy dramatic parts.

While preparing for the Cherubini opera, Callas decided that it was imperative for her to begin dieting. She weighed about two hundred pounds and only by shading her neck with dark makeup could she suggest the gaunt jaw-line which she felt was necessary for dramatic roles such as Medea. In a 1967 broadcast interview she recalled her first *Medeas* and her decision to lose weight:

> I was doing *Medea* then and . . . my first instinct was saying that the face is too fat and I can't stand it. Because I needed the chin for expression in certain very hard phrases and cruel phrases, or tense phrases. And I felt—as a woman of the theater that I was and am—that I needed these neck lines and the chin lines to be very thin and very pronounced. So I was annoyed, I darkened the color and all that, but it's nonsense. You can't *do* that . . . And then I was tired of playing a game like—for instance—playing a beautiful young woman and I was a heavy, uncomfortable woman to move around . . . And I felt, now, if I'm going to do things right—I studied all my life to put things right musically—why don't I just diet and put myself into a certain condition that I'm presentable.

Callas's first *Medea* in Milan took place on December 10, 1953. The only previous production at La Scala (the Italian première) had been during the 1909–10 season. At that time it met with a frigid press reception, although Puccini, who was present at the *prima,* declared that *Medea* was "a real masterpiece." The cast for the 1953 revival included Fedora Barbieri as Neris and Gino Penno as Jason. The great Italian conductor Victor de Sabata had been scheduled to conduct, but ill health forced him to cancel ten days before the first performance. Leonard Bernstein was in Italy for a series of orchestral engagements and La Scala officials pleaded with him to step in for De Sabata. Although he was exhausted from his long concert tour and had acute bronchitis, he examined the totally unfamiliar score, fell in love with it, and agreed to conduct it.

Bernstein felt that cuts should be made, including some in Medea's part, and he was worried about his first meeting with Callas, who, he had been told, could be difficult about changes made in a score. Years later, during a conversation with John Gruen, he recalled the first rehearsal (*Opera News,* September 1972): "Then came the famous meeting with Callas. To my absolute amazement, she understood immediately the dramatic reasons for the transposition of scenes and numbers, and the cutting out of her aria in the second act. We got along famously—it was perfect. She understood everything *I* wanted, and I understood everything *she* wanted."

During the five years which separated Callas's *Medeas* in Milan and her famous 1958 performances in Dallas, her vocal interpretation changed considerably. At La Scala her Medea was basically an evil, cruel, and somewhat shrewish woman. Some of the jagged vocal lines were not entirely in her voice and lachrymose and whining sounds were produced occasionally without apparent dramatic justification. Much of her portrayal was based on sheer vocal power and the majority of the recitatives were hurled out with unmitigated force. In Dallas she presented a more touching and sympathetic characterization. Her Medea was no longer a cold-blooded murderess, but rather an unjustly wronged woman, abandoned and left to die in disgrace far from her native country. Her pleas to Creonte and Jason were more eloquent and convincing. In the recitatives, only the most important words and phrases were stressed and her infinitely varied tone coloration conveyed every shift of emotion.

Callas was in phenomenally glorious voice in Dallas. It is difficult to imagine greater performances of *Medea.* However, on evidence of the tapes, a few of the high, expansive lines at La Scala were even more thrillingly sung. Particularly memorable in the 1953 *Medea* was the sweep and breath-taking security of the sequential phrase "O Dei del ciel" ("O gods of heaven") in the Act III aria "Del fiero duol," the soaring lines beginning "Atre Furie, volate a me" ("Black Furies, fly to me"), and the staggering power of her final words to Jason, "Al sacro fiume io vo', colà t'aspetta l'ombra mia!" ("I go to the sacred river: there my shade will await you").

The second half of the aria "Del fier duol che il cor me frange" ("Over the proud grief that breaks my heart"), which was deleted at La Scala, was included in an abbreviated version in the Dallas performances, as it had been in the Mercury recording. Gino Penno, the Jason in the Scala broadcast, gave one of the finest performances of his short career, but his singing was not in a class with that of Canadian tenor Jon Vickers, the Jason in the Dallas performances.

In June 1959, Callas sang her only Medeas at Covent Garden. The opera had not been heard in London since 1870 when Terese Tietjens sang the title role. Covent Garden borrowed the Dallas production, which had been designed by John Tsarouchis and staged by Alexis Minotis of the Greek National Theater of Athens. The cast included Jon Vickers and bass Nicola Zaccaria, both of whom had sung with Callas in Dallas. Even though seats were the highest price ever at the Royal Opera House, Londoners waited in line for four days for the tickets to go on sale and the five performances were sold out in a few hours after the box office opened. The final performance was attended by Queen Elizabeth.

George Louis Mayer, in a lengthy review of the second *Medea,* wrote of the visual aspect of Callas's characterization (*American Record Guide,* August 1959):

> From her first appearance, standing between two huge pillars, and wrapped in a huge cape which exposes nothing but her eyes, heavily rimmed with black and filled with well-composed hatred to her last, when the temple in which she has murdered her children tumbles to the ground showing her in a snake-entwined chariot with their corpses at her feet, Callas builds her performance into one powerful line of ever-increasing tension. It is the kind of performance which spoils one for anything less from the opera stage.
>
> Huge flowing capes follow her movements and illuminate her moods, creating images which haunt the memory. A cape is gathered together with a sweep of the arm while she stalks the stage plotting her next maneuver. It stretches behind her while she bends and sways imploringly to Creon for a little time to spend with her children—and time to consolidate her hatred into one devastating course. Its movements accompany her deceitful tenderness to Jason as she strokes his body with caressing fingers which a moment before were clenched into fists. Again, it coils behind her like a serpent as, kneeling, she sways forward, slapping the ground with the palms of her hands, praying to her gods for the strength to execute the most monstrous of her plans—that of killing the children—just after having yielded to tenderness and mercy in her first attempt to take their lives in one of the most moving scenes of the opera. The manner in which she pushed them off as they appeared and ran to her with her chilling cries of *Lontan! Lontan, serpenti! via da me!* and then gradually calmed herself to the beginning of *O figli miei* showed Callas at the peak of her powers and illustrated her dramatic range at its fullest, all within a moment . . .

And just as it is with her broad movements and the character she creates as a whole, so is it with the details. Her eyes seemingly can match the thought of the moment and reveal the next move simultaneously. She can tower as a pillar of outraged fury one moment and lie in a heap the next. Part of her plea to Creon is sung from the floor and addressed to his big toe. In addition, the range of her hand movements, already so celebrated in all her roles, is given full play in *Medea*. She can even make and wave a fist, an action few divas could afford to make.

For several years, Callas had wanted to sing *Medea* in the ancient amphitheater of Epidaurus. In August 1961, she appeared with the Greek National Opera Company in two performances of the opera in the open-air theater, before audiences estimated at twenty thousand each night. Callas donated her fee to a scholarship fund for young singers and the city of Athens bestowed on her their Gold Medal. Her final *Medeas* took place in Milan in May and June of 1962. They were to be her last appearances at La Scala.

Callas, with Fedora Barbieri as Neris, during the dress rehearsal for her first *Medea,* Florence, May 1953. The negative for this photograph, along with most of the photographic documentation of Callas's appearances in Florence, was destroyed in the flood of 1966, and only scattered prints are now preserved in private collections. Levi. Collection of Santiago Rodríguez

Medea at the Teatro dell'Opera, Rome, January 1955. Medea pleads with Creon (Boris Christoff) to allow her to remain in Corinth one more day. Oscar Savio

Medea, London, June 1959: Callas's use of the jaw and neck lines for hard or cruel phrases.
London Express News and Features

The incomparable hands.
London Express News and Features

La Scala, Milan, December 1961, Act I: "Dei tuoi figli." Medea entreats Jason (Jon Vickers) to return to her. Piccagliani

Callas as Alceste, queen of Pharae, La Scala, Milan, April 1954. Piccagliani

Alceste

CALLAS considered the operatic season of 1953–54 to be her crowning year at La Scala. Although opening night honors went to Renata Tebaldi, who received a new production of Catalani's *La Wally,* Callas, who had opened the two previous seasons, could hardly have felt slighted. She had been promised three new productions with world-famous conductors: Cherubini's *Medea* with Leonard Bernstein (substituting for the ailing Victor de Sabata), Donizetti's *Lucia di Lammermoor* with Herbert von Karajan, and Christoph Willibald Gluck's *Alceste* with Carlo Maria Giulini.

In her first two Scala seasons, Callas had divided the Milanese public into two camps. Her detractors said that her voice was ugly and she could not maintain the same tonal quality from one phrase to the next. Her admirers stated that her voice was an expressive, limitless instrument capable of infinite tonal shadings. "I had struggles in Italy," Callas recalled years later. "I think they found a new element in me. What they considered bel canto was just a beautiful voice singing, whereas with mine they just had to work their minds a little more. They had emotions that they didn't feel before. I was going against the so-called 'tradition' which was *then* not so good . . . the tradition of high, long-held notes and overdone phrases" (from a 1967 interview with Edward Downes).

By the time of her first *Alceste* on April 4, 1954, Callas had become the most glamorous and controversial soprano of La Scala. *Alceste,* written in 1767, had never been staged at La Scala. In the opera, loosely based on a play by Euripides, Queen Alceste offers her life to the gods so that they might spare her husband who, they have decreed, must die. The gods in turn reward her love by staying the power of death. La Scala's management did not expect Gluck's somber, unadorned melodies and old-fashioned plot to generate much excitement at the box office, and only four performances were scheduled. Composer and critic Riccardo Malipiero wrote of the production (*Opera,* June 1954):

> The desire to create a spectacle and the fear of not quite bringing it off have obviously played upon the mind of the producer. The whole thing is too much weighted down. The drama of *Alceste* is above all personal and intimate: it is the drama of two beings desperately involved in an attempt to sacrifice themselves one for the other . . . Here instead we are confronted, almost all the time, with a mass of people who have nothing to say, who are purely decorative, who intrude into a drama which does not concern them . . . The result is a series of short promenades, parades and rhythmic steps all devoid of any significance.

Callas was highly praised by the press, both for her singing and the nobility of her acting. Particularly memorable was her delivery of the aria "Ah! malgré moi mon faible coeur partage" (sung in an Italian translation). In the stately opening section in which Alceste expresses her fears, Callas molded and caressed Gluck's expansive lines, employing the richest colors of her voice. During the fast concluding section, her voice rang out with steadily increasing urgency. In the lengthy recitative which introduces the final scene, she demonstrated one of her greatest gifts—the ability to make the declamatory passages as vital and effective as the subsequent arias.

Callas's only appearances in the part of Alceste were four performances in sixteen days. Riccardo Malipiero wrote in *Opera:* "As Alceste, Maria Meneghini Callas was once again a most fascinating singer. Although the part is less suited to her than others of which she has been a supreme interpreter, she touched most moving heights, sang with exquisite line and with most moving tone and telling expression." Mario Quaglia reported in the *Corriere del Teatro* (April 15, 1954) that "she excelled in personifying the protagonist in a stupendous fashion, artfully interpreting the role with remarkable skill and with exquisite adaptability of voice—deeply moving in the dramatic passages, soft and persuasive in sentimental expressions."

Alceste, Act I, scene 2, as designed by Pietro Zuffi for La Scala, Milan. Alceste asks her subjects to follow her to the temple to pray that the king's life may be spared. Piccagliani

Don Carlo

AFTER singing four performances of *Aida* at the Teatro San Carlo in Naples in the spring of 1950, Callas was invited to learn the role of Elisabetta di Valois in Verdi's *Don Carlo* for the opening of the theater's 1950–51 season. She prepared the part under Serafin, but her throat became inflamed during rehearsals and she was forced to cancel all scheduled appearances for three weeks. Maria Pedrini opened the season in her place.

Callas's only performances of *Don Carlo* took place at La Scala in April 1954. Broadcast tapes exist of her Scala *Medea, Lucia,* and *Alceste* from the same season, but her complete *Don Carlo* is not known to exist in sound. The cast, under the direction of Antonino Votto, included Ebe Stignani as Eboli, Mario Ortica as Don Carlo, Enzo Mascherini as Rodrigo, and Nicola Rossi-Lemeni as Philip II.

Stignani, judging by reviews of the first night, earned the greatest personal triumph of the evening. Ortica, making his official debut in the title role (he had previously substituted for Mario del Monaco in *La Wally* when he was a student at the Scala opera school), received mixed notices. Callas's physical appearance (enhanced by Nicola

Callas as Elisabetta di Valois in Act I, scene 2, of La Scala's production of the four-act version of *Don Carlo*. Milan, April 1954. Piccagliani

Benois' magnificent costumes) elicted as much comment as her singing. Her five performances coincided with the end of her rigorous program of dieting. During her heaviest period she weighed 212 pounds. She now weighed less than 140 pounds. Critics praised Callas for her regal bearing in the passive role of Elisabetta, but there were some reservations about a lack of tenderness in her interpretation. Riccardo Malipiero wrote in *Opera* (June 1954): "Perhaps Callas's voice is not quite suited to Verdi's music; for this wonderful singer, so confident in difficult passages and powerful in dramatic passages, lacks the sweetness and softness necessary in moments of abandon . . ."

On several occasions EMI wanted to add *Don Carlo* to their catalog of opera recordings with Callas, but they found it impossible to assemble all of the singers of the projected cast at the same time. A final

Act II, scene 2: Rodrigo (Enzo Mascherini) and Elisabetta listen as Carlo addresses his father, Philip II of Spain (Nicola Rossi-Lemeni), on behalf of the oppressed people of Flanders. La Scala, Milan, April 1954. Piccagliani

series of recording sessions was scheduled to begin in Paris on October 16, 1962, but the project was abandoned after EMI once again encountered casting problems. Though Callas never committed the entire role of Elisabetta to disc, in September 1958 she recorded the last act aria "Tu che le vanità." She also included the piece on her 1959 concert programs, a couple of which were broadcast and taped. In February 1964, she recorded the Act II romanza "Non pianger, mia compagna." In recording sessions beginning in November and December of 1972, she and Giuseppe di Stefano taped the Act II duet "Io vengo a domandar" for Philips. Although Callas never considered performing any mezzo-soprano roles on stage—with the exception of Carmen—she included Eboli's aria "O don fatale" on a few concert programs in the early 1960s and recorded it for EMI in February 1964.

Don Carlo, Act III, scene 1: Callas and Ebe Stignani, as Eboli, La Scala, Milan, April 1954. Piccagliani

Callas and Giuseppe di Stefano in costume for the Garden Scene in *Mefistofele,* Verona Arena, July 20, 1954. This was their only appearance together in Boïto's opera.

Piccagliani

Mefistofele

IN July 1954, Callas appeared in three performances of Arrigo Boïto's *Mefistofele,* given in the outdoor Arena of Verona. Nicola Rossi-Lemeni sang the title role and the part of Faust was taken by Ferruccio Tagliavini on the first night and by Giuseppe di Stefano in the two subsequent performances. These were Callas's only appearances in Boïto's masterpiece.

Mefistofele is primarily a bass vehicle and the role of Margherita is fairly short. The soprano sings in only two of the seven scenes, but a powerful interpreter can make a great impression in the garden scene quartet, the well-known aria "L'altra notte," the duet "Lontano, lontano," in which Margherita and Faust reflect on the happiness they might have had, and the highly effective death scene, beginning "Spunta l'aurora palida," in which Margherita sings of her imminent death and prays for salvation.

The reviews state that the *prima* was excellent, an international capacity crowd filled the Arena, and the performance was temporarily halted by rain after the second act, but little else is known about it. Apparently none of the *Mefistofeles* were broadcast and they are not known to exist in sound. Although Callas's career coincided with the development and dissemination of home tape recorders and many of her broadcasts exist in good sound, compact portable machines suitable for "in-the-house" taping were still in their infancy in 1965 when she made her unofficial operatic farewell, and thus only a handful of her non-broadcast performances are preserved.

Callas recorded "L'altra notte" for EMI eight weeks after her Verona performances and included the aria on several recital programs which exist on tape. Early in 1952, she had signed a contract with Cetra to record four complete operas: *La Traviata, La Gioconda, Manon Lescaut,* and *Mefistofele*. The projected cast for the Boïto opera included Ferruccio Tagliavini and Nicola Rossi-Lemeni. Several months later Callas signed an exclusive contract with EMI. After recording *Gioconda* and *Traviata* for Cetra, she was released from her contract. She later recorded *Manon Lescaut* with Giuseppe di Stefano for EMI, but her portrayal of Margherita was never committed to disc. Cetra eventually recorded *Mefistofele* with Marcella Pobbe as Margherita and Giulio Neri in the title role.

Callas singing the Act III aria "L'altra notte in fondo al mare," Verona Arena, July 1954.
Piccagliani

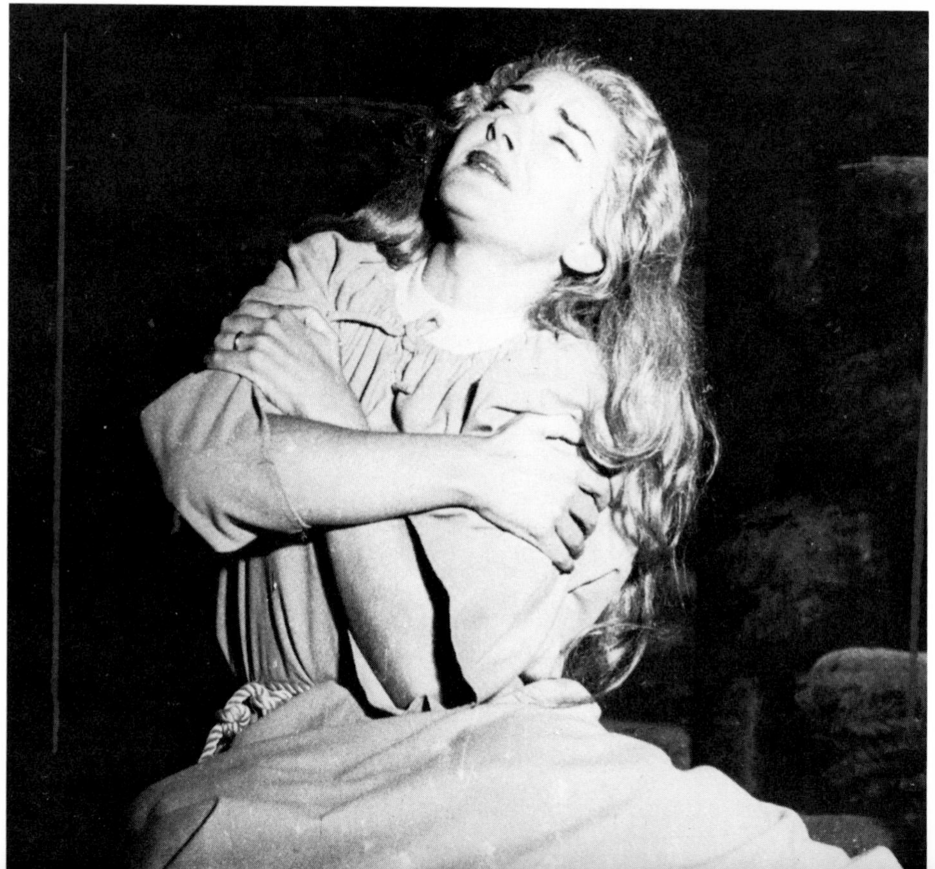

The death of the deranged Margherita: "Enrico, mi fai ribrezzo" ("Enrico, you fill me with loathing"). Verona Arena, July 1954. Piccagliani

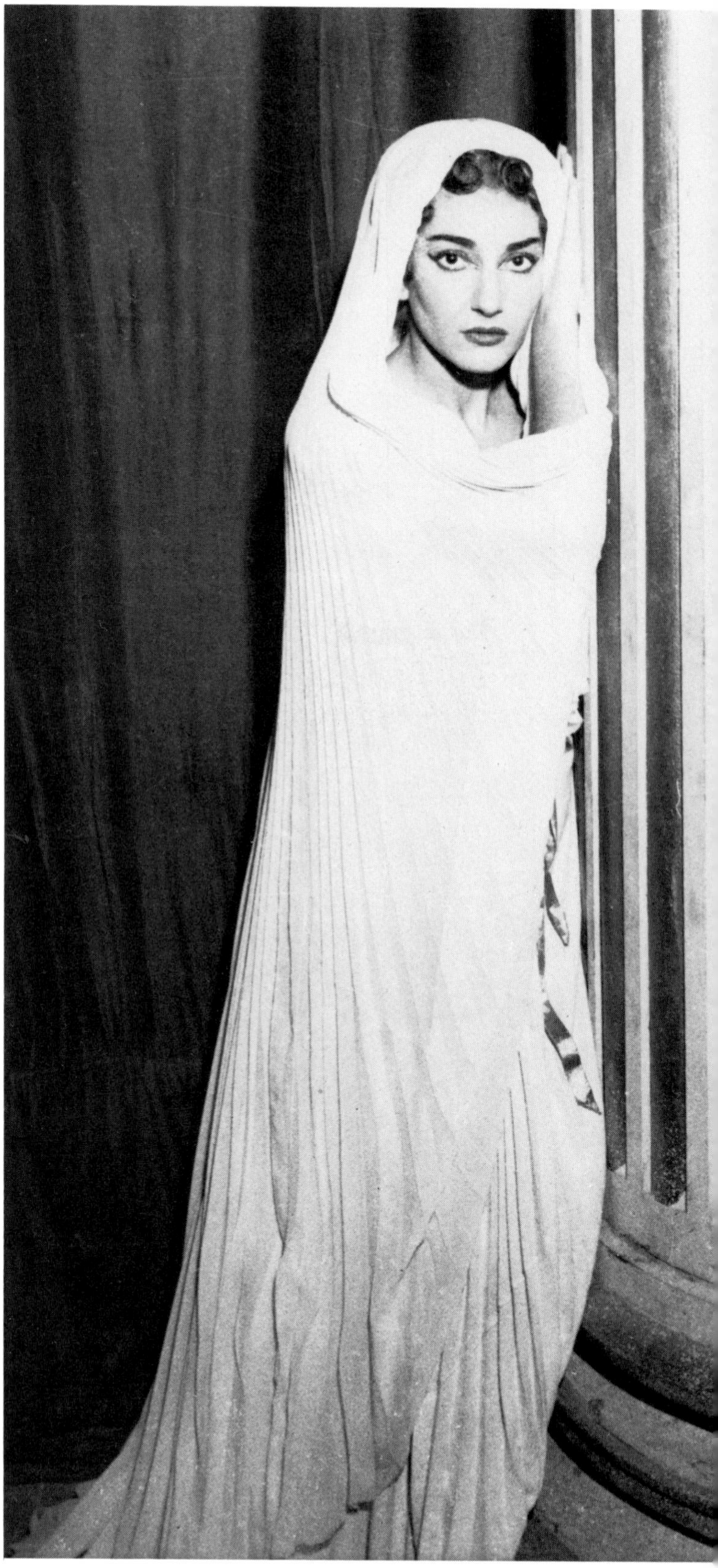

La Vestale

GASPARO SPONTINI'S *La Vestale* was chosen to open the 1954–55 Scala season after an absence of twenty-five years from the repertory. The official reason for the revival was the 180th anniversary of the composer's birth. The unofficial reason was that Callas had asked for the opera. *La Vestale,* set in ancient Rome, concerns a Vestal virgin who is condemned to death for falling in love and allowing the sacred flame to go out in the temple. Although the opera contains two magnificent arias for the soprano, it has received few performances in this century because of the old-fashioned plot and the classic severity of the music.

La Scala's management decided to mount a lavish production even though the opera was slated to be shelved after only five performances. Tickets went quickly as rumors circulated about the revival. The sets and costumes were budgeted at an unprecedented eighty million *lire* (approximately $140,000). A raked stage was built over the existing one and massive three-dimensional sets were constructed.

Callas had met Luchino Visconti in 1950 when she was rehearsing *Il Turco in Italia* at Rome's Teatro Eliseo. From their conversations, she and Visconti discovered that they shared similar views about the

Callas as Giulia in *La Vestale,* La Scala, Milan, December 1954. Piccagliani

dramatic possibilities of opera and a close friendship evolved. Four years later Callas asked Visconti to help her with *Vestale* and he agreed to direct her in the role of Giulia. Franco Corelli, Italy's newest tenor sensation, was signed to make his Scala debut opening night opposite Callas. The most exciting news for the Milanese public was that Arturo Toscanini had returned to Milan and was sitting in on the rehearsals, discussing points of musical interpretation with Callas and conductor Antonino Votto. It was widely known that Toscanini was one of the strongest supporters of La Scala's popular star Renata Tebaldi.

The opening night performance, which was broadcast and taped, was played for all of the passion to be found in Spontini's score. In the most fiery passages, Callas's voice rang out with a searing intensity reminiscent of her Medea. Corelli was praised as much for his height and build as for his powerful voice and Ebe Stignani (a veritable Scala institution) was cheered in the mezzo-soprano role. The production was generally admired by the public, but anachronistic touches were pointed out by critics. Riccardo Malipiero wrote in *Opera* (March 1955):

> The sets were by Pietro Zuffi, who has drawn his inspiration from the true Roman scene: they had that vast impression of grandeur that one still gets today on visiting the *Fori Traianei.* And it must be admitted that they were rather beautiful, even if debatable, with their gilded capitals, which reminded one more of the 18th century of Piermarini rather than of pre-Christian Rome. Even more surprising were the costumes. A frightful conglomeration of colours, designs and styles, they had, apart from the white tunics of the *vestali,* nothing whatever to do with Roman dress. There were feathered headgear, pantaloons, and yards of ribbon.

The highlight of the evening for many came during an Act II curtain call. When Callas stepped to the footlights, she was greeted by a downpour of carnations torn from the garlands that decorated the boxes. Although she is myopic and cannot distinguish faces in the audience, she was told from backstage that Toscanini was in the stage box to her right. She bowed to Toscanini, picked up a flower from the stage and took it to his box. The applause for both Callas and Toscanini was deafening.

Peter Hoffer reported in *Music and Musicians* (February 1955): "Maria Callas sang the lead, and it is said that it was only due to her insistence that the work was put on at all. Be that as it may, the role of Giulia is the perfect one for her, covering the entire vocal range and allowing much freedom for acting. She also looked superb. It is a pleasure to watch her, and one begins to believe at last in the action on the stage."

After five performances in twelve days, the opera left Callas's active repertoire. She recorded the arias "Tu che invoco," "O Nume tutelar," and "Caro oggetto" for EMI in June 1955, and included "Tu che invoco" on her 1958 and 1959 concert programs.

La Vestale, Act I: The high priestess (Ebe Stignani) reminds Giulia to heed her sacred vows.
Piccagliani

La Vestale, Act II: Giulia and Licinius (Franco Corelli) declare their love in the temple of Vesta.
Piccagliani

Andrea Chénier

UMBERTO GIORDANO'S *Andrea Chénier,* written in 1896 and set at the time of the French Revolution, was Callas's first Scala venture into the *verismo* repertory. Verdi's *Il Trovatore* had been announced, but at the last minute tenor Mario del Monaco urged the management to substitute *Chénier* as a personal vehicle. His request could not be taken lightly. He was at the height of his popularity and an enormous box-office draw. He had sung the title role with great success at La Scala in 1949 and 1950, and at the Metropolitan Opera three weeks before the Scala *prima* on January 8, 1955.

Callas agreed to learn the part of Maddalena di Coigny within five days, but the role was destined to be one of her least successful undertakings and she dropped it from her repertoire after six performances. In the five months preceding her *Chénier* appearances, she recorded two complete operas (*La Forza del Destino* and *Il Turco in Italia*), two aria recitals, made her United States debut in Chicago, and opened the Scala season in a new role. Her grueling schedule and the concentrated rehearsals for *Chénier* took their toll on her voice. At the first performance, which was broadcast, her voice showed signs of fatigue

Callas as Maddalena di Coigny in the first act of *Andrea Chénier,* as designed for La Scala by octogenarian Alexandre Benois, January 1955. Piccagliani

and some of her sustained notes had a pronounced beat in the tone. Her detractors waited until the end of her big aria, "La mamma morta," to show their disapproval, and she was booed. In a 1957 radio interview, Callas commented on the mixed opinions she had come to expect after her performances: "It is a matter of loving my kind of voice or not. Some people say I have a beautiful voice. Some people say I have *not.* It is a matter of opinion. Some people say I have a unique voice, and some people say it's just a whole big lie. That is *also* a matter of opinion. The only thing I *can* say is that people who don't like me can just not come and hear me. Because I—when I don't like something—I just don't bother about it."

Callas's approach to the role was untraditional. She attempted to add subtleties to the role which were not warranted by the score and her vocal acting was not entirely successful. In Act I, several unattractive sounds resulted when she tried vocally to portray a mocking and frivolous young girl. In the heavily orchestrated passages, she refused to push her voice and the sound did not always cut through the orchestra.

One of Callas's most effective innovations came at the end of the third act. When Chénier is condemned to death, the composer indicated that Maddalena should cry out desperately, "Andrea, Andrea, rivederlo!" ("Andrea, I must see him!"). Although Giordano did not indicate specific notes, Callas sang her words to the high soaring melody of the orchestra.

Riccardo Malipiero wrote in *Opera* (March 1955): "With [Mario del Monaco] was Maria Meneghini Callas, rather wasted I thought in this part which she nevertheless sustained with dignity." In the opinion of Mario Quaglia (*Corriere del Teatro,* January 15, 1955): "Maria Meneghini Callas, in the silken gowns of Maddalena di Coigny, imparted amorous rapture and delicate abandon to the role, projecting with admirable talent the rich and plentiful sounds of her extended range."

With the exception of her six appearances in *Chénier,* the 1954–55 Scala season was an unbroken series of personal triumphs for Callas. She was given a record number of new productions—three directed by Luchino Visconti (*La Vestale, La Sonnambula,* and *La Traviata*) and one directed by Franco Zeffirelli (*Il Turco in Italia*).

Andrea Chénier, Act III: Maddalena tells Gérard (Aldo Protti) of her suffering during the Revolution and of the death of her mother. La Scala, Milan, January 1955.

Piccagliani

Callas as Amina in Act II of Luchino Visconti's production of *La Sonnambula* for La Scala, March 1955.

Piccagliani

La Sonnambula

CALLAS first portrayed the challenging role of Amina in Vincenzo Bellini's *La Sonnambula* on March 5, 1955. Although she had studied the nineteenth-century bel canto style of singing with Elvira de Hidalgo and Tullio Serafin, Bellini's 1831 pastorale proved to be unusually difficult for her to sing without apparent strain. Unlike Montserrat Caballé, for whom *pianissimo* singing is effortless, Callas found it taxing to scale down the natural volume of her voice for an entire performance.

After the enormous success of the Callas-Bernstein *Medeas* at the beginning of 1954, the Scala management had made numerous attempts to lure the young conductor back to Milan. He agreed to conduct the Bellini opera (his only excursion into conducting the bel canto repertory to date) after being assured of ample rehearsal time. Luchino Visconti was signed as director.

Amina, the heroine of the opera, is an orphan in a Swiss village. Unknown to her fiancé Elvino, she walks in her sleep. One evening, some villagers discover her asleep in a stranger's bed, but eventually her fiancé observes her walking in her sleep over a fragile bridge and is convinced of her fidelity. Dramatically, Callas emphasized the ingenuousness and innocence of the character. She moved with the grace of a ballerina. (Her hair style was based on that worn by the Scala ballerina Carla Fracci, then at the beginning of her international career.)

Visconti chose to present the opera as a semi-stylized period piece. In the nineteenth-century tradition of presenting ballet divertissements on the same program with an opera, *La Sonnambula* was followed by two short ballets—Mikhail Fokine's *Le Spectre de la Rose* and Esmée Bulnes's *Suite,* both with Carla Fracci. *La Sonnambula* was presented ten times in 1955 and the first act of one performance was televised.

Bernstein recalled the *Sonnambula* production in an interview with John Gruen (*Opera News,* September 1972):

> . . . it was something marvelous, the closest to a perfect opera performance I've ever witnessed. The time expended on its preparation—the care, the choices that were made, the work Maria and I did together on cadenzas and embellishments and ornamentations —was enormous. I remember hours of sitting with Visconti in the costume warehouses of La Scala, picking feathers for the caps of the chorus! I had eighteen orchestra rehearsals for a score that is usually done in one rehearsal, because the orchestra doesn't have too much more to do than a series of arpeggios, but those arpeggios were something never to be forgotten. And Callas was just glorious. She was now half the size she had been in *Medea*—it was the time of her famous transformation of girth. Well, it was beautiful!

Callas was in excellent voice for the *prima,* having had a month without performances for rest and preparation. Bernstein's conducting was characterized by expansive tempos for the arias and duets and almost frantic tempos for the choruses. Callas's opening aria, "Come per me sereno," was sung with a full, lovely tone. The cabaletta, "Sovra il sen," was taken at a brisk pace and was delivered as a virtuoso showpiece, with Callas tearing through the sixteenth-note running passages at breakneck speed. The imaginative embellishments included a leap of an octave and a third up to high C and staccato arpeggios up to high D and E flat. Callas ended the aria with a downward cadenza to low A flat in chest, followed by a secure, if somewhat steely, high E flat.

In the exquisite duet "Prendi l'anel ti dono," tenor Cesare Valletti sang with an ardor, elegance of line, and beauty of tone that easily rivaled the legendary 1933 recording by Tito Schipa and Toti dal

Monte. Bellini assigned the melody to the tenor, and Callas scaled her voice down, allowing Valletti's lighter tone to predominate. The subsequent arioso and duet however had little to commend it. Valletti, handicapped during his entire career by a short upper range, omitted the high C's. Callas's music was almost entirely deleted.

The tenor part in the opera, originally written to exploit the phenomenal upper extension of Giovanni Battista Rubini, has been traditionally transposed down. The "Son geloso" duet, written in the key of G but normally performed a full tone down, was transposed down only a half tone for the 1955 Scala production. In the exposed solo trill and cadenza up to high C sharp, Valletti had to resort to falsetto, but the series of trills in thirds was beautifully executed by both artists and they ended with a unison high C sharp.

One of the evening's highlights came at the beginning of the Act II quartet, "Lisa, mendace anch'essa." Valletti sang with ravishing tonal beauty. Later, Callas's "Ah! non credea" was taken very slowly and sung with a steady flow of beautiful tone, slightly veiled to suggest that she was singing in her sleep. The aria was sung simply and without any of the traditional trills.

During the final cabaletta, when Amina wakes, the stage and house lights were gradually raised until the entire theater was brilliantly lit (a Visconti touch). Callas launched into the "Ah! non giunge" with great force and brilliance, and her voice took on its normal metallic cutting edge. The highly ornamented finale was tossed off in a fearless and spontaneous manner reminiscent of her singing in Rossini's *Armida* in 1952. Riccardo Malipiero wrote in *Opera* (May 1955):

> *Sonnambula* had not been seen at the Scala for many years, and the management did handsomely by it . . . Bernstein lingered dangerously over certain parts of the work, and pushed rather too impetuously in others, risking a disintegration of stage and pit—but nevertheless succeeded in revealing the beauty of a score which normally receives but scant attention. Callas's Amina had something of the same quality; she is, as all know, a great artist and a perfect actress, and despite the strange lapses from her astounding vocal best, it was impossible not to yield to her Amina.

La Scala revived the production two years later on March 2, 1957.

The two major changes (neither for the better) were Nicola Monti as Elvino and Antonino Votto as conductor. Callas's Amina had changed considerably. Her tone was lovelier, lighter, and more youthful. Critics who in 1955 had found her to be somewhat coy and affected, now praised her naturalness and total freedom on the stage.

The major flaw in the Votto performances was an over-all lack of spontaneity. Tempos were slow, Monti's thin and rather white voice added little tonal variety to the duets and ensembles, and Callas's florid singing was controlled to the point of sounding cautious. Some of the more brilliant ornaments of 1955 were omitted. In Callas's "Sovra il sen," Bernstein had omitted one stanza and Votto extended the cut to two verses. Although Votto transposed the "Son geloso" duet down a whole tone from the original score, Monti omitted his cadenza up to high C. In the Bernstein performances, Callas sang the stretto section after "Son geloso" up an octave, giving added brilliance to the finale, but it was performed as written in the revival. The Bernstein ornaments and variations were retained, save a couple of changes, for "Ah! non giunge," but Callas sang the music lightly and carefully. In a period of nineteen days, six performances were given at La Scala and the production was committed to disc at the Basilica Santa Euphemia in Milan.

Olivier Merlin, in his 1961 book *Le Bel Canto,* relates an amusing anecdote, perhaps apocryphal, concerning Callas's reaction to a hostile *Sonnambula* audience after a vocal mishap. Amina's opening music is sung without accompaniment. The soprano must receive the pitch offstage or listen to the end of the preceding chorus. Although Callas generally has reliable relative pitch, one evening she made her entrance and began singing a half tone below the correct pitch. When the orchestra joined her in a different key, part of the audience began whistling. She did not take a curtain call after the first act. In the second and final act, she was spellbinding and the audience gave her an ovation. She coldly appeared before the curtain and received the applause: both arms outstretched ("your bravos . . ."), her arms crossed on her chest ("I accept . . ."), and then both arms behind her back ("and do with them as I please"). After a couple of seconds of silence, she walked off the stage to a new storm of whistles and boos.

—*La Sonnambula*—

In July 1957, Callas appeared twice as Amina in Cologne, Germany. The following month her final performances of *Sonnambula* were given in Scotland at the Eleventh Edinburgh Festival. Although she was exhausted and asked La Scala to substitute another soprano, the theater's officials insisted that she sing. Harold Rosenthal summarized her performances (*Musical America,* October 1957):

> *Sonnambula,* with Maria Callas as Amina, was given the honor of opening the operatic series [of the festival]. The soprano was in varying voice throughout her appearances, and after four Aminas she had to cancel her fifth, as she was not well. According to reports, opening night found her in far from good voice. The second and third performances, which were broadcast, displayed the singer at her very best and very worst; in the fourth, which I heard, the soprano was in excellent voice, and her performance ranked with her Normas in London of last winter.
>
> This is not to say the voice was always perfectly produced, or that all the sounds she made fell pleasantly on the ear; but the musicianship, intelligence and intensity with which she invests her roles were in evidence throughout the evening, and her singing of "Come per me sereno" in the first scene and "Ah! non credea" in the last were intensely moving. Dramatically her interpretation was a tour de force: by very nature Miss Callas is an imperious figure more suited to the great tragic roles of the lyric stage, and yet although Amina is a Giselle-like figure, the soprano was able by her personality to make us believe in the figure she created.

La Sonnambula, Act I, scene 2: Amina awaits the arrival of her fiancé, Elvino. La Scala, Milan, March 1955. Piccagliani

Madama Butterfly

IN February 1954, the Lyric Opera of Chicago (then called Lyric Theatre) presented two "calling card" performances of *Don Giovanni,* with Nicola Rossi-Lemeni, Eleanor Steber, Bidù Sayão, and Leopold Simoneau. Chicago had been without a resident opera company for eight years and Carol Fox, daughter of a wealthy Chicago furniture manufacturer, Lawrence Kelly, a real estate agent and insurance broker, and conductor Nicola Rescigno organized the two performances to encourage financial backing for their new company.

With the success of *Don Giovanni,* Carol Fox left for Europe to line up artists for a three-week fall season. After signing Giulietta Simionato, Giuseppe di Stefano, and Tito Gobbi, she visited Callas in Verona and invited her to make her United States debut in Chicago. The two got along well, and Callas agreed to sing two performances each of *Norma, La Traviata,* and *Lucia,* for $2,000 a performance ($1,200 more than Rudolf Bing's maximum offer at that time).

Callas made her United States debut as Norma on November 1, 1954. Her appearances received unqualified raves in the press and prolonged ovations from the Chicago audiences. For the 1955 season, the three

Callas before her first *Madama Butterfly.* With director and consultant Hizi Koyke, Chicago Civic Opera House, November 11, 1955.

founders of the company returned to Europe to sign her for their second season. After discussing repertory, casting, and terms, Callas agreed to sing in *I Puritani, Il Trovatore,* and *Madama Butterfly* (her first Cio-Cio-San on any stage).

In 1948, Edward Johnson, then general manager of the Metropolitan Opera, had offered Callas the role of Butterfly after she had auditioned for him. Callas turned down the part, explaining that she was too heavy for the role (210 pounds) and that she did not consider Butterfly to be an ideal debut role. When Carol Fox and Lawrence Kelly discussed the role with Callas, she had lost seventy-five pounds and felt that visually she could now do justice to the role. She was also scheduled to record the opera with Herbert von Karajan three months before the Chicago season.

Callas sang her first Cio-Cio-San on November 11, 1955, with Giuseppe di Stefano and baritone Robert Weede. The production aimed at creating the atmosphere of the Kabuki Theater. Callas received qualified praise from the critics. Claudia Cassidy wrote (*Opera,* March 1956):

> This was an intimate *Butterfly,* brushed almost from the start by the shadow of tragedy to come. Not even its love duet was the flood of melody to send pulses pounding. Rather it set the mounting ardor of the man against the muted ecstasy of the woman. This is not the only way to sing such Puccini—in memory of magnificent love duets I do not say it is even the best way. But with Callas and Di Stefano on the stage, it is a way of warm Puccini persuasion.
>
> Many an experienced operagoer felt that way about the entire performance, feeling (with a touch of awe) that Callas had worked out the complicated and taxing role to its geisha fingertips. My own regard for her talents goes higher than that. As a decoration she was exquisite, with the aid of another Butterfly beauty of older days, Hizi Koyke, who staged the performance. As a tragic actress, she had the unerring simplicity, the poignant power of that thrust to the heart of the score. But in the first scene she missed the diminutive mood, which is that Butterfly's essence. This was charming make-believe, but it was not Cio-Cio-San, nor was it the ultimate Callas.

Roger Dettmer wrote (Chicago *American,* November 12, 1955):

> In Act I, [the voice] was that of a scared little girl—so willed by its user—when the opera started moving for her. Act II, set three years later, found still traces of the little girl voice, but one darkened by hollow hope and spasms of despair. The final act brought us the tragic heroine—abandoned by her common-law husband and about to have their child taken from her. And here was yet another Callas, unlike any previous characterization—Japanese in movement and mannerism, but deserted Woman epitomized.
>
> Give her further performances and Mme Callas can be the "Butterfly" supreme in our time . . . Ideally, the Callas Butterfly (or anyone's, faithful both to the libretto and to the score) is scaled for an intimate house—the Piccola Scala, for example. Such a setting would require a measure less coyness of expression and deportment in the first act, but it would reward all present with the subtle Callas conception of a beloved but fiendishly difficult role—a potentially great conception, and one that yet may find maturity before another week has passed here.

The announcement of an extra performance brought a record crowd to the Lyric Opera's box office. The line for tickets stretched the length of the theater, around the corner, and over the Washington Street bridge to the Daily News Building. The 3,600-seat house was sold out ninety-eight minutes after the ticket windows opened.

After three performances of *Butterfly,* Callas never showed interest in performing the role again. None of the Chicago *Butterflys* are known to exist in sound, but reviews of the stage performances indicate that her conception of the role closely followed her commercially recorded performance, taped a couple of months earlier. Purely as a tour de force of vocal acting, Callas's performance is one of the most subtle interpretations preserved on disc. Each nuance and vocal color specified in the score is scrupulously observed. Callas's Butterfly is an uncompromising interpretation, meant for people who can follow every word of the text.

In a casual hearing, many of Puccini's most beautiful melodies are apparently thrown away, but an examination of the text invariably reveals the validity of Callas's approach to the role. The "Un bel dì" is no longer the hit tune of the opera, but rather a touching narrative delivered by Cio-Cio-San to her maid. Callas breathes new life into many phrases which other interpreters pass over lightly. In Act I, her de-

Callas's Act I entrance in *Madama Butterfly,* with Giuseppe di Stefano as Pinkerton. Chicago, November 1955.

Courtesy of the Lyric Opera of Chicago

scription of the inquiries into adopting Pinkerton's religion is sung with an inner fervor and eloquence that is extraordinarily moving. Throughout the opera, Callas stresses Butterfly's ingenuousness and child-like faith, making the ultimate realization of her abandonment all the more unbearable. Callas's Butterfly is unique among her interpretations in that it is a personal drama to be overheard, rather than a full-blown operatic performance projected to an audience.

Il Barbiere di Siviglia

THE 1955–56 Scala season was virtually a Callas festival for the soprano's admirers in Milan. She appeared in almost forty performances of *Norma, La Traviata,* and two operas new to her repertoire—Rossini's *The Barber of Seville* and Giordano's *Fedora. The Barber of Seville* proved to be her second and last comic role. La Scala's previous production had been in 1952, with conductor Victor de Sabata and a highly praised cast which included Giulietta Simionato, Ferruccio Tagliavini, and Gino Bechi. For the new production, the management assembled an equally impressive cast, with Tito Gobbi in the title role and the Peruvian tenor Luigi Alva (in his Scala debut) as the count. Carlo Maria Giulini, the theater's principal conductor, presided in the pit.

The February 16, 1956, *prima* found all the principals in excellent voice. Although Callas sang her music in the original mezzo-soprano keys (with the exception of "Contro un cor," which was performed up a tone), several of the low phrases in ensembles were transposed up, placing them in the middle of her voice. She also included some of the variations usually sung only by high sopranos. "Una voce poco fa"

As Rosina in La Scala's 1956 staging of *Il Barbiere di Siviglia,* with costumes and scenery designed by Mario Velloni Marchi. Piccagliani was surprising for the natural mezzo-soprano color which she gave to the aria and her free use of chest voice. In the ensuing recitative in which Rosina complains to Figaro about her lack of freedom, it was evident that Callas's approach to the role was unorthodox. Her shrewish delivery made Rosina appear to be rather bitchy and ill-tempered. A high point of the evening was the brilliantly executed duet "Dunque io son." Gobbi's florid singing equaled Callas's for ease and rhythmic subtleties, and she ended the duet with a solid high D.

Callas followed the recent practice of singing Rossini's original piece "Contro un cor" in the lesson scene. Until the 1950s, audiences could expect to hear almost anything short of "Danny Boy." (At an 1884 Metropolitan Opera gala performance which included Act II of *The Barber of Seville,* Marcella Sembrich astounded the audience by singing Heinrich Proch's "Air and Variations" and the Russian National Anthem during the lesson scene, returning to play part of a Charles Auguste de Beriot violin concerto and a Chopin piano piece, and, for an encore, singing "Ah! non giunge" from *La Sonnambula.*) Callas's "Contro un cor" was dramatic and brilliant, underscoring the "love versus tyranny" theme of the text. In the section beginning "Cara immagine ridente," during which Rosina surreptitiously declares her love for Lindoro who is disguised as her music teacher, Callas's singing became warmer and more playful. After the applause subsided at the end of the scene, Alva sang his words "Bella voce! bravissima" ("Beautiful voice! Excellent"). The audience spontaneously broke into applause and stopped the performance.

Callas's Rosina received mixed reviews. Some critics felt that her powerful personality drew the audience's attention away from Figaro, the central character of the plot. Peter Hoffer wrote (*Music and Musicians,* April 1956): ". . . Rossini's masterpiece *The Barber of Seville* drew full houses and caused something of a controversy. Callas's Rosina was far from a conventional conception and most of the critics were up in arms. She played her as a coquette who 'knows the ropes' and even flouted tradition to the extent of doing a few steps of a dance in which she showed off her ankles. But the voice is in splendid condition and she sings charmingly." In a more negative vein, Claudio Sartori commented in *Opera* (April 1956): "Maria Callas made an excitable, nervous, overpowering Rosina, and her familiar unevenness of emission made one regret, rather than forget, the great interpreters of the past."

It can be stated unequivocally that Callas's wealth of tonal shadings and spontaneity of interpretation—two of her greatest attributes—were never fully captured in her commercial recordings. Seemingly in response to criticism that her voice was unpleasant or even ugly, Callas generally underplayed her vocal acting in the recording studios and emphasized a consistently more attractive tone. Both her uncanny ability to illuminate words and her impeccable phrasing are clearly in evidence in all of the recordings, but the electricity of her stage performances is rarely captured. The 1956 Scala *Barbers* and the EMI commercial recording, taped a year later, differ considerably. Callas's voice is more evenly produced in the studio performance—except for some strain on the sustained high notes—and the interpretation is more subdued and refined. Phrases are less ornamented and fewer transpositions are made, resulting in a purer reading of the score. Chest tones are lightly touched.

Standard cuts were made in both performances, but in the recording, Callas sings a decorated version of her final solo lines which begin "Costò sospiri e pene" (deleted at La Scala). Alceo Galliera, the conductor of the EMI set, led a well-controlled reading of the score, but failed to equal the elasticity and vivaciousness of Giulini's interpretation. One particularly felicitous touch in the Giulini version was the dramatically logical use of a harpsichord throughout the lesson scene. An orchestral accompaniment was employed in the recording.

After five performances at La Scala, Callas never sang *Barbiere* again on stage, though "Una voce poco fa" was included in a few of her concert programs. During the 1959 Dallas opera season, Teresa Berganza was scheduled to appear in *Barbiere* opposite Ettore Bastianini, but impending maternity caused her to cancel her engagement. Callas consented to sing in place of Berganza between scheduled performances of *Lucia* and *Medea,* but her first United States appearances as Rosina never materialized. The dates conflicted with an appearance in court at Brescia, Italy, concerning a legal separation from her husband, and Eugenia Ratti sang in Callas's place.

Il Barbiere di Siviglia, Act I, scene 2: Bartolo (Melchiorre Luise) tries unsuccessfully to match wits with his spirited ward. La Scala, Milan, February 1956.

Piccagliani

Act II: Rosina quickly sees through the disguise of the Count (Luigi Alva). La Scala, Milan, February 1956. Piccagliani

Fedora

FOR the final new production of the 1955–56 season, La Scala's management mounted Umberto Giordano's 1898 melodrama *Fedora* for Callas. It had last been heard at the theater in 1948 with Maria Caniglia in the title role and Giacinto Prandelli in the tenor lead. *Fedora* is, after *Andrea Chénier*, Giordano's most successful opera, and it is still popular in Italy. Magda Olivero, Italy's most celebrated interpreter of Fedora, has appeared in more than ten different productions since 1965.

Giordano's opera closely follows the play of the same name by Victorien Sardou, written in 1882 as a vehicle for Sarah Bernhardt. Its three acts are set in St. Petersburg, Paris, and a Swiss village, respectively. Early in the opera, Princess Fedora Romanov swears to avenge the death of her fiancé, who has been murdered by young Count Loris Ipanov. She eventually learns that her fiancé had been unfaithful to her and she falls in love with Loris, but she has already plotted against him and is indirectly responsible for the death of his mother and brother. In the lengthy final scene, when Loris discovers that she is the mysterious woman who has been pursuing him, she takes poison and begs his forgiveness. *Fedora* is a highly effective theater piece when in the hands of

Callas as Fedora, in the costume designed by Nicola Benois for her Act I entrance, La Scala, Milan, May 1956. Piccagliani

Fedora, Act III: Fedora learns that she was indirectly responsible for the death of Loris's mother and brother. La Scala, May 1956. Piccagliani

a vibrant singing-actress. Giordano included many of Sardou's detailed stage directions in the score and much of the opera's impact depends on subtle gestures and facial expressions. Musically, it is weaker than *Andrea Chénier,* but the opera does contain many moments of melodic inspiration and the Act II love duet is as impassioned as any in the *verismo* repertory.

La Scala scheduled six performances for May and June of 1956. The production was directed by Tatiana Pavlova and the cast included Franco Corelli as Loris and Anselmo Colzani as De Siriex. Peter Hoffer reported in *Music and Musicians* (August 1956): "*Fedora* with Callas in the cast meant full houses and a big success. Once again she proved that even if she is not the greatest singer she is certainly one of the world's greatest actresses. However, her voice seems to have mellowed,

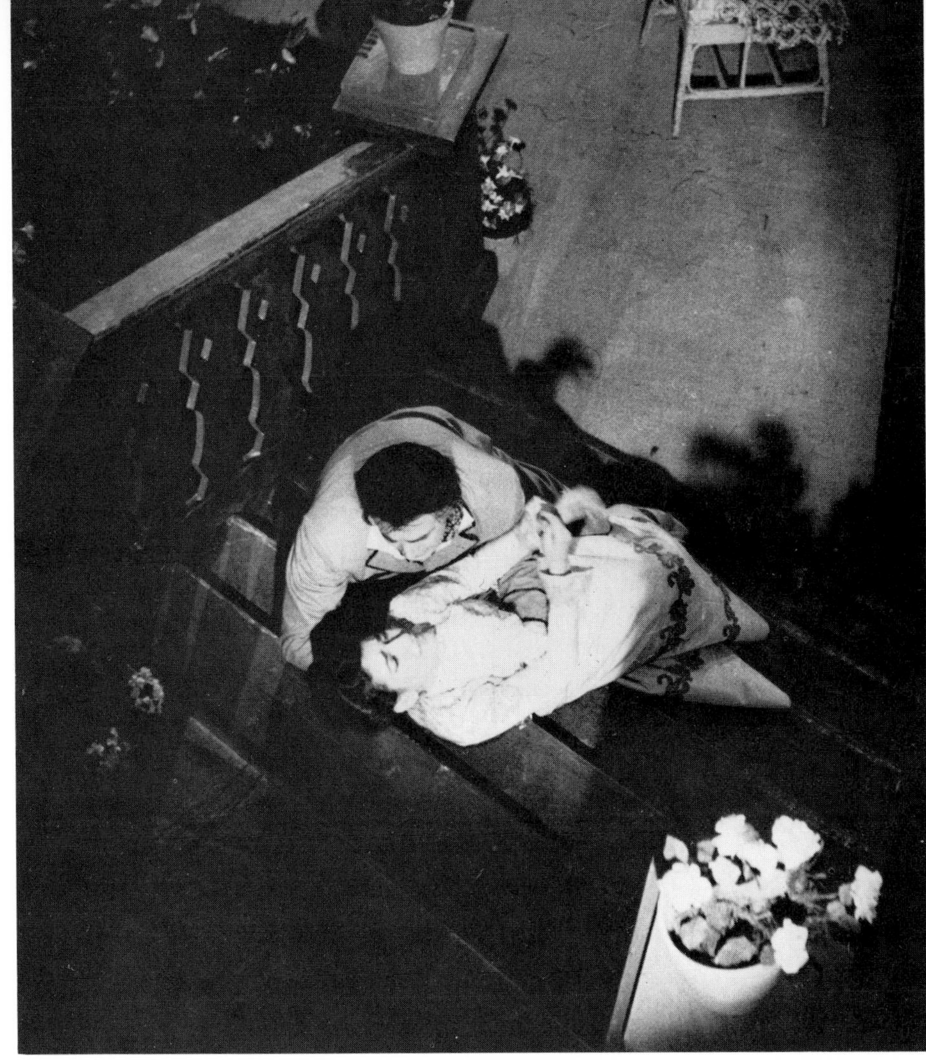

Fedora, having taken poison, asks Loris (Franco Corelli) to forgive her. La Scala, May 1956. Piccagliani

and her upper register has lost some of its strident quality." Claudio Sartori wrote (*Opera,* July 1956): "*Fedora* was also conducted by Gavazzeni, with settings by Benois in which he seemed deliberately to amuse himself with the bad taste of the period. Maria Meneghini Callas and Franco Corelli led the cast, singing and acting with dramatic power, perhaps even overstepping the limits of good style—if indeed good style be desirable in this melodramatic piece."

After six performances in fourteen days, the role left Callas's active repertoire. For over sixteen years, none of Callas's Fedora was generally believed to be preserved in sound (she never recorded any of the music and the Scala revival was not broadcast), but in the spring of 1973 an "in-the-house" tape, reported to be in very poor sound, was made available to a few tape collectors in Europe.

Anna Bolena

GAETANO DONIZETTI'S *Anna Bolena* was revived at La Scala on April 14, 1957. The opera, based on the last days of Anne Boleyn, proved to be one of the greatest triumphs of Callas's career. The work had not been staged at La Scala since 1877 and the management decided to mount a lavish production to coincide with Milan's annual International Trade Fair. Luchino Visconti was director, Nicola Benois designed the massive sets and sumptuous costumes, and Gianandrea Gavazzeni, Italy's foremost Donizetti authority, was the conductor. Vocal fireworks were insured by the casting of Giulietta Simionato as Anne Boleyn's rival, Jane Seymour. Given the slightest opportunity, the diminutive mezzo-soprano could be counted on to steal the show—both vocally and dramatically—from any singer. The other principals included the Bolognese tenor Gianni Raimondi and bass Nicola Rossi-Lemeni.

Callas, in her nineteenth Scala role, had reached the point in her career where she was vocally, physically, and dramatically at her peak. Less than a year later, increasing signs of vocal and physical fatigue would not be uncommon. In *Bolena,* Callas brought every vocal

Callas as the tormented Anne Boleyn in La Scala's 1957 staging of the Donizetti opera. Piccagliani

color at her command into play in order to convey the conflicting emotions of the tormented Anne. The opening night audience immediately sensed Callas's appearance from an ominous tremolo in the strings. Magnificently gowned, Callas slowly descended the long, broad staircase of Windsor Castle. The deliberately cold settings of Benois—in an impersonal black and white—contributed to the sombre mood of the opera.

During her opening aria, delivered softly and introspectively near the front of the stage, it was apparent to the audience that Callas was in exceptional vocal form. Though Anne's remembrance of happier days with Henry was appropriately delivered in light, pure tones, most memorable was Callas's sudden shift to her richest, most vibrant sounds for the phrase, "Son calde ancor le ceneri del mio primiero amore!" ("The embers of my first love smolder still!"). In the cabaletta in which Anne warns Jane Seymour never to be seduced by the empty splendor of a royal throne, Callas caressed and shaped the intricate lines with an ease that belied their difficulty. Every note was clearly defined in her downward runs and scales—the celebrated Callas "string of pearls."

The powerful Act I finale contained many notable examples of Callas's use of the voice to heighten the effect of the text—the disembodied tones on "Ove sono? . . . ove sono?" ("Where am I?") as Anne regains consciousness after having fainted; the hauntingly beautiful *mezza voce* for Anne's plea to Henry, "Lascia che il core oppresso torni per poco in sè" ("Allow my oppressed heart to regain its composure"); and the force and vehemence of "Giudici! ad Anna! . . . Giudici! . . . ad Anna!") (Judges? . . . for Anne? . . . Judges!"), when Henry tells her she will be tried for adultery.

In the final scene of the opera, set in the Tower of London, Callas projected Anne's mental instability through the use of constantly shifting vocal colors. When Anne asked the ladies-in-waiting, "Piangete voi?" ("You are weeping?"), the tone was weak and colorless. "Il crin m'ornate del mio serto di rose" ("Adorn my head with my crown of roses") was delivered with ineffable sweetness. A delicate thread of sound was employed for Anne's plaintive request that she be allowed to return to her homeland ("Al dolce guidami castel natio"). For the brilliant cabaletta finale, beginning "Coppia iniqua, l'estrema vendetta" ("Wicked couple, supreme revenge"), Callas's tone—in sharp contrast with her singing earlier in the scene—took on an almost unbearable intensity. Violently, yet always on the note, Callas hurled out Anne's final lines. "Vendetta" was delivered with raw chest tones which must have chilled the blood of many Italians who were following every word of the text. Before the final notes of the orchestra had sounded, hundreds in the audience were standing and cheering Callas for what many now consider to be her greatest interpretation at La Scala.

Anna Bolena, Act I, scene 1: Callas singing the soft cavatina of recollection, "Come, innocente giovane," La Scala, April 1957. Piccagliani

Iphigénie en Tauride

IPHIGÉNIE EN TAURIDE was composed for the Paris Opéra and first produced in 1779. Based on an adaptation faithful to the Euripides tragedy, it is generally acknowledged to be Christoph Willibald Gluck's finest work. In *Iphigénie,* he successfully reconciled his dramatic and lyrical styles, creating a powerful series of grand arias, choruses, and dances of considerable musical invention.

The opera was first staged at La Scala in 1937, when Victor de Sabata led a cast headed by Maria Caniglia and Armando Borgioli. The Scala management decided to end their 1956–57 season with a sumptuous revival. Minor cuts were made in Gluck's score and it was presented in two acts rather than the usual three, in an Italian translation which closely followed the original French text. Callas agreed to learn the role for four performances, even though she felt that classical operas—with the exception of Cherubini's *Medea*—were old-fashioned and could easily become boring for the public. Luchino Visconti was signed to direct his fifth production with Callas. Visconti and scenic designer Nicola Benois placed the opera in the middle of the eighteenth century and created an elaborate décor in the rococo style of Giuseppe

As Iphigénie in Luchino Visconti's production of Gluck's opera, La Scala, Milan, June 1957.
Piccagliani

Galli Bibiena. A spacious permanent set was constructed for both acts, with double columns, loggias, statues, and a high staircase at background center, behind which a sea was visible. The altar of Diana was placed under one of the porticoes.

An elaborate lighting system was devised, both to give variety to the basic set and to create the shadowy apparition of Clytemnestra and the luminous appearance of the goddess Diana in the final scene. Nino Sanzogno, known primarily for his interpretations of contemporary music, was chosen as conductor and the choreography was assigned to Alfredo Rodríguez.

It was evident after the first few minutes of the June 1, 1957, performance that the dramatic rather than the lyrical aspects of the score would be emphasized. Sanzogno drew rich sonorities from the Scala orchestra, but his consistently loud dynamic level and high pitch of intensity soon became monotonous. Callas made her impressive entrance during the storm scene which opens the opera. She walked up the staircase, looked out over the turbulent sea, and suddenly ran down the stairs, with twenty-five yards of cloak trailing behind and a wind machine at her back, reaching the bottom in time to launch into Iphigénie's opening plea in which she asks the gods to contain their fury.

She was in excellent voice for the *prima*. Her recitatives had the ring of nobility and the broad, arching phrases of her arias were projected with strength. One of the interpretive high points of the evening was her deeply felt delivery of the soliloquy in which Iphigénie, having learned of her father's death, bitterly invites the gods to delight in her anguish. The subsequent aria "O malheureuse Iphigénie"* was sung with a rich, beautiful tone, but emotionally Callas seemed to be outside of the piece and her dynamic level was curiously unvaried. When she recorded the aria in French six years later for the album "Callas in Paris," she achieved a more expansive and sustained line by taking longer phrases in the same breath, but the notes above the staff were no longer effortless. Her most brilliant and free singing came during Iphigénie's invocation to Diana, "Je t'implore et je tremble."

The remainder of the cast ranged from acceptable to mediocre. Bari-

* Although the opera was sung in Italian translation, the arias are referred to here by their more standard French titles.

tone Anselmo Colzani, who was to sing over one hundred performances of operas by Puccini, Giordano, and Cilèa with the Metropolitan during the next decade, sang Thoas, king of Tauris, in a *verismo* style. Dino Dondi, miscast in the high baritone part of Iphigénie's brother Orestes, was handicapped by pitch problems and a lack of the requisite vocal elegance. Tenor Francesco Albanese struggled valiantly with the high tessitura of Pylades' music, but twenty years of singing had robbed the voice of its freshness and his high notes were constricted. *Iphigénie en Tauride* was followed by Aleksandr Glazunov's *The Seasons,* performed by the graduating students of La Scala's ballet school.

Iphigénie's opening invocation to the gods.
Iphigénie en Tauride, Act I, scene 1.
La Scala, June 1957. Piccagliani

Iphigénie refuses the demands of King Thoas (Anselmo Colzani) for a human sacrifice. Act I, scene 2. La Scala, June 1957. Piccagliani

Un Ballo in Maschera

IN 1940, at the Olympia Theater in Athens, Callas appeared as Amelia in a student performance of Act III of Giuseppe Verdi's *Un Ballo in Maschera.* Seven years later, shortly after her Italian debut in Verona, she was invited by La Scala to audition for their forthcoming production of *Ballo,* which was scheduled for April 1948. After the audition, artistic director of the theater Mario Labroca told her that she should work to eradicate certain vocal defects, but he also assured her that she would be considered for the soprano lead. When the cast was eventually announced, the part had been given to Elisabetta Barbato, then nearing the peak of her career. Callas was not to sing at La Scala until April 1950, when she made her unofficial debut in *Aida.*

In 1956, EMI decided to add *Ballo* to their rapidly growing catalog of complete opera recordings. The majority of their Italian opera releases of the 1950s were recorded with soloists, orchestra, and chorus of La Scala and released under the official emblem of the theater. Callas, Giuseppe di Stefano, Tito Gobbi, and Fedora Barbieri were chosen for the principal roles under the direction of conductor Antonino Votto. The soloists were in excellent voice for the recording ses-

Un Ballo in Maschera at La Scala, Milan, December 1957. Ulrica's dwelling, Act I, scene 2: Amelia asks heaven to release her from her hopeless love.

Piccagliani

sions of September 1956, but Votto, while scrupulously observing all of Verdi's dynamic markings, failed to mine the full dramatic possibilities of the score.

Callas's five professional stage appearances in *Ballo* took place at La Scala in December 1957. Amelia was one of the twenty-four major roles which were to leave her active repertoire after six or fewer performances.

Verdi originally based his opera on the 1792 assassination of King Gustav III of Sweden, but because of political censorship he was obliged to change the locale and characters. Gustav became Riccardo, Count of Warwick and governor of Boston. Director Margherita Wallmann and scenic designer Nicola Benois retained the Boston setting for the 1957 Scala production, but changed the period from the late eighteenth century to the seventeenth century. A basic two-level set served for all the scenes except the second act. Painted tapestries, curtains, and fishnets were used to vary the unit set of rough, wooden constructions. In direct contrast, the costumes were of extraordinary sumptuousness. The second act set consisted of the remains of a ship and a row of gallows.

The opening night *Ballo* was broadcast and now exists as one of the most inspired Verdi performances preserved in sound. Callas's Amelia at La Scala and the one on the EMI recording were vocally similar, but her stage interpretation reflected a greater subtlety in her handling of the text. Di Stefano's voice had become darker in the fifteen months following the recording, and his low notes at the *prima* were of unusual richness. Ettore Bastianini was cast as Renato. The young baritone from Siena was usually content with pouring out beautiful sounds, while seldom attempting to create a three-dimensional character. However, his cold personality, lush voice, and brilliant top notes were ideal for the part of Renato. His singing of "Eri tu," the Act III aria of revenge and despair, earned him the most prolonged ovation of the evening. Although few opera houses have the financial means to cast major international stars in brief but important roles, La Scala assigned the part of the sorceress Ulrica to Giulietta Simionato. She was electrifying in her Act I *scena* and her supercharged portrayal set a level of intensity that was matched throughout the evening by the other principals.

Even with a quartet of exceptional singers in top form, a performance can fail to catch fire when a routine hack wields the baton in the orchestra pit. Gianandrea Gavazzeni—one of La Scala's most imaginative conductors—was clearly "up" for the opening night *Ballo*. Although some critics and members of the audience felt that he came close to drowning out the singers on a few occasions, his feeling for symphonic sonority, highlighting of instrumental counter-melodies, razor-sharp attacks, and full-blooded, romantic approach to the score added up to an impassioned reading that ignited the performance on stage.

Callas's most vivid solo singing came in "Ecco l'orrido campo," the Act II aria sung at the foot of the gallows. Both her ability to convey a feeling of terror through vocal means and the icy security of her top tones were unforgettable. Surprisingly, when Callas recorded the selection for an aria recital in 1964 (a time when the highest passages should have taxed her) she sang longer phrases than those of the Scala performance. Instead of breathing after the aria's climactic high C, she sang the entire phrase in one breath. Callas was less effective in "Morrò, ma prima in grazia," the third act aria in which Amelia asks her husband to allow her to see her son for the last time. It was sung sensitively, but lacked the optimum poignancy and ravishing tonal beauty brought to it more recently by Montserrat Caballé. In the ensuing scene, Oscar, the page, invites the conspirators to Riccardo's masked ball. Callas surely must be one of the few dramatic sopranos to echo Oscar's trills with greater precision than those sung by the *soprano leggiero* in the role of the page.

Only at the end of the opera did Callas's Scala performance fall short of her commercially recorded interpretation. She showed signs of fatigue and Gavazzeni's slow, sustained tempos during the ensemble prayer taxed her breath control. The EMI recording sessions were spread over nine days, affording Callas the opportunity to sing the final scene in fresh and beautiful voice.

Ernest de Weerth summarized her performance in *Opera News* (January 6, 1958):

> As soon as the turbulent Maria Meneghini Callas appeared, extravagantly costumed as ever, we realized that she had set her stamp on Amelia. She was in voice and sang superbly. Callas is never dull.

When not held in check she is prone to exaggeration; when guided by an intelligent and trusted *régisseur,* her acting is convincing and exciting. Her personality is without doubt the most imposing on the operatic stage today. Others may have more beautiful voices, but at the moment there is only one Callas, just as there was only one Mary Garden.

The masked ball, Act III, scene 3: Amelia warns Riccardo (Giuseppe di Stefano) that there is a plot against his life. La Scala, Milan, December 1957.

Piccagliani

Il Pirata

VINCENZO BELLINI'S *Il Pirata,* which had premièred at La Scala, Milan, in 1827, was chosen for the final new production of the 1957–58 Scala season. The work had received only three previous productions in this century—in Rome in 1935 (with Beniamino Gigli and Iva Pacetti), Catania in 1951, and Palermo in 1958. When Callas returned to her artistic home in the spring of 1958 for five performances of *Anna Bolena* and five of *Pirata,* she found La Scala's management openly hostile. She had received an enormous amount of adverse criticism from the press because of two recent "scandals," and Antonio Ghiringhelli, the theater's superintendent, pointedly ignored her.

In August 1957, La Scala had agreed to give four performances of *La Sonnambula* at the Edinburgh Festival in Scotland. Callas had stated that she was exhausted and could not appear. The secretary general of La Scala told her that the guarantee of her name was the basis for the contract. Although Callas was not in her best voice, she sang the four performances for which she was contracted, but refused to appear in a fifth performance which had been added to the schedule at the last minute. When the newspapers announced that she had walked out on the

Callas in a costume designed by Piero Zuffi for La Scala's revival of *Il Pirata,* May 1958. Piccagliani

performance, she demanded that Ghiringhelli release a statement explaining that she was never scheduled for a fifth performance, but he refused.

Four months later Callas was slated to open the Rome season in *Norma.* She caught a cold while rehearsing in the unheated theater, but with medication she felt she could sing the performance. During the first act she began to lose her voice and people in the audience shouted, "Go back to Milan!" and "You cost us a million lire!" After a forty-five-minute intermission during which the management pleaded with her to continue—if only to act out the role—the performance was canceled. President Giovanni Gronchi was in the audience and the newspapers felt that Callas's cancellation was a personal insult to Italy's president.

Ghiringhelli, angry about her refusal to sing the fifth Edinburgh *Sonnambula* and the bad press from the Rome cancellation, ignored Callas even during the *Pirata* rehearsals. In an article for *Life* magazine (April 20, 1959), Callas wrote: "If the theater of which you are a guest adds to the tension [of a performance] by continual harassment and rudeness, art becomes physically and morally impossible. For my self-defense and dignity, I had no choice but to leave La Scala."

Callas announced that the five performances of *Pirata,* beginning on May 19, 1958, would be her final appearances at La Scala. In order to leave as *prima donna assoluta,* Callas knew she had to equal her previous successes. Also, her *Piratas* (with Franco Corelli and Ettore Bastianini) followed a month of outstanding performances, which included *L'Elisir d'Amore* with Giuseppe di Stefano and Renata Scotto, *Die Walküre* with Birgit Nilsson, Leonie Rysanek, Hans Hotter, and conductor Herbert von Karajan, and the Italian première of Janáček's *The Cunning Little Vixen.* If her enemies had hoped for some vocal disaster, they were disappointed. Claudio Sartori reported in *Opera* (August 1958): "Maria Callas's interpretation was flawless. Never perhaps has a singer been better adapted by her own means of expression to play the part of Imogene; and never avoided so well those strongly dramatic accents so as to limit herself almost entirely to the meaningful recitatives (which Mme Callas knows how to utter in the only convincing way) and to those lyrical mezza-voce sections, meditative and with slackened tempo, which have become a predominating characteristic of her interpretations . . ."

The day before her third *Pirata,* Callas underwent a painful operation. She wrote in *Life:*

> Only my doctors and a few intimate friends knew about it, for by then I had learned that Callas is not allowed to postpone a performance—or even to have a cold. For six days after the operation I was in pain, for I am allergic to narcotics and cannot have them. I had no sleep and almost nothing to eat. On Sunday, the day after the operation, I sang *Il Pirata.* On Wednesday I sang it again. Saturday was to be my final night, and I hoped to create for the public and myself a final warm memory of our long association.
>
> For the special occasion a group of young men decided that they wanted to throw flowers to me at the end of the performance, and they asked permission. It was granted. But that night when they arrived with their flowers, the order had been changed; no flowers were to be thrown . . . As I walked for the last time out of the theater that had been my operatic home for seven years, the young men were standing out in the street, throwing their flowers for me. They had finally found a place where they could say goodby.

On January 27, 1959, Callas appeared in a concert version of *Il Pirata* in Carnegie Hall. The nonsubscription American Opera Society performance marked the only appearance of her career in Carnegie Hall until her two concerts in 1974. At first her voice showed strain and unsteadiness at the top, but her middle and low notes were rich and secure. By the time Callas ended the lengthy opening scene with a solid high D, her voice had warmed up and she was given a two-minute ovation.

For the seventeen-minute final scene, the lights were lowered and a single spotlight followed Callas as she moved around the stage. Her only prop was a thirteen-foot silk stole which she used in combination with her voice, eyes, and hands to convey the heroine's insanity. Louis Biancolli wrote of her final scene (the New York *World-Telegram and The Sun,* January 28, 1959): "As the other soloists filed out, all the lights but those over the exits and the musicians' desks suddenly went out. Slowly Miss Callas rose, drew close her red stole, and an eerie glow fell on her face. At that ghostly juncture Miss Callas made the most of her strange and haunting timbres. It was something to be left in the dark with the voice of Maria Meneghini Callas."

Although the Scala *Piratas* were not broadcast and are probably lost in sound, the Carnegie Hall performance was professionally taped, thereby preserving Callas in her last major stage interpretation. Ronald Eyer wrote of the New York *Pirata* (*Musical America,* March 1959):

> The voice, which Miss Callas uses more as an extension of her dramatic personality than as a musical instrument, was not always beautiful, at least not in the popular sense in which beauty is equated with the quality of sweetness. Sometimes it was strident, like the tones the late Bronislaw Huberman often saw fit to draw from his violin. But it performed its function, in collaboration with the singer's impeccable musicianship and her unerring sense of authentic drama, in lifting the performance leagues above the kind of surface theatricality that commonly prevails in opera.

Callas in costumes designed by Piero Zuffi for La Scala's revival of *Il Pirata,* May 1958.
Piccagliani

Callas greeting the public after a performance of *Il Pirata,* La Scala, Milan, May 1958. Her curtain calls were as infinitely varied as her performances. Piccagliani

Poliuto

AFTER a thirty-month absence from La Scala, Callas returned to open the 1960–61 season in Gaetano Donizetti's rarely performed opera *Poliuto.* The opera was last staged at La Scala when it opened the 1940–41 season with Beniamino Gigli, Maria Caniglia, and Gino Bechi in the principal roles. Callas had hoped for a relaxed and congenial atmosphere in which to work, but extramusical troubles plagued the production. Luchino Visconti was signed as director, but he resigned in protest against government censorship of his film *Rocco and His Brothers.* He stated he would no longer work in a country where an artist's integrity went unrecognized by men in authority. Herbert Graf, called in to succeed Visconti, was given ten days in which to mount the opera.

Stagehands and musicians next threatened the opening night with a strike in support of a union demand for a twenty per cent increase in musicians' pay. Two days before the première, a concession of half the demanded increase, with the promise of further negotiations, saved the performance.

Donizetti's opera, set in ancient Armenia, concerns Paolina, the daughter of a Roman governor, who embraces Christianity in order to die

As Paolina in the Scala production of Donizetti's *Poliuto,* December 1960. Piccagliani with her husband Poliuto, who is condemned to death because of his religious beliefs. With the exception of the magnificent Act II finale (consisting in part of music which Donizetti salvaged from his unsuccessful *Maria di Rudenz*), the music of *Poliuto* is tuneful but undistinguished. Donizetti wrote the opera in 1838 for the Teatro San Carlo in Naples, but it was not produced because of political censorship. Two years later he drastically revised it for the Paris Opéra. La Scala, in 1960, revived the Naples version, with a few minor cuts, and inserted the overture and an Act I duet for Poliuto and Paolina from the Paris revision. Nicola Benois created massive ochre and gray sets and costumes of gold and amber.

In nine years, Callas opening nights had progressed from interesting musical events to the highlight of the Milan season and, with *Poliuto,* to an international social and musical event. The auditorium was decorated with sixteen thousand carnations for the *prima* of December 7, 1960. A capacity audience of thirty-eight hundred (which included Aristotle Onassis, the Begum Aga Khan, and Prince and Princess Rainier of Monaco) purchased tickets at official prices of up to $65 each, and the black market price for a single ticket was reported by the Associated Press to have reached $800.

Two decades of singing had taken its toll on Callas's voice and her opening night performance reflected the skillful husbanding of her vocal resources and an avoidance of vocal risks above the staff. The high notes were touched but not sustained and the one interpolated high D at the end of Act II was abandoned immediately. Only in the last act, when Callas had to sustain a high B for four measures, did her vocal insecurities become exposed and a trial for both her and the audience.

Callas's most poignant singing came in the second act, beginning with the line "Qual preghiera al ciel rivolgo?" ("What prayer can I offer to heaven?"), where she had an opportunity to sing with the wealth of vocal coloration for which she had become famous. Noel Goodwin reported in the New York *Herald Tribune* (December 18, 1960):

> She still has the capacity to color a phrase with unrivaled dramatic expression, from anger to grief and all points between, but *Poliuto* afforded her scant chance to show it.

> Her movements and gestures, "calculated in the dark and shaped by instinct," as she once said, are still surpassingly grand, in the play of her supplicating or accusing hands, the carriage of her head and body and the scorching flash of her great, black anxious eyes. She commands the stage with consummate technical mastery to underpin a voice which, if it were more comfortable, would likely make her a lesser artist.

A large part of the evening's vocal honors went to Ettore Bastianini and Franco Corelli. Corelli sang with a vocal outpouring combined with a sensitivity of phrasing seldom equaled in his subsequent years at the Metropolitan Opera.

Callas's appearances in *Poliuto* did little to enhance her reputation and on December 21, 1960, she sang her fifth and final performance of the opera. Harold Rosenthal wrote of her third and fifth performances (*Opera,* February 1961):

> Mme Callas was far from being in good voice at the third performance, and although at the fifth the voice was under firmer control, on both occasions her first act was vocally poor. There seemed to be more voice at the singer's disposal than when she was last heard at Covent Garden, but a lot of the time the tone sounded empty and hollow, and she seemed to produce more of those strident top notes than usual. Then suddenly would come a few minutes of sure and exquisite singing, of phrases so full of significance that little thrills would run down the spine.

Andrew Porter wrote of the fourth *Poliuto* (*Musical Times,* February 1961):

> No one will believe me when I say I heard the only performance, of the five she gave, at which Maria Callas found her peak form (a matinée on December 18, for the record). But so it was. She was spellbinding, secure, confident and inspiring confidence. To every role Callas brings something new. To Paolina it was not only beauty of presence, phrase, gesture and inflexion, but an almost physical enactment of the workings of grace, from the first stirrings when this pagan heroine listens to the Christians' hymn, to the supernatural radiance which floods her in the final scene as she resolves to join the Christians in martyrdom.

Paolina was the last part Callas was to learn for the stage. Subsequent

Poliuto, Act I, scene 1: Paolina, concealing herself in a subterranean meeting place, attempts to discover if her husband has converted to Christianity. La Scala, Milan, December 1960. Piccagliani

new roles reported by the press to be under consideration, but eventually rejected, included Orfeo for the Dallas Civic Opera for fall, 1961; the title role in Bellini's *Beatrice di Tenda* for La Scala, May 1961; Valentina in Meyerbeer's *Gli Ugonotti,* also for La Scala, June 1962; and Magda Sorel in Menotti's *The Consul,* to have been produced at the Théâtre des Champs-Élysées in Paris, 1969. One of the most intriguing rumors was a projected Zeffirelli production of Claudio Monteverdi's opera *L'Incoronazione di Poppea* (dating from 1642) to have been staged in Rome in the spring of 1972.

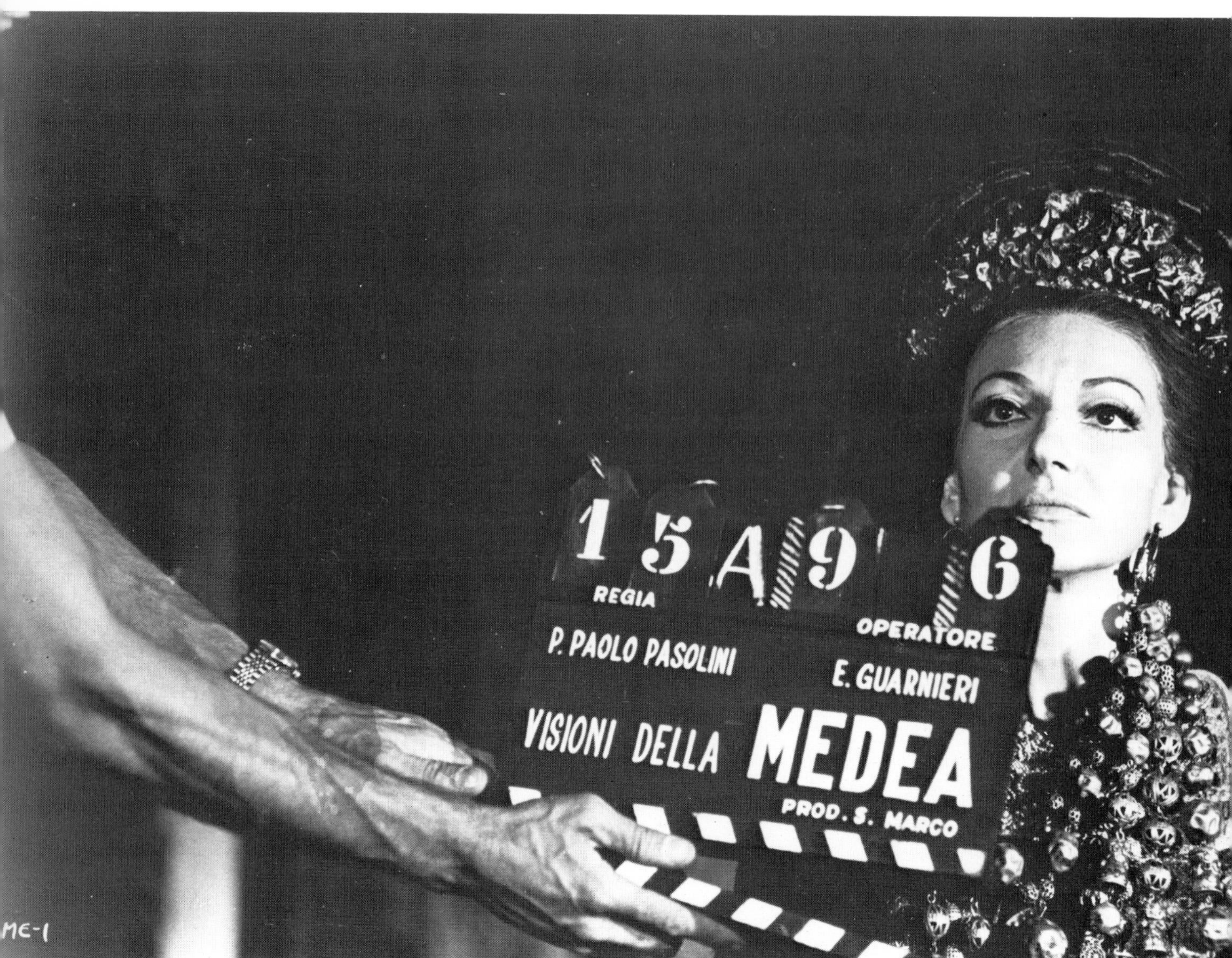

Callas in her film debut. New Line Cinema

Pier Paolo Pasolini's Medea

ALTHOUGH Callas recorded extensively for almost two decades, she could not be persuaded to commit any of her famous interpretations to film. Her husband had wanted her to make a film, but Callas was afraid that the acting appropriate for a stage performance would prove to be unsuitable and overdone for a filmed portrayal. In September 1965, Franco Zeffirelli announced that Callas had agreed in principle to a film version of *Tosca* with Tito Gobbi as co-star, but the project was abandoned. Future generations will be able to study filmed portrayals of Elisabeth Schwarzkopf as the Marschallin in *Der Rosenkavalier,* Cesare Siepi in the title role of *Don Giovanni,* and Tito Gobbi as Figaro in *The Barber of Seville,* but the full visual impact of Callas in *La Traviata, Norma,* and Cherubini's *Medea* is now lost.

Film debuts considered by Callas but rejected include *Macbeth* with Michelangelo Antonioni or Mauro Bolognini as director, film versions of works by Edgar Allan Poe and Max Dreyer, two projects by American-born director Joseph Losey, and the role of Maria in Carl Foreman's 1961 film *The Guns of Navarone.* In October 1968, Franco Rossellini suggested a nonmusical version of *Medea* with Pier Paolo Pasolini as director. Callas had seen Pasolini's *The Gospel According to St. Matthew* and *Oedipus Rex* and had liked them. She later read Pasolini's poetry and met with him to discuss the film.

"Before I did my screen test for *Medea,*" Callas said in an interview for the *Observer Review* (February 8, 1970), "I invited Pasolini to dinner. I said: 'If I do this film, and any time my treatment of the role or my performance in general causes problems for you, do not go to anybody else—come right away and tell *me*. I shall try to do what you want. You are the director. I am the interpreter, and I shall try to make the role my own only to give it back to the public.'"

At the time of filming, Pasolini said of Callas (*Opera News,* December 13, 1969): "It's from personal qualities in Callas that I realized I could make *Medea*. Here is a woman, in one sense the most modern of women, but there lives in her an ancient woman—mysterious, magical—whose sensibilities create a tremendous inner conflict for her." "I've always thought," Callas said at the time of the Pasolini interview, "that my cinema debut would be no easy matter. For the first time it was necessary to have something special, a character in whom I could feel totally involved. In the past I've refused excellent proposals for films because they only half interested me. When Franco Rossellini [*Medea*'s producer] and Pasolini proposed this one, I had no doubt. I immediately understood that this was the occasion I'd been waiting for, and I was determined not to let it slip by. Then, in the first weeks of work, I had the confirmation that my choice was no mistake. I discovered a group of colleagues exceptionally united in a common effort by a force that they all found to be immensely worth while."

The film was dubbed in three languages—Italian, French, and English—and the Italian version received its American première at Hunter College in New York on June 22, 1971. The Italian version later opened in New York on October 28, 1971, for a regular run.

Callas on her conception and filming of the role:

> Medea is a victim of circumstances, a priestess-goddess who is swept away by her passionate love of Jason and dedicates herself to him with the same intensity that she once brought to her religious duties. When Jason discards her, she is completely at a loss in a world of strangers, and she is forced—out of desperation—to commit ter-

As Medea in Pier Paolo Pasolini's film, 1971. United Press International

rible acts. But you must remember that in Medea's religion the killing of her children meant that they would become immortal. She does go mad, of course, but it's a kind of static, internal madness—no yelling or screaming until the absolute end. The emotional scenes were not particularly difficult; it took me perhaps one minute to get into the proper mood. Then I just looked past the cameras and played to the stage-hands and the extras. They were my public. (*The New Yorker,* April 24, 1971)

What the critics said:

To a generation like mine, still burning with the memory of Judith Anderson's Medea, Maria Callas, given one-twentieth of Miss Anderson's dialogue, creates a portrait of the Queen of Colchis that is every bit as memorable and fascinating . . . In the final half hour of the film, Mme. Callas goes to work and achieves what it took all evening for Miss Anderson to do. Returning to her old gods, her magic returns, the sun and the moon speak to her again, and with all of the Furies unleashed, weeping, cursing, loving, hating, she destroys Creon and his daughter, her children and herself, leaving Jason with his gold.

Nobody should be surprised that Callas can act and magnificently so, but that Pasolini should evoke such a performance from her in a film debut is a credit to him. Little more than a presence for the first half of the film (though your eyes never leave her), when she emerges from the landscape to express every emotion of great tragedy, she is incredible. (Bernard Drew, Gannett News Service, October 1971)

Attired in a long, clinging embroidered robe, decked with ropes of barbaric ornaments falling to her feet, [Callas] abandons her body to its own grief, flinging herself to the ground, grovelling with anguish and fury in contortions of pain accented by extraordinary grace—a hypnotic performance such as one rarely sees even attempted nowadays, and endowed with true magnetic power. It is a virtuoso corporeal and psychological triumph . . . It can be said that in this new *Medea* there is contained acting of a supreme dramatic achievement, which will rank the film as a rare work of cinematographic art. (Genêt, "Letter from Paris," *The New Yorker,* February 21, 1970)

Callas, during her final master class at the Juilliard School, New York City, works with three singers on the final trio from *La Forza del Destino*. Eugene Kohn is pianist.

Louis Péres

Master Classes

IN New York between October 1971 and March 1972, Callas conducted two series of twelve master classes (the March 6 class was canceled because she was sick) in the Juilliard School's opera theater. The classes were given on Mondays and Thursdays. The invitation had come from Peter Mennin, the school's director, and critic and opera historian Irving Kolodin. Over three hundred singers auditioned and Callas selected twenty-six. Half the singers were students at Juilliard and the fee was included in their general tuition. Non-Juilliard students were required to pay a $240 tuition fee for the entire series.

Juilliard had advertised, in a single announcement in the New York *Times* at the end of the summer, that a limited number of observers would be allowed. The initial response was modest, probably for a variety of reasons. There was the chance that the classes might not materialize. Callas had been engaged to work with advanced singers at the Curtis Institute in Philadelphia in February 1971 and had departed after only two days. (In an interview published in *The New Yorker* two months later, she stated that the eighteen students were not prepared for advanced training.) The relatively early hour of the classes (5:30

P.M.) made it difficult for some people. Many simply did not see or understand the one announcement.

When the sessions began, there were less than two hundred observers in the thousand-seat theater. As word about the classes circulated, the demand for tickets quickly increased, but Juilliard refused to sell subscriptions or single tickets after the first series began. Through a variety of ruses, including counterfeit passes, the most persistent Callas admirers gained admittance. For the last few sessions, there was nearly a capacity audience. Juilliard changed its policy for the second series and allowed the sale of both subscriptions and single tickets, and attendance was large for the whole series.

In an interview held after her first session, Callas told John Gruen (the New York *Times,* October 31, 1971):

> . . . I would like to pass on to the young ones what I myself have learned—what I've learned from the great conductors I've worked with, from my teachers, and especially from my own research, which has not stopped to this day. I suppose I have a natural insight into music. I am able to read, so to speak, between the notes. I take the trouble to see what lies beneath a composer's work. We must never forget that we are interpreters, that we are there to serve the composer, and to discharge a very delicate task. This is a great responsibility.

Callas walked on stage at precisely five-thirty for each class. The stage was bare save for a grand piano, a high stool, and a desk with the scores for that session. Applause was invariably silenced with a wave of her hand. She was not the Maria Callas usually described in magazine articles: "the living legend," the *bête noire* of impresarios, or a member of the international jet-set. She was a sincere, complete professional who commanded respect, but also a woman who gave the impression of being shy and vulnerable. The singers were seated in the first two rows. Callas would either ask, "Well, who feels like singing?" or call a specific student. She usually worked with five singers during the two-hour sessions. The material was drawn mainly from the Italian and French operatic repertoires. After a few classes, it was made clear to the audience that she would not allow any spontaneous applause or any other audience reaction to interrupt her work with the students.

Callas made occasional annotations in her copies of the scores as the students sang their arias initially without interruption. A phrase-by-phrase coaching usually followed. Almost invariably, she requested a quicker, more pointed delivery of the introductory recitatives. Her coaching followed the basic principles of good singing and musicianship: do not slide into notes, always sing *on* the pitch, maintain a smooth legato and resonate the tone, thoroughly understand the text and the mood which is to be conveyed, perform all the embellishments as written (students who were unable to execute trills were instructed to begin studying them), do not over-embellish, give the notes their proper time value, and be rhythmically precise. It was difficult for some of the singers to shed faults and mannerisms which had become an integral part of their technique, but the progress made in fifteen or twenty minutes was very often phenomenal. During the first run-throughs of the pieces, the singers were often stiff and ill-at-ease. The readings tended to be perfunctory and colorless. After a few minutes of discussion and repetition of phrases, they began to sense the inner life of the music and delivered their lines with conviction and a feeling of emotional involvement.

Callas was warm, relaxed, and considerate with the students, but she insisted on a serious approach to their work. She was frank, but never condescending or reproachful. Her long stage experience made her aware of the problems and difficulties which they were encountering, and she always managed to put them at ease with affectionate or humorous exchanges. Although she stated before the first series that the classes would be devoted to interpretation rather than vocal technique, she found it necessary to urge a few students to work on their tone production. Some of the men were handicapped by a constricted vocal production and most of the women either had weak chest tones or were afraid to use them.

Callas worked largely by example. She was at Juilliard to guide students rather than to perform, but many in the audience had never heard her in person (in the previous fourteen years, in New York, she had sung only two *Toscas* at the Metropolitan, a concert performance of *Il Pirata* at Carnegie Hall, and two arias from *Carmen* at Madison Square Garden) and they were there to hear anything that she might do. She sang many of the pieces almost in their entirety, but rarely in sections lasting more than fifteen seconds. The phrases were occasionally taken down an octave, but generally were sung as written. At times she sounded tired, but frequently she was in excellent voice. In an attempt to convey the passion of the conclusion of "D'amour l'ardente flamme" from Hector Berlioz's *La Damnation de Faust,* she sang the final stanza with full intensity. Her singing at Juilliard was considerably more beautiful and vibrant than in her 1963 recording of the same music.

Her illustration of a musical point was not limited to the use of her voice. All of the apparently instinctive dramatic possibilities of her eyes, hands, and facial expressions were brought into play. While a tenor was singing the aria "Guardate! Come io piango ed imploro" ("Look at me! How I weep and implore you") from *Manon Lescaut,* Callas silently "sang" the aria with him and facially conveyed Des Grieux's despair.

Callas had previously recorded the majority of the soprano arias which were examined and consequently the greatest musical revelations came during her work with the male singers. Particularly memorable were her eloquent singing of the *cantabile* section beginning "E voi, piuttosto" in the "Prologue" from *I Pagliacci,* the dramatic strength of "Nemico della patria" from *Andrea Chénier,* and the way in which she captured the heartless cynicism of the "Credo" from *Otello.* Her singing of these baritone arias not only revealed the interpretive subtleties possible in this music, but also indicated the quickness of her musical perception in repertoire she had never performed.

Possibly her most overwhelmingly powerful singing came after a discussion of the "Cortigiani" from *Rigoletto.* She told the young baritone that Rigoletto "should be fiercely savage, like a blind animal here." With her left hand, she suddenly set an extraordinarily fast tempo for the pianist and launched into the lines beginning "Cortigiani, vil razza dannata" ("Courtiers, despicable, condemned breed"). As she hurled out the short, vituperative phrases—her hands curved toward her like talons and her face reflecting the jester's terror and rage—the observers in the audience were frozen in their seats. Those who had only read of the electricity generated by Callas at her most intense were experiencing for the first time the full impact of her interpretive gifts. At the conclusion of the section, which lasted less than a minute, many in the audience were in tears.

She told the students at the end of the final class: "Whether I keep on singing or not doesn't make any difference," and she urged them to continue working and to apply what they had learned. Without waiting for an audience response, she quickly walked off the stage.

Coaching Romanian soprano Eugenia Moldoveanu, winner of the Third International Madama Butterfly Competition, Osaka Festival Hall, Japan, May 1973.
Courtesy of Matahiko Okada

An early photograph of Callas in concert, Teatro Verdi, Trieste, April 21, 1951.

The "Mad Scene" from Ambroise Thomas's *Hamlet,* Royal Festival Hall, London, September 23, 1959. Callas suggested Ophelia's madness by allowing the shoulder straps of her gown to slip down. For the "Sleepwalking Scene" from *Macbeth,* which followed on the program, Callas concluded the *scena* by walking off the stage as she would have in a staged performance.

London Express News and Features

Tatania Palast, Berlin, October 23, 1959.
Harry Croner

Städtische Saalbau, Essen, March 19, 1962. Although Callas's operatic appearances in Germany were limited to two performances each in Berlin and Cologne, her four concert tours, between 1959 and 1973, took her to nine other cities in Germany.
Collection of Winfried Stiffel

Deutsche Oper, Berlin, May 17, 1963. Heinz Köster

Carnegie Hall, New York, March 5, 1974. Beverley Gallegos

With Giuseppe di Stefano and pianist Robert Sutherland, March 1974.

Luis Péres

Callas, Louise Caselotti, Nicola Rossi-Lemeni (standing), and a fellow passenger, sailing for Italy on the S.S. *Rossia,* June 1947. Courtesy of Louise Caselotti

Palacio de Bellas Artes, Mexico City, July 12, 1951: Callas, her husband Giovanni Battista Meneghini (at right), and friends attending a performance of *L'Elisir d'Amore* with tenor Cesare Valletti. Collection of Carlos Díaz Du-Pond

Callas and Giuseppe di Stefano embrace after Act II of their first *Lucia* at La Scala, Milan, January 18, 1954. Their artistic collaboration, both on stage and in the recording studio, has spanned over two decades. Piccagliani

The eminent German conductor Karl Böhm, in Naples for a series of performances of *Tannhäuser* at the Teatro San Carlo, visiting with Callas in her dressing room during a March 1956 performance of *Lucia di Lammermoor*. The two musicians were never to appear together in performance. Troncone

Sightseeing in Edinburgh, Scotland, 1957.
Piccagliani

Soprano Elisabeth Schwarzkopf, one of Callas's closest friends, visits during the intermission of a performance of *La Sonnambula* at La Scala, Milan, March 1957. Four months later they returned to La Scala to record together in *Turandot* for EMI.
Piccagliani

Callas and Sir Winston Churchill on Aristotle Onassis' yacht *Christina,* August 1959. United Press International

Callas and Aristotle Onassis, at the beginning of their nine-year romance, leaving a Milan night club, September 1959. United Press International

Arriving at Tempelhof, Berlin, for a concert at the Tatiana Palast, October 1959.
Harry Croner

With Maestro Tullio Serafin during a recording session for their stereo remake of *Norma* for EMI, September 1960. Piccagliani

Callas receives an affectionate greeting from her favorite director, Luchino Visconti. Piccagliani

Film-maker Marcel Pagnol, Princess Grace of Monaco, Italian director Vittorio de Sica, and Callas at Monte Carlo's Sporting Club, during the Second International Television Festival, January 22, 1962. United Press International

Callas and Joan Sutherland, costumed as Marguerite de Valois, during a break in the dress rehearsal for La Scala's 1962 all-star production of Meyerbeer's *Gli Ugonotti.* Piccagliani

Callas waving good-bye to admirers outside of the Royal Opera House, London, after a gala performance of *Tosca* which was to be her final operatic stage appearance, July 5, 1965. Eight years later, on October 25, 1973, she returned to the stage as a concert artist. United Press International

Callas visits with Greek soprano Elena Suliotis at Carnegie Hall, New York, during the intermission of the American Opera Society's concert performance of *Norma,* November 9, 1967. Although Callas appeared in almost ninety performances of *Norma,* this was her first hearing of the opera as a member of the audience.

Collection of Gregg Newbern

Callas, a member of the international jury at the Fourth Tchaikovsky Competition, acknowledges cheers from the audience in Moscow, June 23, 1970.

United Press International

On the David Frost Show, December 10, 1970. For ninety minutes, in her first appearance on an American talk-show, Callas discussed her career and personal beliefs.
Courtesy of Group W Productions

Opening night at La Scala, Milan, December 7, 1971: Antonio Ghiringhelli, general manager of the theater, watches as Callas cuts the ribbon on new technical equipment. Piccagliani

Countess Wally Castelbarco, Arturo Toscanini's daughter (second from left), and Callas join in the applause for the cast at the conclusion of La Scala's revival of *I Vespri Siciliani,* Milan, December 7, 1971. Piccagliani

Callas and Giuseppe di Stefano, co-directors of *I Vespri Siciliani* at Turin's Teatro Regio, with conductor Fulvio Vernizzi, during a round-table discussion held the day after the controversial *prima* of April 10, 1973.
Courtesy of the *Gazzetta del Popolo,* Torino

Relaxing on a private island in the Aegean Sea, July 1970. "Here is a woman, in one sense the most modern of women, but there lives in her an ancient woman —mysterious, magical—whose sensibilities create a tremendous inner conflict for her" (Pier Paolo Pasolini, 1969). United Press International

III

Performance Annals by Arthur Germond

Foreword

MARIA CALLAS is generally acknowledged to be one of the most important operatic performers of the twentieth century. The full impact of her performances could only be experienced by both hearing her and seeing her in the opera house. Some of this impact is preserved in her many commercial recordings and in private recordings made from live performances. Photographs also preserve a measure of her stage presence. Another aspect of her career can be preserved in a record of what she sang, when and where she sang, and who sang with her. This performance list attempts to make available such a record.

In addition to providing a simple list of the details of Callas's performances, this list also provides some interesting insights into her career. In the first three years of her international career (1947–1949) Callas sang ten different operatic roles. By 1956 all of these roles except one, Norma, had been dropped from her repertoire, never to be sung on stage again. Among the roles dropped, most of them in the dramatic soprano category, were Isolde, Brünnhilde, Kundry, La Gioconda, Aida, and Turandot. Norma, the exception cited above, was the one role that remained continuously in her repertoire throughout these years. It is not surprising, therefore, to find that Norma is the role she sang most often, a total of eighty-eight times in eighteen cities. For comparison, Rosa Ponselle, the pre-eminent Norma of an earlier era, appears to have sung the role some thirty-six times in nine cities.

As an example of how strongly Callas stamped her own personality upon her roles, one finds that even in roles which she sang infrequently she became the standard by which later singers were judged. The role of Lady Macbeth was sung five times only, all at La Scala, Milan, in a period of less than two weeks. Over twenty years later an American critic would lament, when reviewing the singers who had recorded the role, that Callas had not committed her interpretation to a commercial recording. *Anna Bolena* has been revived several times since Callas first sang the role in 1957, and every singer who has sung that role since then has been compared to Callas. Callas sang that role twelve times in two seasons, all at La Scala. When *I Vespri Siciliani* opened the rebuilt Teatro Regio in Turin in 1973, with Callas directing, it was remarked that the most successful performances of that work in memory were those in which Callas sang. Callas sang *I Vespri Siciliani* four times at the 1951 Florence May Festival and seven times at La Scala the following December and January.

The number of people who actually could have heard Callas in roles such as these must have been small, yet these performances remained vivid memories for many of them, to be commented upon in later years, making them seem almost as important in her career as Norma, Tosca, Lucia, or Violetta, roles which she sang many times and in many cities around the world. To some extent, also, her fame in these roles can be attributed to the circulation of private recordings of the live performances so that people who never saw any of these performances could still experience some of their force.

Callas's operatic career extended from 1940 to 1965. She began appearing in major roles in mid-1941 or 1942. Between September 1945 and August 1947 she did not perform at all on stage. Her career as a leading singer, allowing for the interval in which she did not appear, therefore covered some twenty-one years. During these years she sang over 560 opera performances (526 between 1947 and 1965 and, according to a statement she made in an interview, a possible 30 to 40 additional between 1941/42 and 1945). Up through 1965 Callas also made fifty-four stage appearances (concerts and the like) and eighteen radio and television appearances, along with recording twenty-six complete operas and eleven LP recitals. Callas's career cannot be termed notable simply in terms of the number of performances sung. Many singers, both contemporary and in the past, have sung many more performances over a similar number of years. Enrico Caruso, for example, in a twenty-six-year career sang over 1,500 operatic performances, but then the fame of both Caruso and Callas is not based on numbers of performances sung.

Previous published works about Callas have been marred by inaccuracies. Anyone who compares this performance list with other books and articles will find a number of discrepancies. Several writers have stated that Callas first sang *Norma* in Buenos Aires in June 1949, unaware that she had already performed it in Florence the preceding November. In several places it is stated that she sang *Aida* at the Caracalla Baths in Rome in August 1948, when in fact the opera was *Turandot* and the performances were in July. Her first commercial recordings, three 78-rpm records made for Cetra, have always been placed immediately after the March 1949 RAI concert in which she sang the same arias that were recorded. However, numbers engraved on the records themselves turn out to be the recording dates and establish that these recordings were made in the following November. Every book and article that I have seen which gives the date for Callas's Italian debut at the Arena in Verona gives the date as August 3, 1947. Information supplied me by the Verona Arena, however, gives the date as August 2. Attempting to determine which date was correct, I found a brief news item in the *Corriere della Sera* of Milan for August 3, 1947. The item was datelined "Verona, Aug. 2 (night)" and stated that the season at the Arena opened "this evening" with a performance of *La Gioconda,* and among the cast members listed is Maria Callas. August 2, 1947, therefore, is the correct date for Callas's Italian debut and the beginning date of her international career. Granted that the difference of one day is a small matter, but still it is worth while to be accurate in giving one of the most significant dates in Callas's career.

It would be too much to hope that my own list is entirely free from error, despite the effort to make it completely accurate. In the interests of accuracy, I have gone wherever possible to firsthand sources and checked all sources against each other. Most of the opera houses in which she sang have been contacted to verify the dates and casts of her performances. A special effort was made to secure the dates and casts of the repeat performances which followed her first appearance of the season in each opera. Obtaining this information was especially difficult in many cases since, while the first performance would be reviewed and widely publicized, the subsequent performances would generally be ignored in most books and publications. Wherever possible, performance information supplied by the opera houses or derived from books and periodicals was checked against contemporary newspapers, if they were available, to confirm casts and performance dates. In the process of collating information for the same performance, I have found that information supplied by opera houses from their archives or in official publications is occasionally inaccurate. A few examples of errors of this sort may be of interest, especially if someone wishes to compare some of the performance information in this list against the various sources that are cited. The Teatro Massimo Bellini, Catania, in a letter to me which listed the *prima* dates of each of the performances sung by Callas in Catania, gave the date for her first *La Traviata* there as March 8, 1952. This same date appears in the generally authoritative listing "La Callas in Italia" by Dr. Carlo Marinelli which appeared in *Discoteca.* In fact, however, the March 8 performance never took place. It had to be canceled because Callas was ill with influenza. The second scheduled performance on March 12 thus became the *prima.* This information was found in the March 8, 1952, issue of the Catanian newspaper *La Sicilia.* A clipping of the announcement was sent to me by the Biblioteca Universitaria of Catania which also sent me the details of all the repeat performances at Catania as drawn from local newspaper announcements. The *Cronache del Teatro S. Carlo,* the official performance annals published by the Teatro San Carlo, Naples, lists four performances of *Lucia di Lammermoor* for the spring of 1956: March 22, 24, 27, and April 7. The cast is listed for the first performance, and no change from this cast is shown for any of the later performances. Callas is shown in the first performance, so by implication she sang all four. A letter from the archivist of the Teatro San Carlo indicated that Callas sang only the first three performances, and this was verified by a news item in the *Corriere della Sera* of March 28, 1956, which said that on the previous night Callas had made her farewell appearance at the San Carlo before an audience which crowded the theater to its limits. Research in the archives of La Scala has corrected some of the casts listed in *La Scala 1946–1956,* a book published by the La Scala theater. A number of other examples of a similar nature could be noted, but I hope that the examples mentioned here will indicate the effort that has been made to insure accuracy in this list. In a few instances where it was impossible to resolve discrepancies between sources, I have made my own judgment about which source was likely to be correct.

There is one instance, however, in which I have been forced to rely on conjecture, since complete performance information could not be obtained. Somewhat surprisingly this performance occurred in Callas's 1974 American tour with Giuseppe di Stefano, a tour for which it would be expected that information would be readily available. In fact, determining the selections sung in the concerts on this tour proved to be almost as difficult as determining the details of performances in small cities in Italy that took place twenty or more years earlier. I was successful in obtaining the selections for all the concerts except that in Portland, Oregon. Despite a number of inquiries the precise program in this city could not be established, so I have augmented the few details obtained from newspaper reviews with such other selections as seemed probable based on the concerts which preceded and followed it.

The sources used in compiling this list are cited in the following section.

I hope that this record of the performances of a career unique in the operatic world of our time will be of interest and value to all those who respect and admire Maria Callas.

ACKNOWLEDGMENTS AND SOURCES

The compilation of this list extended over several years. Many people have assisted in its preparation by furnishing information and suggestions. I would like to express here my gratitude for their help and acknowledge their contributions. Any errors are my own responsibility and, of course, corrections would be most gratefully received.

For supplying essential information I want to thank the opera houses and libraries in the following cities:

Bergamo	Teatro Gaetano Donizetti
Bologna	Biblioteca Comunale
Brescia	Biblioteca Queriniana
Cagliari	Teatro Massimo
Catania	Biblioteca Universitaria
	Teatro Massimo Bellini
Florence	Biblioteca Nazionale Centrale
	Teatro Comunale
Genoa	Biblioteca Universitaria
	Teatro Comunale dell'Opera
Naples	Teatro San Carlo
Palermo	Teatro Massimo
Paris	Bibliothèque et Musée de l'Opéra
Parma	Teatro Regio
Pisa	Biblioteca Universitaria
Reggio Calabria	Biblioteca Sandicchi
Rio de Janeiro	Teatro Municipal
Rovigo	Accademia dei Concordi
Trieste	Civico Museo Teatrale
Turin	Biblioteca Civica
	Teatro Regio
Udine	Biblioteca Comunale "Vincenzo Joppi"
Venice	Teatro La Fenice
Verona	Arena

I am indebted to the following individuals for their help:

Messrs. Michael Allen and John Hughes of EMI in London and Mr. Walter Legge, former director of classical recording for that company, for information about the published EMI (Angel) recordings, and to Mr. John Watson of EMI's International Classical Division for researching the unpublished recordings.

Mr. J. Graham Baker of Penistone, Sheffield, England, for checking innumerable details and providing many worthwhile leads.

Signora Renata Bertelli of the RAI office in Rome for information about several of Callas's RAI broadcasts.

Mr. Armando Bona of New York City for checking and correcting on the basis of theater archives at La Scala, Milan, and the Teatro Carlo Felice, Genoa, the information that I had compiled about performances in those cities.

Mr. Charles Jahant of Hyattsville, Maryland, for his assistance in uncovering details of Callas's early career in Greece through his research in the holdings of Greek newspapers at the Library of Congress. His work was of great value in clarifying the basic facts of these years and greatly simplified my own work among these papers at the Library of Congress.

Miss Shirley Manley of New York City for information about the Juilliard master classes.

Dr. Carlo Marinelli of Rome for furnishing me detailed information about Callas's performances in Rome. In addition, his list "La Callas in Italia (1947–1961)" (*Discoteca,* October 1972) which showed where Callas had performed in Italy provided a useful confirmation of my own research as well as details of a few performances that I had not until then known about.

Mr. Harold Rosenthal, editor of *Opera,* for responding with information to a number of my inquiries.

Mr. Martin Sokol of New York City for his research work for me at the Library of Congress and for helpful suggestions at various stages of the compilation of this list.

At various points in compiling this list I circulated draft copies to a number of knowledgeable Callas fans, friends, and authorities. Among them I would especially like to mention Mr. John Ardoin of Dallas, Texas, Mrs. Dario Soria and Messrs. Leo Lerman, Robert H. Reid, and Richard Striker, all of New York City, and Mr. Michael Scott of London. For their assistance on specific points, comments, suggestions, and encouragement I am most grateful. Misses May and Olive Haddock of Leeds, England, Signor Silvio Maionica of Milan, Signor Luciano di Cave of Rome, and Mrs. Howard Pritz of Columbus, Ohio, helped in answering questions about specific details.

The books, periodicals, and newspapers consulted in preparing this list are shown below:

Books

Armani, Franco (editor), *La Scala, 1946/1956,* Milan, 1957
Armani, Franco (editor), *La Scala, 1946/1966,* Milan, 1967
Callas, Evangelia (in collaboration with Lawrence G. Blochman), *My Daughter—Maria Callas,* New York, Fleet Publishing Corporation, 1960; London, Leslie Frewin Publishers, 1967 (with additional chapter by Blochman)
Cronache del Teatro S. Carlo, Naples, 1968
Davis, Ronald, *Opera in Chicago,* New York, Appleton-Century-Crofts, 1966
Galatopoulos, Stelios, *Callas: La Divina,* Elmsford, N.Y., London House & Maxwell, 1970
Gatti, Carlo, *Il Teatro alla Scala nella storia e nell' arte (1778–1963),* 2 vols., Milan, 1964 (with *Cronologia completa degli spettacoli e dei concerti a cura di Giampiero Tintori*)
Jellinek, George, *Callas: Portrait of a Prima Donna,* New York, Ziff-Davis Publishing Company, 1960
Pinzauti, Leonardo, *Il Maggio Musicale Fiorentino,* Florence, 1967
Seltsam, William H., *Metropolitan Opera Annals: First Supplement, 1947–1957,* New York, The H. W. Wilson Company, 1957; *Second Supplement, 1957–1966,* New York, The H. W. Wilson Company, 1968

Periodicals

Discoteca (Milan)
Gramophone (London)
Music and Musicians (London)
Musical America (New York)
Musical Courier (New York)
Oggi (Milan)
Opera (London)
Opera News (New York)
L'Opera; rassegna internazionale del teatro lirico (Milan)
Opéra; la revue de l'art lyrique (Paris)
The Saturday Review (New York)
La Scala, Rivista dell'Opera (Milan)

Newspapers

Amsterdam: *De Telegraaf*
Athens: *Deutsche Nachrichten in Griechenland*
'E Vradyne
Le Messager
Atlanta: *The Atlanta Constitution*

Barcelona: *La Vanguardia Española*
Berlin: *Der Tagesspiegel*
Bonn: *General-Anzeiger*
Boston: *Boston Evening Globe*
Brussels: *Le Soir*
Buenos Aires: *La Prensa*
Chicago: *Chicago Today*
Chicago Tribune
Cincinnati: *The Cincinnati Enquirer*
Cologne: *Kölnische Rundschau*
Dallas: *The Dallas Morning News*
The Dallas Times Herald
Detroit: *The Detroit News*
Düsseldorf: *Rheinische Post*
Frankfurt: *Frankfurter Allgemeine*
Hamburg: *Hamburger Abendblatt*
Kansas City: *Kansas City Star*
Lisbon: *O Século*
London: *Daily Herald*
The Financial Times
The Times
Los Angeles: *Los Angeles Herald-Examiner*
Los Angeles Times
Madrid: *A B C*
Arriba
Marca
Ya
Mannheim: *Mannheimer Morgen*
Mexico City: *El Universal*
Miami: *The Miami News*
Milan: *Corriere del Teatro*
Corriere della Sera
Montreal: *La Presse*
The Montreal Star
Munich: *Süddeutsche Zeitung*
New York City: *The New York Times*
Variety
Paris: *France-Soir*
Le Figaro
Le Monde
Philadelphia: *Philadelphia Inquirer*
Portland: *The Oregonian*
The Oregon Journal
Rome: *Il Tempo*
St. Louis: *St. Louis Post-Dispatch*
San Francisco: *San Francisco Chronicle*
São Paulo: *O Estado de São Paulo*
Seattle: *The Seattle Times*
Stuttgart: *Stuttgarter Zeitung*
Toronto: *The Toronto Star*
Vancouver: *The Province*
The Vancouver Sun
Washington, D.C.: *The Evening Star*
The Washington Post and Times-Herald
Washington Star-News
Wiesbaden: *Wiesbadener Kurier*
Zürich: *Neue Zürcher Zeitung*

Many of the music critics of the newspapers shown above have also provided me with additional details not covered in their reviews. I wish to thank them collectively for their courteous and helpful replies to my letters.

The two biographies of Maria Callas which are listed above, by George Jellinek and Stelios Galatopoulos, despite a number of inaccuracies and omissions, provided a most valuable general background and chronology of her career.

—Performance Annals—

ARRANGEMENT

The list of performances of Maria Callas has been divided into three parts, coinciding with the stages of her career. Part One covers the years 1938–1945, the period when she was singing in Greece. The details of this period are not well established in all cases, so the performance information is given in narrative form, citing discrepancies where they occur. Part Two covers the years 1947–1965, the period of her international career. Performances during these years are given complete. Part Three covers the years 1965–1974. Except at the end of this period, Callas did not sing in public but did become involved in film, master classes, and directing. From the fall of 1973 through the fall of 1974 she returned to the stage in a concert tour with Giuseppe di Stefano. These activities are all listed.

Performances are listed in chronological order. The date of the performance is given first, followed by the city and the opera house or concert hall, and, finally, the particulars of the performance—the name of the opera together with the cast or, in the case of concerts, the arias sung on the program. Only appearances in which Callas sang are listed. Excluded are radio interviews, television appearances, etc.

Where pertinent, following the name of the city and the house, added in parentheses is the name of the organization under whose auspices the performance took place, for example the Opera Nacional in Mexico City and the Civic Opera Company in Dallas. In the cast list, the role sung by Callas always appears first; however, her name is not entered before the role, as are the names of the other cast members, since the constant repetition of her name seemed superfluous. When Callas appeared in a concert, radio broadcast, or telecast with other artists, these artists are listed by name, but the selections they presented are omitted. Information about the production, such as whether it was a new production for Callas or the name of the director, is given only when the director is of special note (Zeffirelli or Visconti, for example).

The names of the operas and the titles of the arias sung in concerts are given in the language in which they were presented, e.g. *La Walkiria* or *Tristano e Isotta*—Morte di Isotta instead of *Die Walküre* or *Tristan und Isolde*—Liebestod. Where the original, or more familiar, title may not be obvious, it has been added in parentheses. It should be noted that all of Callas's operatic performances on stage after she left Athens in 1945 were sung in Italian (she did record *Carmen* in French). In concert programs and recordings she sang some arias in French and one, "Ocean! Thou mighty monster" from *Oberon,* in English.

The following symbol and abbreviation are used in the list:

* An asterisk after the date indicates that all or part of this performance exists on tape or private recording.
c. Conductor.

—Performance Annals—

LIST OF PERFORMANCES OF MARIA CALLAS

Part One
1938 – 1945

The years 1938 to 1945 cover the period of Maria Callas's career in Greece when she was a student and when she first began to sing professionally on stage. Part of this period was during wartime when Greece was under German and Italian occupation. Information about her performances during these years is meager, and sources of information frequently are in conflict about dates and details. Information for the following summary of Callas's performances from 1938 through 1945 is drawn from a variety of sources.

First are the recollections of Maria Callas herself and of her mother, Mrs. Evangelia Callas. A detailed interview with Callas concerning her years in Greece was published in the Italian periodical *Oggi* (issue of January 10, 1957). In addition Callas has made comments on this period in a number of newspaper and radio interviews. In the following summary, Callas's statements are taken from the *Oggi* interview unless identified otherwise. Mrs. Evangelia Callas published her recollections in 1960 in her book *My Daughter—Maria Callas.* The recollections of both Callas and her mother have the value of being firsthand accounts by the principals involved in these events. At the same time it should be kept in mind that such recollections understandably may be subject to error regarding events which occurred fifteen to twenty years earlier.

Next are the biographies of Callas by George Jellinek (*Callas: Portrait of a Prima Donna*) and Stelios Galatopoulos (*Callas: La Divina*). Both books are secondary sources, and the brief descriptions which they provide of the events of these years are not annotated, nor are the sources used identified. It is difficult, therefore, to evaluate the reliability of these accounts.

Last among the sources are Athens newspapers for these years. These newspapers provide the only contemporary record of these performances. Various problems are encountered, however, when using these newspapers. Holdings in the United States of Athens newspapers for this period are far from complete. There are frequent gaps of days, weeks, and even months, and all too often the papers relevant to Callas's career are lacking. The newspaper accounts themselves suffer various shortcomings. Reviews and announcements during the war years were much curtailed because shortages of newsprint had reduced the papers to only a few pages. Apart from reviews of major events, the space provided for "entertainment" news generally was a half column or less which simply provided for a listing of musical events, plays, and movies for that day. Casts for most performances are not listed. In addition, the announcement of a performance is not proof that the performance took place since postponements are rarely noted. The newspapers consulted were the Greek language *'E Vradyne* and *Akropolis,* the German language *Deutsche Nachrichten in Griechenland* (a paper published for the occupying German authorities), and the French language *Le Messager.*

On the basis of the information provided by these sources, the performance history of Callas's career from 1938 through 1945 is described below. Discrepancies between the various sources are indicated.

1. Student Performances

In September 1937, Callas was admitted to the Ethnikon Odeon (National Conservatory), where she became a pupil of Maria Trivella. Her first appearance in a full-length operatic role was as Santuzza in a student performance of *Cavalleria Rusticana.* The date given for this performance varies. Callas states that it took place in October or November of 1938 when she was "less than fifteen years old." In another reference to the *Cavalleria* performance, she told interviewer Harry Fleetwood: "After six months [with Trivella] I debuted in concerts . . . And then, after a year, I debuted in *Cavalleria.*" Jellinek, almost certainly basing his information on Callas's *Oggi* interview, gives November 1938 as the date. Galatopoulos places the performance five months later, in April 1939. Her mother writes that Callas was fifteen at the time of the performance, which, if she is precise, would place the performance after December 4, 1938, the date of Callas's fifteenth birthday.

During this period a concert at Parnassus Hall, on May 22, 1939, given by pupils of Mme. Trivella, was announced in Athens newspapers with Callas being mentioned among the participants.

In the fall of 1939, Callas ended her studies at the National Conservatory and enrolled in the more prestigious Odeon Athenon (Athens Conservatory). She continued her vocal studies there with Elvira de Hidalgo. In 1940 she sang the title role in a student performance of *Suor Angelica,* which was presented with piano accompaniment. This performance of the Puccini opera is cited by Mrs. Callas, Jellinek, and Galatopoulos. Additional student performances in the title role of *Aida* and as Amelia in *Un Ballo in Maschera* are mentioned by Galatopoulos. There is also a newspaper notice of a radio performance on April 3, 1940, by five singers, among whom are Callas, Irma Kolassi, and Arda Mandikian.

2. *First Professional Stage Appearance—Boccaccio*

Maria Callas's first professional stage appearance was in Franz von Suppé's operetta *Boccaccio,* in which she sang one of the smaller parts, the role of Beatrice. One article about Callas states that she sang the leading role of Fiammetta, but Callas is explicit in the *Oggi* interview that the role was Beatrice, and her mother's recollections are consistent with her statement. The performance undoubtedly took place sometime during 1940; however, there is some variance in the sources on this point. Callas states that her success in the student performance of *Cavalleria* led to her being chosen "a few months afterwards" to sing in *Boccaccio* at the National Lyric Theater in Athens. Her mother writes that "soon after" the *Cavalleria,* when Maria was "still not yet sixteen," she made her appearance at the National Lyric Theater in *Boccaccio.* Since the *Cavalleria* performance most likely occurred in the fall of 1938, the statements of both Callas and her mother appear to place the *Boccaccio* performance sometime in 1939, a fact supported by her mother's statement of Callas's age as not yet sixteen, that is before December 4, 1939. In another part of her book, however, Mrs. Callas dates the performance to when her daughter was "still sixteen," which would make the year 1940. Jellinek, without mentioning the year, says she was a "sixteen-year-old student" at the time of the performance. Galatopoulos gives a precise date—November 27, 1940, but he does not cite the source for his statement. The Athens newspaper *Le Messager* carries announcements for a number of performances of *Boccaccio* at the Pallas Theater between January 26 and March 9, 1940. These are the earliest performances of the operetta that can be traced in newspapers of this period. The review of the first performance does not mention Callas, but then only the singers in the major roles are mentioned. Since newspapers for the fall of 1940 are lacking, and thus an exact determination cannot be made, it is quite possible that *Boccaccio* was revived later that year, so the date given by Galatopoulos is plausible. A date in the fall of 1940 would also be consistent with Callas's having gained the additional stage experience from the student performances mentioned above before making her professional debut.

Following *Boccaccio,* Callas may have sung secondary roles in other operas. Mrs. Callas remarks that her daughter was paid to sing small parts at the Royal Theater.

Among the discrepancies found in the different sources is the title of the company with which Callas sang in Athens. In *Oggi,* Callas consistently calls it the Royal Opera (Teatro Reale dell'Opera). Mrs. Callas calls it the Royal Theater, Jellinek and Galatopoulos the Athens Opera. The official title of the company was the National Lyric Theater (in Greek, Ethnikon Theatron—Lyrike Skene). The "Lyric" designation was used to distinguish the company from the other branch of the National Theater which presented spoken drama. In newspaper announcements it is always referred to as the National Theater or the Lyric Stage (Lyrike Skene). The German language newspaper at first uses the term Nationaltheater and then eventually changes to the name Staatsoper. It is possible that before the war the company enjoyed royal patronage and thus was also called the Royal Opera. Use of the title "royal" during the German occupation, when the Greek king and the royal government were in exile, would undoubtedly have been proscribed. The company was formed in 1940. It does not seem to have had a permanent home since it performed in a number of theaters around Athens. Performances almost invariably were presented in Greek.

3. *First Major Role—Tosca*

In April 1941 the Germans invaded and overran Greece. With the occupation of Athens, all public places were closed. Galatopoulos writes that a few months afterwards the Germans allowed the theaters to reopen, and at this time De Hidalgo arranged for Callas to become a permanent member of the Athens Opera.

All sources agree that the first major role that Callas assumed after becoming a permanent member of the company was the title role in *Tosca.* Beyond this, however, the sources present conflicting details. Callas states that after the *Boccaccio,* the director of the Royal Opera chose her for *Tosca,* and rehearsals lasted more than three months prior to the opera's being presented to the public. After mentioning this performance, she turns to her memories of the German occupation, specifically of the hardships experienced in the winter of 1941–42. With the *Boccaccio* occurring, presumably, late in 1940, and the German occupation beginning in April 1941, her chronology here clearly implies that the *Tosca* occurred in 1941, probably in the first part of the year. Mrs. Callas gives the date as July 1941, and she says that her daughter was called upon to substitute for the soprano originally scheduled to sing the role. A July 1941 date would appear to be not long after the theaters were reopened following the German occupation.

Galatopoulos, however, states that the *Tosca* performance occurred on July 4, 1942, that is, a whole year later than the date given above. He also states that Callas substituted for a singer who had suddenly become indisposed. Jellinek repeats this story also and, like Galatopoulos, gives the date as July 1942.

The sources cited above are generally consistent as to the month, July, in which the *Tosca* took place, but differ as to the year. Unfortunately, newspapers for the summer of 1941 are missing, so one source which could resolve the discrepancy is unavailable. Newspapers are available for the summer of 1942, however, and they shed some light on this problem. The papers show that there were no performances of *Tosca* in July 1942. *Tosca* was, however, performed later that summer. The newspapers *'E Vradyne* and *Deutsche Nachrichten* both carry notices toward the middle of July 1942 announcing a forthcoming season of opera to be given by the National Theater. These announcements give a list of the leading singers in the company, and among the names listed is M. Kalogeropoulou. (This is the original form of her name which she used in Greece at this time.) The repertory listed for the company consisted of four works: *Tzouitta* (*Giuditta*), *La Traviata, 'E Eythyme Hera* (*The Merry Widow*), and *Tosca.* The season opened with *Giuditta* on July 16 at the open-air theater at Dragatsaniou Street, Klanthmonos Place. *Tosca* was first presented on August 27 and performed twelve more times: August 28, 30, September 2, 4, 6, 8, 10, 12, 14, 16, 24, and 27. A review of the first performance (August 27) gives the cast as Maria Kalogeropoulou (Tosca), Antonios Delendas (Cavaradossi), and T. Xereles (Scarpia). The performance of September 8 is also reviewed since it marked the debut of the tenor Ludovic Kurusopoulos in the role of Cavaradossi. Callas is again noted as a member of the cast along with L. Vasilakis (Scarpia) and the conductor S. Vasilakis. The review also notes that, contrary to custom, this performance was sung in Italian. Cast information on other *Tosca* performances in this series is not provided by the newspapers so it is impossible to determine which other performances Callas might have sung. It seems likely, though, that she sang in most of them.

On the basis of the information available, it seems most probable that Callas first sang *Tosca* in July 1941, and that the performances in August and September 1942 mark her resumption of the role. The following facts point toward this conclusion. Callas's name appears on the roster of the leading singers of the company at the beginning of the 1942 season, implying that she has already attained some standing and is not a relatively unknown student who has yet to make her mark in public. If Callas did not sing Tosca in 1941, then the August 27, 1942, performance would appear to be the likely contender for her first Tosca. The review of this performance does not indicate that she is singing the role for the first time. Lastly, as noted in the following section, during August 1942 and necessarily prior to the first *Tosca* on August 27, Callas with other artists of the company gave several concerts in Salonika. Galatopoulos states that these concerts were arranged by an Italian general who was impressed by the efforts of the Athens Opera artists, "no less of Maria herself." For this to be the case, Callas would have to have achieved prominence well before August 1942.

Mrs. Callas notes that the other singers in her daughter's first *Tosca* were the tenor Thellentas and the baritone Cerelis. Undoubtedly, these are the same singers, Delendas and Xereles, who again appeared in the opera in August 1942.

4. Opera Concerts in Salonika

Mrs. Callas and Galatopoulos both describe a visit to Salonika by Callas and other artists of the Athens Opera, who gave a series of Italian operatic excerpts, with piano accompaniment, for an audience consisting mostly of Italian soldiers. Mrs. Callas dates these concerts to the summer of 1942 and Galatopoulos more specifically as August 1942.

5. Performances in 1943

The 1942–43 fall-winter season of the National Theater consisted of three operas: *Aida, La Gioconda,* and *Don Giovanni.* Callas's name, however, does not appear on the roster of singers for this season, so, presumably, she did not appear in any of these operas.

The 1943 summer season of the company consisted of four works: *Carmen, Tosca, 'E Hora toy Meidiamagos* (*The Land of Smiles*), and *Eis Nukta in Venetia* (*A Night in Venice*). The usual announcement which lists the roster of singers for the season does not appear in any of the newspapers that are available (again there are numerous gaps), so it cannot be stated for certain that Callas appeared during this season. It seems likely that Callas did sing in the *Tosca* performances since she was associated with that opera in preceding seasons. *Tosca* is announced for July 17, 19, 21, 23, and 25, but no casts are given, and, again, the newspaper which would have contained the review of the first performance is among those missing.

The appearance of Franz Lehár's *The Land of Smiles* in this season is interesting since on two occasions Callas listed this work as among those in which she had sung in Athens. She mentioned this operetta once in a radio interview with Harry Fleetwood and once in an interview for *Opera News,* but in her *Oggi* article it is not mentioned, nor is it mentioned in any other source. Mrs. Callas referring to the *Opera News* interview, which appeared prior to the writing of her book, stated, "I have no recollection of *The Land of Smiles* or of Maria's singing in this Lehár operetta." Again there are no papers available with reviews to give the cast of a performance. If Callas did sing in this operetta, it would have been either the leading role of Lisa or, more likely, the supporting part of Mi.

Mrs. Callas and Galatopoulos mention that in this year Callas again journeyed to Salonika, this time to give two solo recitals. Mrs. Callas gives the date as the summer of 1943, and Galatopoulos gives the month as August. Galatopoulos also gives the location as the White Tower Theater, and he states the concerts consisted of Italian arias and lieder by Schubert and Brahms.

6. *Performances in 1944*

The newspaper holdings for 1944, fortunately, are quite complete and provide definitive information about the performances in this year, performances which are among the most interesting of Callas's early career.

The 1944 season of the National Theater opened at the Olympia Theater on April 1, 1944, with the opera *Rhea* by the Greek composer Spiro Samara. Callas first appeared in this season on April 22, 1944, in the Greek première of Eugen d'Albert's *Tiefland.* The cast as given in the review in *Deutsche Nachrichten* on the following day was as follows: Maria Kalogeropoulou (Marta), Zoe Vlachopoulou (Nuri), Antonios Delendas (Pedro), Evangelios Mangliveras (Sebastiano), G. Moulas (Tommaso), Z. Remoundou (Pepa), M. Kourachani (Antonia), A. Bourdakou (Rosalia), L. Mavrakis (Nando), and Ch. Athinaios (Moruccio), with Leonidas Zoras conducting. Additional performances were scheduled for April 23, 27, 30, May 4, 7, and 10. Mrs. Callas, Jellinek, and Galatopoulos all correctly date the *Tiefland* to the spring or April 1944, though Galatopoulos gives a date of April 1943 when he first refers to the performance.

Following *Tiefland,* Callas next appeared in *Cavalleria Rusticana.* The opera, given on a double bill with Petro Petridis' *The Shopkeeper,* was first performed on May 6, 1944, at the Olympia Theater. The review in *Deutsche Nachrichten* again gives the cast: Maria Kalogeropoulou (Santuzza), Antonios Delendas (Turiddu), T. Tsoumbris (Alfio), M. Kourachani (Lola), and A. Bourdakou (Lucia), with T.

Karalivanos conducting. The opera was repeated May 9, 14, 16, 19, 23, 28, June 1, and 8. An additional performance on June 16 was announced with a new cast in which another soprano was assigned the role of Santuzza. Whether Callas sang all of the other performances is uncertain since the newspaper announcements do not list the day-by-day casts. Jellinek places this *Cavalleria* early in 1943, and Galatopoulos gives the date as January 1943. Mrs. Callas, referring to the student performance of *Cavalleria* in 1938, mistakenly states that this was the "only time Maria sang *Cavalleria Rusticana* in Athens."

The May 24, 1944, *Deutsche Nachrichten* carries a review of a concert broadcast from the "Staatsoper." Among the performers mentioned is Maria Kalogeropoulou singing "Casta Diva" from *Norma.* Very possibly this concert marks the first time that she sang in public any part of the role which was to become most closely associated with her.

In the summer of 1944, the National Theater presented a season of opera in the ancient open-air theater of Herodes Atticus, below the southwest slope of the Acropolis. Callas sang in two of the productions: *'O Protomastoras* and *Fidelio.*

'O Protomastoras (*The Master Builder*) is an opera by Manolis Kalomiris, the director of the National Conservatory, set to the text of an early play by Nikos Kazantzakis. The opera had its world première in March 1916 and was revived in 1930 in a concert performance during the one hundredth anniversary celebrations of Greek independence. The opera was revived again on July 29, 1944. Among the performers listed in the announcement on the day of this performance is Maria Kalogeropoulou. The review of the performance in *Deutsche Nachrichten,* however, fails to mention Callas and two others who are listed in the announcement, all of whom apparently sang relatively minor roles. For the record the cast was: Antonios Delendas (The Master Builder), Z. Remoundou (Smaragda), Evangelios Mangliveras (The Sovereign), N. Galanou (The Singer), A. Bourdakou (The Old Mother), and P. Choidas (The Peasant). The performance was conducted by the composer. M. Koronis and M. Doumanis are the other singers, besides Callas, listed in the announcement but not mentioned in the review. *'O Protomastoras* was repeated on July 30, August 1, 3, 5, and 6. Neither Callas nor Jellinek makes any mention of an appearance in this opera,

which is understandable if Callas sang only a minor role. Galatopoulos states, however, that Callas undertook the leading role of Smaragda. Furthermore, he states that she sang this role in the world première, which, according to him, took place in March 1943. Mrs. Callas also states that her daughter sang the soprano lead in this opera. She dates the performance, along with that of *Fidelio,* which immediately followed, to the summer of 1941, in what is obviously a lapse of memory or a misunderstanding on the part of her collaborator who helped with the book. A production of the opera in 1943, certainly not the world première though, is possible but highly unlikely. The review in *Deutsche Nachrichten* states that only now, after this performance, is the opera first truly appreciated, a statement which implies that there were no other recent successful performances. In addition, it does not seem likely that Callas would consent to sing a minor role in an opera in which earlier she had undertaken the leading role. It is possible that Callas sang the role of Smaragda in one of the performances after July 29. However, *Deutsche Nachrichten* at this time notes most major cast changes and no such announcement appears for *'O Protomastoras,* so this possibility is remote.

On August 14, 1944, Beethoven's *Fidelio* received its Greek première in the amphitheater of Herodes Atticus. The review in *Deutsche Nachrichten* mentions only Callas and the tenor Delendas. However, from the newspaper announcement on the day of the première, the cast can be reconstructed as follows: Maria Kalogeropoulou (Leonora), Antonios Delendas (Florestan), Zoe Vlachopoulou (Marzelline), Evangelios Mangliveras (Don Pizarro), G. Moulas (Rocco), G. Kokolios (Jaquino), A. Tzeneralis (Don Fernando), and Hans Hörner, conductor. *Fidelio* was repeated on August 15 and 17, undoubtedly with Callas. An announcement for a performance on August 19 lists an entirely new cast. Subsequent performances on August 22, 24, and 25 were most likely also sung by the new cast. Galatopoulos and Jellinek both give the date for *Fidelio* as September 1944. Jellinek also states that the performance was sung in German, but in a 1967 interview with Edward Downes, Callas mentioned that she had sung *Fidelio* in Greek.

7. *Performances in 1945*

Callas said in *Oggi* that after *Fidelio* the opera management gave her three months' leave. In October 1944 the German army withdrew from Greece and the exiled government returned. In December fighting broke out between Communist and anti-Communist forces and for most of that month Athens was a battleground for the contending forces. Mrs. Callas wrote that for twenty days she and Maria were virtually confined to their apartment. In February 1945, when the theaters were reopened after order had been restored, the director of the opera told Callas that several of her older colleagues threatened to strike unless she were demoted to second soprano. Callas was offered a new contract but, finding the terms unacceptable, she decided to return to the United States. In order to raise money for the trip she gave a recital. Both Mrs. Callas and Galatopoulos place the concert in July 1945 at the Rex Theater. Mrs. Callas says the concert consisted of Italian arias and German lieder. Callas states that before her departure she wanted to give a last proof of her ability and sang the soprano lead (Laura) in Karl Millöcker's operetta *The Beggar Student* (*Der Bettelstudent*). Galatopoulos dates the performance as August 1945. Mrs. Callas, mistakenly referring to *The Beggar Student* as *The Student Prince* by Romberg, wrote that the performance took place the night before her daughter left for the United States. In another part of her book, Mrs. Callas mentions that Maria sailed from Greece in mid-July, which would place the performance at that time. The Athens newspapers show the first performance of *'O Zitianos Foititis* (*The Beggar Student*) by the National Theater to be on September 6, at the theater on Avenue Alexander. Additional performances took place almost nightly into October. Presumably Callas sang in the first performance on September 6. Whether she sang in any of the subsequent performances cannot be determined, but her mother's comment seems to indicate only one performance. At most she could have sung only the first few performances (September 7, 8, 10), since she seems to have arrived in New York at the end of September after a trip which must have taken several weeks.

In an interview with Claudia Cassidy (*Chicago Tribune,* November 21, 1954), Callas summed up her Athens career with the statement "I sang thirty or forty performances, in *Tosca, Fidelio, Tiefland, Cavalleria Rusticana, Boccaccio.*"

Part Two
1947 – 1965

1947

Aug. 2	Verona, Arena	*La Gioconda:* (La Gioconda); Elena Nicolai (Laura); Anna Maria Canali (La Cieca); Richard Tucker (Enzo); Carlo Tagliabue (Barnaba); Nicola Rossi-Lemeni (Alvise); Eraldo Coda (Zuane); Aristide Baracchi (Isepo); Luigi Nardi (Singer); Tullio Serafin, c.
Aug. 5	"	*La Gioconda:* Same cast as Aug. 2.
Aug. 10	"	*La Gioconda:* Same cast as Aug. 2.
Aug. 14	"	*La Gioconda:* Same cast as Aug. 2.
Aug. 17	"	*La Gioconda:* Same cast as Aug. 2.
Dec. 30	Venice, Teatro La Fenice	*Tristano e Isotta:* (Isolde); Fiorenzo Tasso (Tristan); Fedora Barbieri (Brangaene); Raimondo Torres (Kurvenal); Boris Christoff (King Mark); Attilio Barbesi (Melot); Uberto Scaglione (Steersman); Guglielmo Torcoli (Shepherd); Ottorino Begali (Sailor's Voice); Tullio Serafin, c.

1948

Jan. 3	Venice, Teatro La Fenice	*Tristano e Isotta:* Same cast as Dec. 30.
Jan. 8	"	*Tristano e Isotta:* Same cast as Dec. 30.
Jan. 11	"	*Tristano e Isotta:* Same cast as Dec. 30.
Jan. 29	"	*Turandot:* (Turandot); José Soler (Calaf); Elena Rizzieri (Liù); Bruno Carmassi (Timur); Emilio

		Gherardini (Ping); Alfredo Mattioli (Pang); Giuseppe Nessi (Pong); Guglielmo Torcoli (Altoum); Attilio Barbesi (Mandarin); Nino Sanzogno, c.
Jan. 31	"	*Turandot:* Same cast as Jan. 29.
Feb. 3	"	*Turandot:* Same cast as Jan. 29.
Feb. 8	"	*Turandot:* Same cast as Jan. 29.
Feb. 10	"	*Turandot:* Same cast as Jan. 29.
Mar. 11	Udine, Teatro Puccini	*Turandot:* (Turandot); José Soler (Calaf); Dolores Ottani (Liù); Silvio Maionica (Timur); Carlo Togliani (Ping); Sante Messina (Pang); Alfredo Mattioli (Pong); Guglielmo Torcoli (Altoum); Pasquale Lombardo (Mandarin); Oliviero de Fabritiis, c.
Mar. 14	"	*Turandot:* Same cast as Mar. 11.
Apr. 17	Trieste, Politeama Rossetti	*La Forza del Destino:* (Leonora); Giuseppe Vertecchi (Don Alvaro); Benvenuto Franci (Don Carlo); Cesare Siepi (Padre Guardiano); Ottavio Serpo (Fra Melitone); Anna Maria Canali (Preziosilla); Mario Parenti, c.
Apr. 20	"	*La Forza del Destino:* Same cast as Apr. 17.
Apr. 21	"	*La Forza del Destino:* Same cast as Apr. 17.
Apr. 25	"	*La Forza del Destino:* Same cast as Apr. 17.
May 12	Genoa, Teatro Grattacielo	*Tristano e Isotta:* (Isolde); Max Lorenz (Tristan); Elena Nicolai (Brangaene); Raimondo Torres (Kurvenal); Nicola Rossi-Lemeni

		(King Mark); Cesare Oliva (Melot); Rinaldo Grattarola (Steersman); Giorgio Gallo (Shepherd); Mario Berti (Sailor's Voice); Tullio Serafin, c.
May 14	″	*Tristano e Isotta:* Same cast as May 12.
May 16	″	*Tristano e Isotta:* Same cast as May 12.
July 4	Rome, Terme di Caracalla	*Turandot:* (Turandot); Galliano Masini (Calaf); Vera Montanari (Liù); Giuseppe Flamini (Timur); Mario Borriello (Ping); Nino Mazziotti (Pang); Fernando delle Fornaci (Pong); Blando Giusti (Altoum); Gino Conti (Mandarin); Oliviero de Fabritiis, c.
July 6	″	*Turandot:* Same cast as July 4.
July 11	″	*Turandot:* Same cast as July 4.
July 27	Verona, Arena	*Turandot:* (Turandot); Antonio Salvarezza (Calaf); Elena Rizzieri (Liù); Nicola Rossi-Lemeni (Timur); Luigi Borgonovo (Ping); Luciano della Pergola (Pang); Mariano Caruso (Pong); Luigi Nardi (Altoum); Attilio Barbesi (Mandarin); Antonino Votto, c.
Aug. 1	″	*Turandot:* Same cast as July 27 except Era Tognoli (Liù).
Aug. 5	″	*Turandot:* Same cast as July 27 except Disma de Cecco (Liù).
Aug. 9	″	*Turandot:* Same cast as July 27 except Disma de Cecco (Liù).
Aug. 11	Genoa, Teatro Carlo Felice	*Turandot:* (Turandot); Mario del Monaco (Calaf); Vera Montanari

		(Liù); Silvio Maionica (Timur); Saturno Meletti (Ping); Giorgio Gallo (Pang); Cesare Masini-Sperti (Pong); Alfredo Poggianti (Altoum); Angelo Questa, c.
Aug. 14	"	*Turandot:* Same cast as Aug. 11 except Antonio Salvarezza (Calaf).
Sep. 18	Turin, Teatro Lirico	*Aida:* (Aida); Roberto Turrini (Radames); Elena Nicolai (Amneris); Raffaele de Falchi (Amonasro); Ernesto Dominici (King); Marco Stefanoni (Ramfis); Wladimiro Lozzi (Messenger); Tullio Serafin, c.
Sep. 19	"	*Aida:* Same cast as Sep. 18 except Irma Colasanti (Amneris).
Sep. 23	"	*Aida:* Same cast as Sep. 18.
Sep. 25	"	*Aida:* Same cast as Sep. 18 except Irma Colasanti (Amneris).
Oct. 19	Rovigo, Teatro Sociale	*Aida:* (Aida); Roberto Turrini (Radames); Miriam Pirazzini (Amneris); Enzo Viaro (Amonasro); Romeo Morisani (King); Andrea Mongelli (Ramfis); Cesare Masini-Sperti (Messenger); Umberto Berrettoni, c.
Oct. 21	"	*Aida:* Same cast as Oct. 19.
Oct. 24	"	*Aida:* Same cast as Oct. 19.
Nov. 30	Florence, Teatro Comunale	*Norma:* (Norma); Mirto Picchi (Pollione); Fedora Barbieri (Adalgisa); Cesare Siepi (Oroveso); Lucia Danieli (Clotilde); Massimo Bison (Flavio); Tullio Serafin, c.
Dec. 5	"	*Norma:* Same cast as Nov. 30.

1949

Jan. 8	Venice, Teatro La Fenice	*La Walkiria:* (Brünnhilde); Giovanni Voyer (Siegmund); Ernesto Dominici (Hunding); Raimondo Torres (Wotan); Jolanda Magnoni (Sieglinde); Amalia Pini (Fricka); Natalia Cavallaro Giorgi (Helmwige); Ada Bertelle (Gerhilde); Miti Truccato Pace (Ortlinde); Luciana de Nardo Fainelli (Rossweisse); Maria Amadini (Grimgerde); Mafalda Masini (Waltraute); Giacinta Berengo Gardin (Siegrune); Antonietta Astolfi Seveso (Schwertleite); Tullio Serafin, c.
Jan. 12	"	*La Walkiria:* Same cast as Jan. 8.
Jan. 14	"	*La Walkiria:* Same cast as Jan. 8.
Jan. 16	"	*La Walkiria:* Same cast as Jan. 8.
Jan. 19	"	*I Puritani:* (Elvira); Antonio Pirino (Arturo); Ugo Savarese (Riccardo); Boris Christoff (Giorgio); Silvio Maionica (Gualtiero); Guglielmo Torcoli (Bruno); Mafalda Masini (Enrichetta); Tullio Serafin, c.
Jan. 22	"	*I Puritani:* Same cast as Jan. 19.
Jan. 23	"	*I Puritani:* Same cast as Jan. 19.
Jan. 28	Palermo, Teatro Massimo	*La Walkiria:* (Brünnhilde); Giovanni Voyer (Siegmund); Bruno Carmassi (Hunding); Giulio Neri (Wotan); Jolanda Magnoni (Sieglinde); Lucy Cabrera (Fricka); Giuseppina Sani, Luisa Malagrida, Rosa Bianca di Bella, Maria Rosato, Maria Teresa Man-

		dalari, Emilia Curiel, Maria Cannizzaro, Lucy Cabrera (Valkyries); Francesco Molinari-Pradelli, c.
Feb. 10	"	*La Walkiria:* Same cast as Jan. 28.
Feb. 12	Naples, Teatro San Carlo	*Turandot:* (Turandot); Renato Gigli (Calaf); Vera Montanari (Liù); Mario Petri (Timur); Mario Borriello (Ping); Luciano della Pergola (Pang); Gianni Assante (Pong); Gianni Avolanti (Altoum); Giuseppe Maranini (Mandarin); Jonel Perlea, c.
Feb. 16	"	*Turandot:* Same cast as Feb. 12.
Feb. 18	"	*Turandot:* Same cast as Feb. 12.
Feb. 20	"	*Turandot:* Same cast as Feb. 12.
Feb. 26	Rome, Teatro dell'Opera	*Parsifal:* (Kundry); Hans Beirer (Parsifal); Cesare Siepi (Gurnemanz); Marcello Cortis (Amfortas); Carlo Platania (Titurel); Armando Dadò (Klingsor); Paolo Caroli and Virgilio Stocco (Knights); Adele Sticchi, Graziella Muzzi, Nino Mazziotti, and Mino Russo (Esquires); Anna Leonelli, Adele Sticchi, Angela Rositani, Amalia Oliva, Miriam di Giove, and Ada Landi (Flower Maidens); Tullio Serafin, c.
Mar. 2	"	*Parsifal:* Same cast as Feb. 26.
Mar. 5	"	*Parsifal:* Same cast as Feb. 26.
Mar. 7	Turin, RAI Auditorium	Radio Broadcast: Concert (with Mario Filippeschi): *I Puritani*—Qui la voce and Vien, diletto; *Aida*—O cieli azzurri; *Norma*—Casta Diva and Ah! bello a me;

		Tristano e Isotta—Morte di Isotta; with the Orchestra of RAI, Turin, Francesco Molinari-Pradelli, c.
Mar. 8	Rome, Teatro dell'Opera	*Parsifal:* Same cast as Feb. 26.
May 20*	Buenos Aires, Teatro Colón	*Turandot:* (Turandot); Mario del Monaco (Calaf); Helena Arizmendi (Liù); Juan Zanin (Timur); Renato Cesari (Ping); Roberto Maggiolo (Pang); Carlos Giusti (Pong); Virgilio Tavini (Altoum); Tullio Serafin, c.
May 29	"	*Turandot:* Same cast as May 20 except Nicola Rossi-Lemeni (Timur).
June 11	"	*Turandot:* Same cast as May 20.
June 17	"	*Norma:* (Norma); Antonio Vela (Pollione); Fedora Barbieri (Adalgisa); Nicola Rossi-Lemeni (Oroveso); Emma Brizzio (Clotilde); Humberto di Toto (Flavio); Tullio Serafin, c.
June 19	"	*Norma:* Same cast as June 17.
June 22	"	*Turandot:* Same cast as May 20.
June 25	"	*Norma:* Same cast as June 17.
June 29	"	*Norma:* Same cast as June 17.
July 2	"	*Aida:* (Aida); Antonio Vela (Radames); Fedora Barbieri (Amneris); Victor Damiani (Amonasro); Jorge Danton (King); Nicola Rossi-Lemeni (Ramfis); Carlos Giusti (Messenger); M. del C. Ecignard (Priestess); Tullio Serafin, c.
July 9	"	Concert (133d Anniversary of the Argentine Declaration of Inde-

		pendence) (Callas and others): *Norma*—Casta Diva (with Nicola Rossi-Lemeni), Tullio Serafin, c.; *Turandot:* Act III—Same cast as May 20 except Nicola Rossi-Lemeni (Timur).
Sep. 18	Perugia, Chiesa di San Pietro	*San Giovanni Battista* (oratorio by Alessandro Stradella): (Herod's Daughter); Rina Corsi (Herod's Mother); Miriam Pirazzini (St. John the Baptist); Amedeo Berdini (The Councilor); Cesare Siepi (Herod); with orchestra, Gabriele Santini, c.
Nov. 8– Nov. 10	Turin, RAI Auditorium	Recordings: *Tristano e Isotta*—Morte di Isotta; *Norma*—Casta Diva and Ah! bello a me; *I Puritani*—Qui la voce and Vien, diletto; with the Orchestra of RAI, Turin, Arturo Basile, c. Released in Italy on Cetra CB 20481, 20482, and 20483, respectively, in May 1950.
Dec. 20*	Naples, Teatro San Carlo	*Nabucco:* (Abigaille); Gino Bechi (Nabucco); Amalia Pini (Fenena); Gino Sinimberghi (Ismaele); Luciano Neroni (Zaccaria); Iginio Riccò (High Priest); Luciano della Pergola (Abdallo); Silvana Tenti (Anna); Vittorio Gui, c.
Dec. 22	"	*Nabucco:* Same cast as Dec. 20.
Dec. 27	"	*Nabucco:* Same cast as Dec. 20.

1950

Jan. 13	Venice, Teatro La Fenice	*Norma:* (Norma); Gino Penno (Pollione); Elena Nicolai (Adal-

		gisa); Tancredi Pasero (Oroveso); Nerina Ferrari (Clotilde); Cesare Masini-Sperti (Flavio); Antonino Votto, c.
Jan. 15	"	*Norma:* Same cast as Jan. 13.
Jan. 19	"	*Norma:* Same cast as Jan. 13.
Feb. 2	Brescia, Teatro Grande	*Aida:* (Aida); Mario del Monaco (Radames); Amalia Pini (Amneris); Aldo Protti (Amonasro); Duilio Baronti (King); Enzo Feliciati (Ramfis); Piero de Palma (Messenger); Alberto Erede, c.
Feb. 6	Rome, Teatro dell'Opera	*Tristano e Isotta:* (Isolde); August Seider (Tristan); Elena Nicolai (Brangaene); Benvenuto Franci (Kurvenal); Giulio Neri (King Mark); Virgilio Stocco (Melot); Gino Conti (Steersman); Mino Russo (Shepherd); Paolo Caroli (Sailor's Voice); Tullio Serafin, c.
Feb. 7	Brescia, Teatro Grande	*Aida:* Same cast as Feb. 2.
Feb. 9	Rome, Teatro dell'Opera	*Tristano e Isotta:* Same cast as Feb. 6.
Feb. 19	"	*Tristano e Isotta:* Same cast as Feb. 6.
Feb. 23	"	*Norma:* (Norma); Galliano Masini (Pollione); Ebe Stignani (Adalgisa); Giulio Neri (Oroveso); Ada Landi (Clotilde); Paolo Caroli (Flavio); Tullio Serafin, c.
Feb. 25	"	*Tristano e Isotta:* Same cast as Feb. 6.

Feb. 26	"	*Norma:* Same cast as Feb. 23.
Feb. 28	"	*Tristano e Isotta:* Same cast as Feb. 6 except Luciano Neroni (King Mark).
Mar. 2	"	*Norma:* Same cast as Feb. 23 except Antonio Cassinelli (Oroveso).
Mar. 4	"	*Norma:* Same cast as Feb. 23 except Antonio Cassinelli (Oroveso).
Mar. 7	"	*Norma:* Same cast as Feb. 23 except Antonio Cassinelli (Oroveso).
Mar. 13	Turin, RAI Auditorium	Radio broadcast: Concert (with Cesare Siepi): *Oberon*—Aria di Rezia (Ocean! Thou might monster); *La Traviata*—Ah, fors'è lui and Sempre libera; *Il Trovatore*—D'amor sull'ali rosee; *Dinorah*—Ombra leggiera; with the orchestra of RAI, Turin, Alfredo Simonetto, c.
Mar. 16	Catania, Teatro Massimo Bellini	*Norma:* (Norma); Mirto Picchi (Pollione); Jolanda Gardino (Adalgisa); Marco Stefanoni (Oroveso); Maria Zagami (Clotilde); Nino Valori (Flavio); Umberto Berrettoni, c.
Mar. 19	"	*Norma:* Same cast as Mar. 16.
Mar. 22	"	*Norma:* Same cast as Mar. 16.
Mar. 25	"	*Norma:* Same cast as Mar. 16.
Apr. 12	Milan, Teatro alla Scala	*Aida:* (Aida); Mario del Monaco (Radames); Fedora Barbieri (Amneris); Raffaele de Falchi (Amonasro); Silvio Maionica (King); Cesare Siepi (Ramfis); Mario Carlin (Messenger); Franco Capuana, c.

Apr. 15	″	*Aida:* Same cast as Apr. 12.
Apr. 18	″	*Aida:* Same cast as Apr. 12 except Aldo Protti (Amonasro).
Apr. 27	Naples, Teatro San Carlo	*Aida:* (Aida); Mirto Picchi (Radames); Ebe Stignani (Amneris); Ugo Savarese (Amonasro); Iginio Riccò (King); Cesare Siepi (Ramfis); Luciano della Pergola (Messenger); Anna Vovola (Priestess); Tullio Serafin, c.
Apr. 30	″	*Aida:* Same cast as Apr. 27.
May 2	″	*Aida:* Same cast as Apr. 27.
May 4	″	*Aida:* Same cast as Apr. 27.
May 23*	Mexico City, Palacio de Bellas Artes (Opera Nacional)	*Norma:* (Norma); Kurt Baum (Pollione); Giulietta Simionato (Adalgisa); Nicola Moscona (Oroveso); Concha de los Santos (Clotilde); Carlos Sagarminaga (Flavio); Guido Picco, c.
May 27	″	*Norma:* Same cast as May 23.
May 30*	″	*Aida:* (Aida); Kurt Baum (Radames); Giulietta Simionato (Amneris); Robert Weede (Amonasro); Ignacio Ruffino (King); Nicola Moscona (Ramfis); Carlos Sagarminaga (Messenger); Rosita Rodríguez (Priestess); Guido Picco, c.
June 3	″	*Aida:* Same cast as May 30.
June 8*	″	*Tosca:* (Tosca); Mario Filippeschi (Cavaradossi); Robert Weede (Scarpia); Gilberto Cerda (Angelotti); Francisco Alonso (Sacristan and Sciarrone); Carlos Sagarminaga (Spoletta); Concha de

		los Santos (Shepherd); Umberto Mugnai, c.
June 10	"	*Tosca:* Same cast as June 8.
June 15	"	*Aida:* Same cast as May 30 except Mario Filippeschi (Radames).
June 20*	"	*Il Trovatore:* (Leonora); Kurt Baum (Manrico); Giulietta Simionato (Azucena); Leonard Warren (Count di Luna); Nicola Moscona (Ferrando); Carlos Sagarminaga (Ruiz); Ana Maria Feuss (Inez); Guido Picco, c.
June 24	"	*Il Trovatore:* Same cast as June 20.
June 27*	"	*Il Trovatore:* Same cast as June 20 except Ivan Petroff (Count di Luna).
Sep. 24	Bologna, Teatro Duse	*Tosca:* (Tosca); Roberto Turrini (Cavaradossi); Rodolfo Azzolini (Scarpia); Giannetto Zini (Angelotti); Giuseppe Noto (Sacristan); N. Castagnoli (Spoletta); Angelo Questa, c.
Oct. 2	Rome, Teatro dell'Opera	*Aida:* (Aida); Mirto Picchi (Radames); Ebe Stignani (Amneris); Raffaele de Falchi (Amonasro); Augusto Romani (King): Giulio Neri (Ramfis); Fernando delle Fornaci (Messenger); Anna Marcangeli (Priestess); Vincenzo Bellezza, c.
Oct. 7	Pisa, Teatro Comunale Giuseppe Verdi	*Tosca:* (Tosca); Galliano Masini (Cavaradossi); Afro Poli (Scarpia); Riccardo Santarelli, c.

Oct. 8	"	*Tosca:* Same cast as Oct. 7.
Oct. 19	Rome, Teatro Eliseo (Associazione Anfiparnaso)	*Il Turco in Italia:* (Fiorilla); Sesto Bruscantini (Selim); Cesare Valletti (Narciso); Anna Maria Canali (Zaida); Angelo Mercuriali (Albazar); Franco Calabrese (Geronio); Mariano Stabile (Prosdocimo); Gianandrea Gavazzeni, c.
Oct. 22	"	*Il Turco in Italia:* Same cast as Oct. 19.
Oct. 25	"	*Il Turco in Italia:* Same cast as Oct. 19.
Oct. 29	"	*Il Turco in Italia:* Same cast as Oct. 19.
Nov. 20–Nov. 21*	Rome, RAI Studios	Radio Broadcast: *Parsifal:* (Kundry); Africo Baldelli (Parsifal); Boris Christoff (Gurnemanz); Rolando Panerai (Amfortas); Dimitri Lopatto (Titurel); Giuseppe Modesti (Klingsor); Aldo Bertocci and Mario Frosini (Knights); Silvana Tenti, Miti Truccato Pace, Mario Frosini, and Aldo Bertocci (Esquires); Lina Pagliughi, Renata Broilo, Anna Maria Canali, Liliana Rossi, Silvana Tenti, and Miti Truccato Pace (Flower Maidens); with the Orchestra and Chorus of RAI, Rome, Vittorio Gui, c. (Act I broadcast on Nov. 20; Acts II and III on Nov. 21.)

1951

Jan. 14	Florence, Teatro Comunale	*La Traviata:* (Violetta); Francesco Albanese (Alfredo); Enzo

		Mascherini (Germont); Giuseppina Angelini (Flora); Carlo Sorel (Duphol); Camillo Righini (Dr. Grenvil); Ivana Ceccherini (Annina); Salvatore di Tommaso (Gastone); Giorgio Giorgetti (D'Obigny); Tullio Serafin, c.
Jan. 16	"	*La Traviata:* Same cast as Jan. 14.
Jan. 20	"	*La Traviata:* Same cast as Jan. 14.
Jan. 27*	Naples, Teatro San Carlo	*Il Trovatore:* (Leonora); Giacomo Lauri-Volpi (Manrico); Cloe Elmo (Azucena); Paolo Silveri (Count di Luna); Italo Tajo (Ferrando); Teresa de Rosa (Inez); Luciano della Pergola (Ruiz); Gerardo Gaudioso (Old Gypsy); Gianni Avolanti (Messenger); Tullio Serafin, c.
Jan. 30	"	*Il Trovatore:* Same cast as Jan. 27.
Feb. 1	"	*Il Trovatore:* Same cast as Jan. 27 except Giuseppe Vertecchi (Manrico).
Feb. 15	Palermo, Teatro Massimo	*Norma:* (Norma); Renato Gavarini (Pollione); Elena Nicolai (Adalgisa); Giulio Neri (Oroveso); Francesca Dalmas (Clotilde); Adelio Zagonara (Flavio); Franco Ghione, c.
Feb. 20	"	*Norma:* Same cast as Feb. 15.
Feb. 28	Reggio Calabria, Teatro Comunale Francesco Cilèa	*Aida:* (Aida); José Soler (Radames); Miriam Pirazzini (Amneris); Antonio Manca-Serra (Amonasro); Gaetano Fanelli (King); Romeo Morisani (Ramfis); Giovanni Amodei (Messenger); Federico del Cupolo, c.

Mar. 12*	Turin, RAI Auditorium	Radio Broadcast: Concert (with Sesto Bruscantini): *Il Franco Cacciatore* (*Der Freischütz*)—Aria di Agata (Leise, leise); *Mignon*—Io son Titania; *Un Ballo in Maschera*—Ecco l'orrido campo . . . Ma dall' arido stelo divulsa; Proch Variations; with the Orchestra of RAI, Turin, Manno Wolf-Ferrari, c.
Mar. 14	Cagliari, Teatro Massimo	*La Traviata:* (Violetta); Giuseppe Campora (Alfredo); Afro Poli (Germont); Rina Cavallari (Flora); Giorgio Onesti (Duphol); Dimitri Lopatto (Dr. Grenvil); Angela Vercelli (Annina): Salvatore di Tommaso (Gastone); Umberto Frisaldi (D'Obigny); Alessandro Maddalena (Giuseppe); Francesco Molinari-Pradelli, c.
Mar. 18	"	*La Traviata:* Same cast as Mar. 14.
Apr. 21	Trieste, Teatro Giuseppe Verdi	Concert (with Tito Schipa, Dolores Wilson, and Mario Tommasini): *Norma*—Casta Diva; *I Puritani*—Qui la voce; *Aida*—O cieli azzurri; *La Traviata*—Ah, fors'è lui and Sempre libera; with the Orchestra Filarmonica Triestina, Armando La Rosa Parodi, c.
May 26*	Florence, Teatro Comunale (Maggio Musicale)	*I Vespri Siciliani:* (Elena); Giorgio Bardi-Kokolios (Arrigo); Enzo Mascherini (Monforte); Boris Christoff (Procida); Bruno Carmassi (Bethune); Mario Frosini (Vaudemont); Mafalda

		Masini (Ninetta); Gino Sarri (Danieli); Aldo de Paoli (Tebaldo); Lido Pettini (Roberto); Brenno Ristori (Manfredo); Erich Kleiber, c.
May 30	"	*I Vespri Siciliani:* Same cast as May 26.
June 2	"	*I Vespri Siciliani:* Same cast as May 26.
June 5	"	*I Vespri Siciliani:* Same cast as May 26.
June 9	Florence, Teatro della Pergola (Maggio Musicale)	*Orfeo ed Euridice* (Haydn): (Euridice); Tyge Tygeson (Orfeo); Boris Christoff (Creonte); Juliana Farkas (Genio); Erich Kleiber, c.
June 10	"	*Orfeo ed Euridice:* Same cast as June 9.
June 11	Florence, Grand Hotel	Concert: *Norma*—Casta Diva; *Dinorah*—Ombra leggiera; *Aida*—O cieli azzurri; Proch Variations; *Mignon*—Io son Titania; *La Traviata*—Ah, fors'è lui and Sempre libera; with piano, Bruno Bartoletti, accompanist.
July 3*	Mexico City, Palacio de Bellas Artes (Opera Nacional)	*Aida:* (Aida); Mario del Monaco (Radames); Oralia Domínguez (Amneris); Giuseppe Taddei (Amonasro); Ignacio Ruffino (King); Roberto Silva (Ramfis); Carlos Sagarminaga (Messenger); Rosita Rodríguez (Priestess); Oliviero de Fabritiis, c.
July 7	"	*Aida:* Same cast as July 3.
July 10	"	*Aida:* Same cast as July 3.
July 15	Mexico City, XEW Studios	Radio Broadcast: Concert: *La Forza del Destino*—Pace, pace,

		mio Dio; *Un Ballo in Maschera*—Morrò, ma prima in grazia; with orchestra, Oliviero de Fabritiis, c.
July 17*	Mexico City, Palacio de Bellas Artes	*La Traviata:* (Violetta); Cesare Valletti (Alfredo); Giuseppe Taddei (Germont); Cristina Girón (Flora); Gilberto Cerda (Duphol); Ignacio Ruffino (Dr. Grenvil); Luz María Farfan (Annina); Carlos Sagarminaga (Gastone); Francisco Alonso (D'Obigny); Oliviero de Fabritiis, c.
July 19	"	*La Traviata:* Same cast as July 17.
July 21	"	*La Traviata:* Same cast as July 17.
July 22	"	*La Traviata:* Same cast as July 17 except Carlo Morelli (Germont).
Sep. 7	São Paulo, Teatro Municipal	*Norma:* (Norma); Mirto Picchi (Pollione); Fedora Barbieri (Adalgisa); Nicola Rossi-Lemeni (Oroveso); Eleuze Pennafort (Clotilde); Mariano Caruso (Flavio); Tullio Serafin, c.
Sep. 9	"	*La Traviata:* (Violetta); Giuseppe di Stefano (Alfredo); Tito Gobbi (Germont); Wanda Bonfin (Flora); Enrico Campi (Duphol); José Perrotta (Dr. Grenvil); Vilma Marini (Annina); Mariano Caruso (Gastone); Ettore Sbrana (D'Obigny); Tullio Serafin, c.
Sep. 12	Rio de Janeiro, Teatro Municipal	*Norma:* (Norma); Mirto Picchi (Pollione); Elena Nicolai (Adalgisa); Boris Christoff (Oroveso); Carmen Pimentel (Clotilde); Gino del Signore (Flavio); Antonino Votto, c.

Sep. 14	"	Concert (Red Cross Benefit) (Callas, Renata Tebaldi, and others): *La Traviata*—Ah, fors'è lui and Sempre libera; *Aida*—O cieli azzurri; with orchestra.
Sep. 16	"	*Norma:* Same cast as Sep. 12.
Sep. 24*	"	*Tosca:* (Tosca); Gianni Poggi (Cavaradossi); Paolo Silveri (Scarpia); Giulio Neri (Angelotti); Guilherme Damiano (Sacristan); Gino del Signore (Spoletta); Antonio Lembo (Jailer); Anna Maria Canali (Shepherd); Antonino Votto, c.
Sep. 28	"	*La Traviata:* (Violetta); Gianni Poggi (Alfredo); Antonio Salsedo (Germont); Anna Maria Canali (Flora); Antonio Lembo (Duphol); Carlos Walter (Dr. Grenvil); Gretel Bruno (Annina); Gino del Signore (Gastone); Ernesto de Marco (D'Obigny); Nino Gaioni, c.
Sep. 30	"	*La Traviata:* Same cast as Sep. 28.
Oct. 20	Bergamo, Teatro Gaetano Donizetti	*La Traviata:* (Violetta); Giacinto Prandelli (Alfredo); Giovanni Fabbri (Germont); Giuliana Ghilardi (Flora); Enrico Campi (Duphol); Aristide Baracchi (Dr. Grenvil); Norma Benetti (Annina); Luciano della Pergola (Gastone); Vito Susca (D'Obigny); Guglielmo Fazzini (Giuseppe); Carlo Maria Giulini, c.
Oct. 23	"	*La Traviata:* Same cast as Oct. 20.
Nov. 3	Catania, Teatro Massimo Bellini	*Norma:* (Norma); Gino Penno (Pollione); Giulietta Simionato

		(Adalgisa); Boris Christoff (Oroveso); Maria Cannizzaro (Clotilde); Nino Valori (Flavio); Franco Ghione, c.
Nov. 6	"	*Norma:* Same cast as Nov. 3.
Nov. 8	"	*I Puritani:* (Elvira); Wenko Wenkow (Arturo); Carlo Tagliabue (Riccardo); Boris Christoff (Giorgio); Leonardo Wolowski (Gualtiero); Nino Valori (Bruno); Maria Cannizzaro (Enrichetta); Manno Wolf-Ferrari, c.
Nov. 11	"	*I Puritani:* Same cast as Nov. 8.
Nov. 13	"	*I Puritani:* Same cast as Nov. 8.
Nov. 16	"	*I Puritani:* Same cast as Nov. 8.
Nov. 17	"	*Norma:* Same cast as Nov. 3.
Nov. 20	"	*Norma:* Same cast as Nov. 3 except Leonardo Wolowski (Oroveso).
Dec. 7	Milan, Teatro alla Scala	*I Vespri Siciliani:* (Elena); Eugene Conley (Arrigo); Enzo Mascherini (Monforte); Boris Christoff (Procida); Giovanni Fabbri (Bethune); Luigi Sgarro (Vaudemont); Mafalda Masini (Ninetta); Luciano della Pergola (Danieli); Vittorio Pandano (Tebaldo); Enrico Campi (Roberto); Gino del Signore (Manfredo); Victor de Sabata, c.
Dec. 9	"	*I Vespri Siciliani:* Same cast as Dec. 7.
Dec. 12	"	*I Vespri Siciliani:* Same cast as Dec. 7.
Dec. 16	"	*I Vespri Siciliani:* Same cast as Dec. 7.

Dec. 19	"	*I Vespri Siciliani:* Same cast as Dec. 7.
Dec. 27	"	*I Vespri Siciliani:* Same cast as Dec. 7 except Argeo Quadri, c.
Dec. 29	Parma, Teatro Regio	*La Traviata:* (Violetta); Arrigo Pola (Alfredo); Ugo Savarese (Germont); Ebe Ticozzi (Flora); Camillo Righini (Duphol); Eraldo Coda (Dr. Grenvil); Maria Varetti (Annina); Vittorio Pandano (Gastone); Oliviero de Fabritiis, c.

1952

Jan. 3	Milan, Teatro alla Scala	*I Vespri Siciliani:* Same cast as Dec. 7 except Giuseppe Modesti (Procida) and Argeo Quadri, c.
Jan. 9	Florence, Teatro Comunale	*I Puritani:* (Elvira); Eugene Conley (Arturo); Carlo Tagliabue (Riccardo); Nicola Rossi-Lemeni (Giorgio); Silvio Maionica (Gualtiero); Alberto Lotti-Camici (Bruno); Grace Hoffman (Enrichetta); Tullio Serafin, c.
Jan. 11	"	*I Puritani:* Same cast as Jan. 9.
Jan. 16	Milan, Teatro alla Scala	*Norma:* (Norma); Gino Penno (Pollione); Ebe Stignani (Adalgisa); Nicola Rossi-Lemeni (Oroveso); Ebe Ticozzi (Clotilde); Mariano Caruso (Flavio); Franco Ghione, c.
Jan. 19	"	*Norma:* Same cast as Jan. 16 except Anna Maria Anelli (Clotilde).
Jan. 23	"	*Norma:* Same cast as Jan. 16 ex-

		cept Anna Maria Anelli (Clotilde).
Jan. 27	"	*Norma:* Same cast as Jan. 16 except Anna Maria Anelli (Clotilde).
Jan. 29	"	*Norma:* Same cast as Jan. 16 except Anna Maria Anelli (Clotilde).
Feb. 2	"	*Norma:* Same cast as Jan. 16 except Anna Maria Anelli (Clotilde).
Feb. 7	"	*Norma:* Same cast as Jan. 16 except Anna Maria Anelli (Clotilde).
Feb. 10	"	*Norma:* Same cast as Jan. 16 except Anna Maria Anelli (Clotilde).
Feb. 18*	Rome, RAI Studios	Radio Broadcast: Concert (with Nicola Filacuridi): *Macbeth*—Vieni! t'affretta!; *Lucia di Lammermoor*—Il dolce suono (Mad Scene—part I); *Nabucco*—Anch'io dischiuso; *Lakmé*—Dov' è l'Indiana bruna (Bell Song); with the Orchestra of RAI, Rome, Oliviero de Fabritiis, c.
Mar. 12	Catania, Teatro Massimo Bellini	*La Traviata:* (Violetta); Giuseppe Campora (Alfredo); Enzo Mascherini (Germont); Nerina Ferrari (Flora); Enzo Cecchetelli (Duphol); Bruno Carmassi (Dr. Grenvil); Berta Vanzi (Annina); Nino Valori (Gastone); Carmelo Mollica (D'Obigny); Paolo Leonardi (Giuseppe); Francesco Molinari-Pradelli, c.

Mar. 14	"	*La Traviata:* Same cast as Mar. 8.
Mar. 16	"	*La Traviata:* Same cast as Mar. 8.
Apr. 2	Milan, Teatro alla Scala	*Il Ratto dal Serraglio* (*Die Entführung aus dem Serail*): (Costanza); Tatiana Menotti (Bionda); Petre Munteanu (Pedrillo); Giacinto Prandelli (Belmonte); Salvatore Baccaloni (Osmin); Nerio Bernardi (Selim); Aldo Talentino (Captain of the Guard); Jonel Perlea, c.
Apr. 5	"	*Il Ratto dal Serraglio:* Same cast as Apr. 2.
Apr. 7	"	*Il Ratto dal Serraglio:* Same cast as Apr. 2 except Franca Duval (Bionda).
Apr. 9	"	*Il Ratto dal Serraglio:* Same cast as Apr. 2 except Franca Duval (Bionda).
Apr. 14	"	*Norma:* Same cast as Jan. 16 except Anna Maria Anelli (Clotilde).
Apr. 26*	Florence, Teatro Comunale (Maggio Musicale)	*Armida:* (Armida); Francesco Albanese (Rinaldo); Alessandro Ziliani (Goffredo); Antonio Salvarezza (Eustazio); Mario Filippeschi (Gernando and Ubaldo); Gianni Raimondi (Carlo); Mario Frosini (Idraotte); Marco Stefanoni (Astarotte); Tullio Serafin, c.
Apr. 29	"	*Armida:* Same cast as Apr. 26.
May 2	Rome, Teatro dell'Opera	*I Puritani:* (Elvira); Giacomo Lauri-Volpi (Arturo); Paolo Silveri (Riccardo); Giulio Neri (Giorgio); Augusto Romani

		(Gualtiero); Paolo Caroli (Bruno); Maria Huder (Enrichetta); Gabriele Santini, c.
May 4	Florence, Teatro Comunale	*Armida:* Same cast as Apr. 26.
May 6	Rome, Teatro dell'Opera	*I Puritani:* Same cast as May 2.
May 11	"	*I Puritani:* Same cast as May 2 except Antonio Pirino (Arturo).
May 29*	Mexico City, Palacio de Bellas Artes (Opera Nacional)	*I Puritani:* (Elvira); Giuseppe di Stefano (Arturo); Piero Campolonghi (Riccardo); Roberto Silva (Giorgio); Ignacio Ruffino (Gualtiero); Tanis Lugo (Bruno); Rosa Rimoch (Enrichetta); Guido Picco, c.
May 31	"	*I Puritani:* Same cast as May 29.
June 3*	"	*La Traviata:* (Violetta); Giuseppe di Stefano (Alfredo); Piero Campolonghi (Germont); Cristina Trevi (Flora); Gilberto Cerda (Duphol); Ignacio Ruffino (Dr. Grenvil); Edna Patoni (Annina); Francesco Tortolero (Gastone); Alberto Herrera (D'Obigny); Umberto Mugnai, c.
June 7	"	*La Traviata:* Same cast as June 3.
June 10*	"	*Lucia di Lammermoor:* (Lucia); Giuseppe di Stefano (Edgardo); Piero Campolonghi (Enrico); Roberto Silva (Raimondo); Carlo del Monte (Arturo); Anna Maria Feuss (Alisa); Francesco Tortolero (Normanno); Guido Picco, c.
June 14	"	*Lucia di Lammermoor:* Same cast as June 10.
June 17*	"	*Rigoletto:* (Gilda); Giuseppe di

		Stefano (Duke); Piero Campolonghi (Rigoletto); Ignacio Ruffino (Sparafucile); Maria Teresa García (Maddalena); Gilberto Cerda (Monterone); Carlos Sagarminaga (Borsa); Edna Patoni (Countess Ceprano); Anna Maria Feuss (Giovanna); Alberto Herrera (Marullo); Francisco Alonso (Count Ceprano); Umberto Mugnai, c.
June 21	"	*Rigoletto:* Same cast as June 17.
June 26	"	*Lucia di Lammermoor:* Same cast as June 10.
June 28	"	*Tosca:* (Tosca); Giuseppe di Stefano (Cavaradossi); Piero Campolonghi (Scarpia); Gilberto Cerda (Angelotti); Francisco Alonso (Sacristan and Sciarrone); Carlos Sagarminaga (Spoletta); Luz María Farfan (Shepherd); Guido Picco, c.
July 1*	"	*Tosca:* Same cast as June 28.
July 19	Verona, Arena	*La Gioconda:* (La Gioconda); Elena Nicolai (Laura); Anna Maria Canali (La Cieca); Gianni Poggi (Enzo); Giovanni Inghilleri (Barnaba); Italo Tajo (Alvise); Attilio Barbesi (Zuane); Vittorio Pandano (Isepo); Danilo Campi (Singer); Antonino Votto, c.
July 23	"	*La Gioconda:* Same cast as July 19.
Aug. 2	"	*La Traviata:* (Violetta); Giuseppe Campora (Alfredo); Enzo Mascherini (Germont); Maria Huder (Flora); Enrico Campi (Duphol);

		Attilio Barbesi (Dr. Grenvil); Ada Bertelle (Annina); Mariano Caruso (Gastone); Danilo Franchi (D'Obigny); Vittorio Pandano (Giuseppe); Francesco Molinari-Pradelli, c.
Aug. 5	"	*La Traviata:* Same cast as Aug. 2.
Aug. 10	"	*La Traviata:* Same cast as Aug. 2
Aug. 14	"	*La Traviata:* Same cast as Aug. 2.
Aug.	Florence, Teatro Comunale	Recording: *Don Giovanni*—Non mi dir; with the Orchestra of the Maggio Musicale Fiorentino, Tullio Serafin, c. (Unreleased EMI recording.)
Sep.	Turin, RAI Auditorium	Recording: *La Gioconda:* (La Gioconda); Fedora Barbieri (Laura); Maria Amadini (La Cieca); Gianni Poggi (Enzo); Paolo Silveri (Barnaba); Giulio Neri (Alvise); Piero Poldi (Zuane and Pilot); Armando Benzi (Isepo); with the Orchestra and Chorus of Radio Italiana, Turin, Antonino Votto, c. Released in Italy on Cetra LPC 1241 and in the United States on Cetra-Soria 1241, both in March 1953; reissued in the United States on Everest-Cetra 419/3 in Jan. 1967.
Nov. 8	London, Royal Opera House, Covent Garden	*Norma:* (Norma); Mirto Picchi (Pollione); Ebe Stignani (Adalgisa); Giacomo Vaghi (Oroveso); Joan Sutherland (Clotilde); Paul Asciak (Flavio); Vittorio Gui, c.
Nov. 10	"	*Norma:* Same cast as Nov. 8.
Nov. 13	"	*Norma:* Same cast as Nov. 8 ex-

		cept John Pritchard, c.
Nov. 18*	"	*Norma:* Same cast as Nov. 8.
Nov. 20	"	*Norma:* Same cast as Nov. 8.
Dec. 7*	Milan, Teatro alla Scala	*Macbeth:* (Lady Macbeth); Enzo Mascherini (Macbeth); Italo Tajo (Banco); Gino Penno (Macduff); Luciano della Pergola (Malcolm); Angela Vercelli (Lady-in-Waiting); Dario Caselli (Physician); Attilio Barbesi (Manservant); Mario Tommasini (Murderer); Ivo Vinco (Herald); Victor de Sabata, c.
Dec. 9	"	*Macbeth:* Same cast as Dec. 7.
Dec. 11	"	*Macbeth:* Same cast as Dec. 7 except Giuseppe Modesti (Banco).
Dec. 14	"	*Macbeth:* Same cast as Dec. 7.
Dec. 17	"	*Macbeth:* Same cast as Dec. 7.
Dec. 26	"	*La Gioconda:* (La Gioconda); Ebe Stignani (Laura); Lucia Danieli (La Cieca); Giuseppe di Stefano (Enzo); Carlo Tagliabue (Barnaba); Italo Tajo (Alvise); Aristide Baracchi (Zuane); Angelo Mercuriali (Isepo); Attilio Barbesi (Singer and Pilot); Mario Tommasini (Barnabite Monk); Antonino Votto, c.
Dec. 28	"	*La Gioconda:* Same cast as Dec. 26.
Dec. 30	"	*La Gioconda:* Same cast as Dec. 26.

1953

Jan. 1	Milan, Teatro alla Scala	*La Gioconda:* Same cast as Dec. 26.

Jan. 3	"	*La Gioconda:* Same cast as Dec. 26.
Jan. 8	Venice, Teatro La Fenice	*La Traviata:* (Violetta); Francesco Albanese (Alfredo); Ugo Savarese (Germont); Fernanda Cadoni (Flora); Camillo Righini (Duphol); Alessandro Maddalena (Dr. Grenvil); Ada Bertelle (Annina); Vladimiro Badiali (Gastone); Uberto Scaglione (D'Obigny); Amedeo Bissòn (Giuseppe); Angelo Questa, c.
Jan. 10	"	*La Traviata:* Same cast as Jan. 8 except Carlo Tagliabue (Germont).
Jan. 15	Rome, Teatro dell'Opera	*La Traviata:* (Violetta); Francesco Albanese (Alfredo); Ugo Savarese (Germont); Maria Huder (Flora); Arturo La Porta (Duphol); Augusto Romani (Dr. Grenvil); Miriam di Giove (Annina); Mino Russo (Gastone); Antonio Sacchetti (D'Obigny); Paolo Caroli (Giuseppe); Piero Passerotti (Messenger); Filiberto Picozzi (Servant); Gabriele Santini, c.
Jan. 18	"	*La Traviata:* Same cast as Jan. 15.
Jan. 21	"	*La Traviata:* Same cast as Jan. 15.
Jan. 25	Florence, Teatro Comunale	*Lucia di Lammermoor:* (Lucia); Giacomo Lauri-Volpi (Edgardo); Ettore Bastianini (Enrico); Raffaele Ariè (Raimondo); Valiano Natali (Arturo); Dina Precini (Alisa); Gino Sarri (Normanno); Franco Ghione, c.

Jan. 28	"	*Lucia di Lammermoor:* Same cast as Jan. 25.
Feb. 5	"	*Lucia di Lammermoor:* Same cast as Jan. 25 except Giuseppe di Stefano (Edgardo).
Feb. 8	"	*Lucia di Lammermoor:* Same cast as Jan. 25 except Giuseppe di Stefano (Edgardo).
Feb.	"	Recording: *Lucia di Lammermoor:* (Lucia); Giuseppe di Stefano (Edgardo); Tito Gobbi (Enrico); Raffaele Ariè (Raimondo); Valiano Natali (Arturo); Anna Maria Canali (Alisa); Gino Sarri (Normanno); with the Orchestra and Chorus of the Maggio Musicale Fiorentino, Tullio Serafin, c. Released in the United States on Angel 3503 in Jan. 1954 and in Great Britain on Columbia 33 CX 1131–32 in March 1954; reissued in the United States on Seraphim IB-6032 in Nov. 1968.
Feb. 19	Milan, Teatro alla Scala	*La Gioconda:* Same cast as Dec. 26 except Giuseppe Modesti (Alvise).
Feb. 23*	"	*Il Trovatore:* (Leonora); Ebe Stignani (Azucena); Gino Penno (Manrico); Carlo Tagliabue (Count di Luna); Giuseppe Modesti (Ferrando); Ebe Ticozzi (Inez); Mariano Caruso (Ruiz); Carlo Forti (Old Gypsy); Angelo Mercuriali (Messenger); Antonino Votto, c.
Feb. 26	"	*Il Trovatore:* Same cast as Feb. 23.

Feb. 28	"	*Il Trovatore:* Same cast as Feb. 23.
Mar. 14	Genoa, Teatro Carlo Felice	*Lucia di Lammermoor:* (Lucia); Giuseppe di Stefano (Edgardo); Enzo Mascherini (Enrico); Giorgio Algorta (Raimondo); Emilio Renzi (Arturo); Franco Ghione, c.
Mar. 17	"	*Lucia di Lammermoor:* Same cast as Mar. 14.
Mar. 24	Milan, Teatro alla Scala	*Il Trovatore:* Same cast as Feb. 23 except Vittorio Pandano (Ruiz).
Mar. 29	"	*Il Trovatore:* Same cast as Feb. 23 except Vittorio Pandano (Ruiz).
Mar. 24–Mar. 30	Milan, Basilica Santa Euphemia	Recording: *I Puritani:* (Elvira); Giuseppe di Stefano (Arturo); Rolando Panerai (Riccardo); Nicola Rossi-Lemeni (Giorgio); Carlo Forti (Gualtiero); Angelo Mercuriali (Bruno); Aurora Cattelani (Enrichetta); with the Orchestra and Chorus of La Scala, Tullio Serafin, c. Released in the United States on Angel 3502 and in Great Britain on Columbia 33 CX 1058–60, both in Nov. 1953.
Apr. 9	Rome, Teatro dell'Opera	*Norma:* (Norma); Franco Corelli (Pollione); Fedora Barbieri (Adalgisa); Giulio Neri (Oroveso); Ada Landi (Clotilde); Paolo Caroli (Flavio); Gabriele Santini, c.
Apr. 12	"	*Norma:* Same cast as Apr. 9.
Apr. 15	"	*Norma:* Same cast as Apr. 9.
Apr. 18	"	*Norma:* Same cast as Apr. 9.
Apr. 21	Catania, Teatro Massimo Bellini	*Lucia di Lammermoor:* (Lucia); Roberto Turrini (Edgardo); Giu-

		seppe Taddei (Enrico); Raffaele Ariè (Raimondo); Angelo Leanza (Arturo); Vita Pennisi (Alisa); Nino Valori (Normanno); Oliviero de Fabritiis, c.
Apr. 23	"	*Lucia di Lammermoor:* Same cast as Apr. 21.
May 7	Florence, Teatro Comunale (Maggio Musicale)	*Medea:* (Medea); Carlo Guichandut (Jason); Gabriella Tucci (Glauce); Mario Petri (Creon); Fedora Barbieri (Neris); Liliana Poli and Maria Andreassi (Handmaidens); Mario Frosini (Captain of the Guard); Vittorio Gui, c.
May 10	"	*Medea:* Same cast as May 7.
May 12	"	*Medea:* Same cast as May 7.
May 19	Rome, Teatro dell'Opera	*Lucia di Lammermoor:* (Lucia); Gianni Poggi (Edgardo); Gian Giacomo Guelfi (Enrico); Antonio Cassinelli (Raimondo); Athos Cesarini (Arturo); Anna Marcangeli (Alisa); Nino Mazziotti (Normanno); Gianandrea Gavazzeni, c.
May 21	"	*Lucia di Lammermoor:* Same cast as May 19.
May 24	"	*Lucia di Lammermoor:* Same cast as May 19.
June 4*	London, Royal Opera House, Covent Garden	*Aida:* (Aida); Kurt Baum (Radames); Giulietta Simionato (Amneris); Jess Walters (Amonasro); Michael Langdon (King); Giulio Neri (Ramfis); Hector Thomas (Messenger); Joan Sutherland (Priestess); Sir John Barbirolli, c.
June 6	"	*Aida:* Same cast as June 4 except Marian Nowakowski (Ramfis).

June 10	"	*Aida:* Same cast as June 4.
June 15	"	*Norma:* (Norma); Mirto Picchi (Pollione); Giulietta Simionato (Adalgisa); Giulio Neri (Oroveso); Joan Sutherland (Clotilde); Paul Asciak (Flavio); John Pritchard, c.
June 17	"	*Norma:* Same cast as June 15.
June 20	"	*Norma:* Same cast as June 15.
June 23	"	*Norma:* Same cast as June 15.
June 26	"	*Il Trovatore:* (Leonora); Giulietta Simionato (Azucena); James Johnston (Manrico); Jess Walters (Count di Luna); Michael Langdon (Ferrando); Leonne Mills (Inez); William McAlpine (Ruiz); Herbert Littlewood (Old Gypsy); Emlyn Jones (Messenger); Alberto Erede, c.
June 29	"	*Il Trovatore:* Same cast as June 26.
July 1	"	*Il Trovatore:* Same cast as June 26.
July 23	Verona, Arena	*Aida:* (Aida); Mario del Monaco (Radames); Elena Nicolai (Amneris); Aldo Protti (Amonasro); Silvio Maionica (King); Giulio Neri (Ramfis); Vittorio Pandano (Messenger); Luciana de Nardo Fainelli (Priestess); Tullio Serafin, c.
July 25	"	*Aida:* Same cast as July 23.
July 28	"	*Aida:* Same cast as July 23 except Mario Filippeschi (Radames).
July 30	"	*Aida:* Same cast as July 23.
Aug. 3–	Milan, Basilica	Recording: *Cavalleria Rusticana:*

Aug. 4	Santa Euphemia	(Santuzza); Giuseppe di Stefano (Turiddu); Rolando Panerai (Alfio); Anna Maria Canali (Lola); Ebe Ticozzi (Lucia); with the Orchestra and Chorus of La Scala, Tullio Serafin, c. (Earlier recording sessions took place June 16–25 without Callas.) Released in the United States on Angel 3509 in April 1954 and in Great Britain on Columbia 33 CX 1182–83 in Oct. 1954.
Aug. 8	Verona, Arena	*Aida:* Same cast as July 23 except Primo Zambruno (Radames); Miriam Pirazzini (Amneris); Giampiero Malaspina (Amonasro); Franco Ghione, c.
Aug. 10– Aug. 21	Milan, Teatro alla Scala	Recording: *Tosca:* (Tosca); Giuseppe di Stefano (Cavaradossi); Tito Gobbi (Scarpia); Franco Calabrese (Angelotti); Melchoirre Luise (Sacristan); Angelo Mercuriali (Spoletta); Dario Caselli (Sciarrone and Jailer); Alvaro Cordova (Shepherd); with the Orchestra and Chorus of La Scala, Victor de Sabata, c. Released in the United States on Angel 3508 in Nov. 1953 and in Great Britain on Columbia 33 CX 1094–95 in Dec. 1953.
Aug. 15	Verona, Arena	*Il Trovatore:* (Leonora); Lucia Danieli (Azucena); Primo Zambruno (Manrico); Aldo Protti (Count di Luna); Silvio Maionica (Ferrando); Barbara Calcina

		(Inez); Vittorio Pandano (Ruiz); Attilio Barbesi (Old Gypsy); Luigi Nardi (Messenger); Francesco Molinari-Pradelli, c.
Sep.	Turin, RAI Auditorium	Recording: *La Traviata:* (Violetta); Francesco Albanese (Alfredo); Ugo Savarese (Germont); Ede Marietti Gandolfo (Flora); Alberto Albertini (Duphol); Mario Zorgniotti (Dr. Grenvil and D'Obigny); Ines Marietti (Annina); Mariano Caruso (Gastone); Tommaso Soley (Giuseppe); with the Orchestra and Chorus of Radio Italiana, Turin, Gabriele Santini, c. Released in Italy on Cetra LPC 1246 and in the United States on Cetra-Soria 1246, both in Sep. 1954; reissued in the United States on Everest-Cetra 425/3 in Jan. 1967.
Nov. 19*	Trieste, Teatro Giuseppe Verdi	*Norma:* (Norma); Franco Corelli (Pollione); Elena Nicolai (Adalgisa); Boris Christoff (Oroveso); Bruna Ronchini (Clotilde); Raimondo Botteghelli (Flavio); Antonino Votto, c.
Nov. 22	"	*Norma:* Same cast as Nov. 19.
Nov. 23	"	*Norma:* Same cast as Nov. 19.
Nov. 29	"	*Norma:* Same cast as Nov. 19.
Dec. 10*	Milan, Teatro alla Scala	*Medea:* (Medea); Gino Penno (Jason); Maria Luisa Nache (Glauce); Giuseppe Modesti (Creon); Fedora Barbieri (Neris); Angela Vercelli and

		Maria Amadini (Handmaidens); Enrico Campi (Captain of the Guard); Leonard Bernstein, c.
Dec. 12	"	*Medea:* Same cast as Dec. 10.
Dec. 16	Rome, Teatro dell'Opera	*Il Trovatore:* (Leonora); Miriam Pirazzini (Azucena); Giacomo Lauri-Volpi (Manrico); Paolo Silveri (Count di Luna); Giulio Neri (Ferrando); Loretta di Lelio (Inez); Adelio Zagonara (Ruiz); Carlo Platania (Old Gypsy); Paolo Caroli (Messenger); Gabriele Santini, c.
Dec. 19	"	*Il Trovatore:* Same cast as Dec. 16 except Fedora Barbieri started the opera as Azucena and was replaced, after becoming indisposed in Act II, by Miriam Pirazzini.
Dec. 23	"	*Il Trovatore:* Same cast as Dec. 16.
Dec. 29	Milan, Teatro alla Scala	*Medea:* Same cast as Dec. 10 except Clara Betner (Second Handmaiden).

1954

Jan. 2	Milan, Teatro alla Scala	*Medea:* Same cast as Dec. 10 except Clara Betner (Second Handmaiden).
Jan. 6	"	*Medea:* Same cast as Dec. 10 except Clara Betner (Second Handmaiden).
Jan. 18*	"	*Lucia di Lammermoor:* (Lucia); Giuseppe di Stefano (Edgardo); Rolando Panerai (Enrico); Giuseppe Modesti (Raimondo); Giuseppe Zampieri (Arturo); Luisa Villa (Alisa); Mario Carlin (Nor-

		manno); Herbert von Karajan, c. (New production directed by Herbert von Karajan.)
Jan. 21	"	*Lucia di Lammermoor:* Same cast as Jan. 18.
Jan. 24	"	*Lucia di Lammermoor:* Same cast as Jan. 18.
Jan. 27	"	*Lucia di Lammermoor:* Same cast as Jan. 18.
Jan. 31	"	*Lucia di Lammermoor:* Same cast as Jan. 18.
Feb. 5	"	*Lucia di Lammermoor:* Same cast as Jan. 18.
Feb. 7	"	*Lucia di Lammermoor:* Same cast as Jan. 18 except Gianni Poggi (Edgardo).
Feb. 13	Venice, Teatro La Fenice	*Lucia di Lammermoor:* (Lucia); Luigi Infantino (Edgardo); Ettore Bastianini (Enrico); Giorgio Tozzi (Raimondo); Giuseppe Zampieri (Arturo); Ebe Ticozzi (Alisa); Guglielmo Torcoli (Normanno); Angelo Questa, c.
Feb. 16	"	*Lucia di Lammermoor:* Same cast as Feb. 13 except Mariano Caruso (Arturo).
Feb. 21	"	*Lucia di Lammermoor:* Same cast as Feb. 13 except Mariano Caruso (Arturo).
Mar. 2	"	*Medea:* (Medea); Renato Gavarini (Jason); Gabriella Tucci (Glauce); Giorgio Tozzi (Creon); Miriam Pirazzini (Neris); Liliana Poli and Maria Andreassi (Handmaidens); Giorgio Santi (Captain of the Guard); Vittorio Gui, c.

		(Florence May Festival production.)
Mar. 4	"	*Medea:* Same cast as Mar. 2.
Mar. 7	"	*Medea:* Same cast as Mar. 2.
Mar. 10	Genoa, Teatro Carlo Felice	*Tosca:* (Tosca); Mario Ortica (Cavaradossi); Gian Giacomo Guelfi (Scarpia); Silvio Maionica (Angelotti); Melchiorre Luise (Sacristan); Luciano della Pergola (Spoletta); Armando Torti (Sciarrone); Rinaldo Grattarola (Jailer); Franco Ghione, c.
Mar. 15	"	*Tosca:* Same cast as Mar. 10.
Mar. 17	"	*Tosca:* Same cast as Mar. 10.
Apr. 4*	Milan, Teatro alla Scala	*Alceste:* (Alceste); Renato Gavarini (Admeto); Paolo Silveri (High Priest); Rolando Panerai (Apollo); Silvio Maionica (Tanato); Giuseppe Zampieri (Evandro); Enrico Campi (Herald); Nicola Zaccaria (Oracle); Carlo Maria Giulini, c.
Apr. 6	"	*Alceste:* Same cast as Apr. 4.
Apr. 12	"	*Don Carlo:* (Elisabetta); Mario Ortica (Don Carlo); Enzo Mascherini (Rodrigo); Nicola Rossi-Lemeni (Philip II); Marco Stefanoni (Grand Inquisitor); Ebe Stignani (Eboli); Antonio Zerbini (Monk); Sandra Ballinari (Tebaldo); Luciano della Pergola (Count de Lerma); Giuseppe Zampieri (Herald); Grete Rapisardi (Voice); Antonino Votto, c.
Apr. 15	"	*Alceste:* Same cast as Apr. 4 ex-

		cept Antonio Zerbini (Tanato).
Apr. 17	"	*Don Carlo:* Same cast as Apr. 12.
Apr. 20	"	*Alceste*: Same cast as Apr. 4 except Antonio Zerbini (Tanato).
Apr. 23	"	*Don Carlo:* Same cast as Apr. 12.
Apr. 25	"	*Don Carlo:* Same cast as Apr. 12.
Apr. 27	"	*Don Carlo:* Same cast as Apr. 12.
Apr. 23–May 3	Milan, Cinema Metropol	Recording: *Norma:* (Norma); Mario Filippeschi (Pollione); Ebe Stignani (Adalgisa); Nicola Rossi-Lemeni (Oroveso); Rina Cavallari (Clotilde); Paolo Caroli (Flavio); with the Orchestra and Chorus of La Scala, Tullio Serafin, c. Released in the United States on Angel 3517 and in Great Britain on Columbia 33 CX 1179–81, both in Nov. 1954; reissued in the United States on Seraphim IC-6037 in Apr. 1969.
May 23	Ravenna, Teatro Alighieri	*La Forza del Destino:* (Leonora); Mario del Monaco (Don Alvaro); Aldo Protti (Don Carlo); Giuseppe Modesti (Padre Guardiano); Renato Capecchi (Fra Melitone); Jolanda Gardino (Preziosilla); Cesare Pasella (Marquis di Calatrava); Lola Pedretti (Curra); Cesare Masini-Sperti (Mastro Trabucco); Franco Ghione, c.
May 26	"	*La Forza del Destino:* Same cast as May 23.
May 25–June 17	Milan, Teatro alla Scala	Recording: *Pagliacci:* (Nedda); Giuseppe di Stefano (Canio); Tito

		Gobbi (Tonio); Nicola Monti (Beppe); Rolando Panerai (Silvio); with the Orchestra and Chorus of La Scala, Tullio Serafin, c. Released in the United States on Angel 3527 in Apr. 1955 and in Great Britain on Columbia 33 CX 1211–12 in Sep. 1955.
July 15	Verona, Arena	*Mefistofele:* (Margherita); Disma de Cecco (Elena); Ferruccio Tagliavini (Faust); Nicola Rossi-Lemeni (Mefistofele); Aurora Cattelani (Pantalis); Maria Amadini (Marta); Giuseppe Zampieri (Wagner); Ottorino Begali (Nereo); Antonino Votto, c.
July 20	"	*Mefistofele:* Same cast as July 15 except Giuseppe di Stefano (Faust); Anna de Cavalieri (Elena).
July 25	"	*Mefistofele:* Same cast as July 15 except Anna de Cavalieri (Elena).
Aug. 17– Aug. 27	Milan, Teatro alla Scala	Recording: *La Forza del Destino:* (Leonora); Richard Tucker (Don Alvaro); Carlo Tagliabue (Don Carlo); Nicola Rossi-Lemeni (Padre Guardiano); Renato Capecchi (Fra Melitone); Elena Nicolai (Preziosilla); Plinio Clabassi (Marquis di Calatrava); Rina Cavallari (Curra); Dario Caselli (A Mayor and A Surgeon); Gino del Signore (Mastro Trabucco); with the Orchestra and Chorus of La Scala, Tullio Serafin, c.

		Released in the United States on Angel 3531 in Apr. 1955 and in Great Britain on Columbia 33 CX 1258–60 in June 1955; reissued in the United States on Seraphim IC-6088 in January 1974.
Aug. 31– Sep. 8	"	Recording: *Il Turco in Italia:* (Fiorilla); Nicola Rossi-Lemeni (Selim); Nicolai Gedda (Narciso); Jolanda Gardino (Zaida); Piero de Palma (Albazar); Franco Calabrese (Geronio); Mariano Stabile (Prosdocimo); with the Orchestra and Chorus of La Scala, Gianandrea Gavazzeni, c. Released in the United States on Angel 3535 in Sep. 1955 and in Great Britain on Columbia 33 CX 1289–91 in Oct. 1955.
Sep. 15– Sep. 21	Watford, England, Town Hall	Recording: Puccini Arias: *Manon Lescaut*—In quelle trine morbide; *Manon Lescaut*—Sola, perduta, abbandonata; *La Bohème*—Mi chiamano Mimì; *La Bohème*—Donde lieta uscì; *Madama Butterfly*—Un bel dì vedremo; *Madama Butterfly*—Tu? tu? piccolo Iddio!; *Suor Angelica*—Senza mamma; *Gianni Schicchi*—O mio babbino caro; *Turandot*—Signore, ascolta; *Turandot*—In questa reggia; *Turandot*—Tu che di gel sei cinta; with the Philharmonia Orchestra, Tullio Serafin, c. Released in Great Britain on Columbia 33 CX 1204 in Dec. 1954

		and in the United States on Angel 35195 in Jan. 1955.
Sep. 15– Sep. 21	"	Recording: Coloratura-Lyric Arias: *Adriana Lecouvreur*—Io son l'umile ancella; *Adriana Lecouvreur*—Poveri fiori; *La Wally*—Ebben? Ne andrò lontana; *Andrea Chénier*—La mamma morta; *Mefistofele*—L'altra notte; *Il Barbiere di Siviglia*—Una voce poco fa; *Dinorah*—Ombra leggiera; *Lakmé*—Dov'è l'Indiana bruna?; *I Vespri Siciliani*—Mercè, dilette amiche; with the Philharmonia Orchestra, Tullio Serafin, c. Released in the United States on Angel 35233 and in Great Britain on Columbia 33 CX 1231, both in Sep. 1955.
Oct. 6	Bergamo, Teatro Gaetano Donizetti	*Lucia di Lammermoor:* (Lucia); Ferruccio Tagliavini (Edgardo); Ugo Savarese (Enrico); Silvio Maionica (Raimondo); Giuseppe Zampieri (Arturo); Lina Rossi (Alisa); Angelo Camozzi (Normanno); Francesco Molinari-Pradelli, c.
Oct. 9	"	*Lucia di Lammermoor:* Same cast as Oct. 6.
Nov. 1	Chicago, Civic Opera House (Lyric Theatre of Chicago)	*Norma:* (Norma); Mirto Picchi (Pollione); Giulietta Simionato (Adalgisa); Nicola Rossi-Lemeni (Oroveso); Gloria Lind (Clotilde); Lawrence White (Flavio); Nicola Rescigno, c.
Nov. 5	"	*Norma:* Same cast as Nov. 1.

Nov. 8	"	*La Traviata:* (Violetta); Leopold Simoneau (Alfredo); Tito Gobbi (Germont); Gloria Lind (Flora); Algerd Brazis (Duphol); Andrew Foldi (Dr. Grenvil); Mary Kreste (Annina); Virginio Assandri (Gastone); Miles Nekolny (D'Obigny); Nicola Rescigno, c.
Nov. 12	"	*La Traviata:* Same cast as Nov. 8.
Nov. 15	"	*Lucia di Lammermoor:* (Lucia); Giuseppe di Stefano (Edgardo); Gian Giacomo Guelfi (Enrico); Thomas Stewart (Raimondo); Lawrence White (Arturo); Mary Kreste (Alisa); Virginio Assandri (Normanno); Nicola Rescigno, c.
Nov. 17	"	*Lucia di Lammermoor:* Same cast as Nov. 15.
Dec. 7*	Milan, Teatro alla Scala	*La Vestale:* (Giulia); Franco Corelli (Licinio); Enzo Sordello (Cinna); Nicola Rossi-Lemeni (Pontifex Maximus); Ebe Stignani (High Priestess); Vittorio Tatozzi (Consul); Nicola Zaccaria (Soothsayer); Antonino Votto, c. (New production directed by Luchino Visconti.)
Dec. 9	"	*La Vestale:* Same cast as Dec. 7.
Dec. 12	"	*La Vestale:* Same cast as Dec. 7.
Dec. 16	"	*La Vestale:* Same cast as Dec. 7.
Dec. 18	"	*La Vestale:* Same cast as Dec. 7.
Dec. 27*	San Remo, Teatro del Casino	Radio Broadcast: Concert (with Beniamino Gigli): *Il Ratto dal Serraglio* (*Die Entführung aus dem Serail*)—Tutte le torture (Martern aller Arten); *Dinorah*—

		Ombra leggiera; *Louise*—Depuis le jour; *Armida*—D'amore al dolce impero; with the Orchestra of RAI, Milan, Alfredo Simonetto, c.

1955

Jan. 8*	Milan, Teatro alla Scala	*Andrea Chénier:* (Maddalena); Mario del Monaco (Andrea Chénier); Aldo Protti (Gérard); Maria Amadini (Contessa); Silvana Zanolli (Bersi); Enzo Sordello (Fléville); Mario Carlin (Abbé); Carlo Forti (Majordomo); Michele Cazzato (Mathieu); Mariano Caruso (Un Incredibile); Enrico Campi (Roucher); Lucia Danieli (Madelon); Vittorio Tatozzi (Fouquier); Giuseppe Morresi (Dumas); Eraldo Coda (Schmidt); Antonino Votto, c.
Jan. 10	"	*Andrea Chénier:* Same cast as Jan. 8.
Jan. 13	"	*Andrea Chénier:* Same cast as Jan. 8 except Angela Vercelli (Bersi); Angelo Mercuriali (Un Incredibile).
Jan. 16	"	*Andrea Chénier:* Same cast as Jan. 8 except Angela Vercelli (Bersi).
Jan. 22	Rome, Teatro dell'Opera	*Medea:* (Medea); Francesco Albanese (Jason); Gabriella Tucci (Glauce); Boris Christoff (Creon); Fedora Barbieri (Neris); Anna Leonelli and Teresa Cantarini (Handmaidens); Antonio Sac-

		chetti (Captain of the Guard); Gabriele Santini, c. (La Scala production.)
Jan. 25	"	*Medea:* Same cast as Jan. 22.
Jan. 27	"	*Medea:* Same cast as Jan. 22.
Jan. 30	"	*Medea:* Same cast as Jan. 22.
Feb. 3	Milan, Teatro alla Scala	*Andrea Chénier:* Same cast as Jan. 8 except Mario Ortica (Andrea Chénier); Giuseppe Taddei (Gérard); Angela Vercelli (Bersi); Ugo Novelli (Roucher).
Feb. 6	"	*Andrea Chénier:* Same cast as Jan. 8 except Mario Ortica (Andrea Chénier); Giuseppe Taddei (Gérard); Angela Vercelli (Bersi); Ugo Novelli (Roucher).
Mar. 5*	"	*La Sonnambula:* (Amina); Cesare Valletti (Elvino); Giuseppe Modesti (Rodolfo); Gabriella Carturan (Teresa); Eugenia Ratti (Lisa); Pierluigi Latinucci (Alessio); Giuseppe Nessi (Notary); Leonard Bernstein, c. (New production directed by Luchino Visconti.)
Mar. 8	"	*La Sonnambula:* Same cast as Mar. 5.
Mar. 13	"	*La Sonnambula:* Same cast as Mar. 5.
Mar. 16	"	*La Sonnambula:* Same cast as Mar. 5.
Mar. 19	"	*La Sonnambula:* Same cast as Mar. 5.
Mar. 24	"	*La Sonnambula:* Same cast as Mar. 5 except Nicola Zaccaria (Rodolfo).

Mar. 30	"	*La Sonnambula:* Same cast as Mar. 5 except Nicola Zaccaria (Rodolfo).
Apr. 12	"	*La Sonnambula:* Same cast as Mar. 5.
Apr. 15	"	*Il Turco in Italia:* (Fiorilla); Nicola Rossi-Lemeni (Selim); Cesare Valletti (Narciso); Jolanda Gardino (Zaida); Angelo Mercuriali (Albazar); Franco Calabrese (Geronio); Mariano Stabile (Prosdocimo); Gianandrea Gavazzeni, c. (New production directed by Franco Zeffirelli.)
Apr. 18	"	*Il Turco in Italia:* Same cast as Apr. 15.
Apr. 21	"	*Il Turco in Italia:* Same cast as Apr. 15.
Apr. 23	"	*Il Turco in Italia:* Same cast as Apr. 15.
Apr. 24	"	*La Sonnambula:* Same cast as Mar. 5.
Apr. 27	"	*La Sonnambula:* Same cast as Mar. 5.
May 4	"	*Il Turco in Italia:* Same cast as Apr. 15.
May 28*	"	*La Traviata:* (Violetta); Giuseppe di Stefano (Alfredo); Ettore Bastianini (Germont); Silvana Zanolli (Flora); Arturo La Porta (Duphol); Silvio Maionica (Dr. Grenvil); Luisa Mandelli (Annina); Giuseppe Zampieri (Gastone); Antonio Zerbini (D'Obigny); Franco Ricciardi (Giuseppe); Carlo Forti (Messen-

		ger); Carlo Maria Giulini, c. (New production directed by Luchino Visconti.)
May 31	"	*La Traviata:* Same cast as May 28 except Giacinto Prandelli (Alfredo).
June 5	"	*La Traviata:* Same cast as May 28 except Giacinto Prandelli (Alfredo).
June 7	"	*La Traviata:* Same cast as May 28 except Giacinto Prandelli (Alfredo).
June 9–June 12	"	Recording: Callas at La Scala: *Medea*—Dei tuoi figli; *La Vestale*—Tu che invoco; *La Vestale*—O Nume tutelar; *La Vestale*—Caro oggetto; with the Orchestra of La Scala, Tullio Serafin, c. Released (along with *La Sonnambula*—Come per me and *I Puritani*—Qui la voce and Vien, diletto from the complete recordings) in the United States on Angel 35304 in Feb. 1958 and in Great Britain on Columbia 33 CX 1540 in June 1958.
June	"	Recording: *La Sonnambula*—Come per me sereno . . . Sovra il sen; *La Sonnambula*—Oh! se una volta sola . . . Ah! non credea mirarti . . . Ah! non giunge; with the Orchestra of La Scala, Tullio Serafin, c. (Unreleased EMI recording.)
June 29*	Rome, RAI Studios	Radio Broadcast: *Norma:* (Norma); Mario del Monaco

		(Pollione); Ebe Stignani (Adalgisa); Giuseppe Modesti (Oroveso); Rina Cavallari (Clotilde); Athos Cesarini (Flavio); with the Orchestra and Chorus of RAI, Rome, Tullio Serafin, c.
Aug. 1– Aug. 6	Milan, Teatro alla Scala	Recording: *Madama Butterfly:* (Cio-Cio-San); Nicolai Gedda (Pinkerton); Lucia Danieli (Suzuki); Mario Borriello (Sharpless); Renato Ercolani (Goro); Mario Carlin (Yamadori); Plinio Clabassi (The Bonze); Enrico Campi (Imperial Commissioner); Luisa Villa (Kate Pinkerton); with the Orchestra and Chorus of La Scala, Herbert von Karajan, c. Released in the United States on Angel 3523 in Nov. 1955 and in Great Britain on Columbia 33 CX 1296–98 in Dec. 1955.
Aug. 10– Aug. 24	"	Recording: *Aida:* (Aida); Richard Tucker (Radames); Fedora Barbieri (Amneris); Tito Gobbi (Amonasro); Nicola Zaccaria (King); Giuseppe Modesti (Ramfis); Franco Ricciardi (Messenger); Elvira Galassi (Priestess); with the Orchestra and Chorus of La Scala, Tullio Serafin, c. Released in the United States on Angel 3525 in Dec. 1955 and in Great Britain on Columbia 33 CX 1318–20 in Jan. 1956.

Sep. 3– Sep. 16	"	Recording: *Rigoletto:* (Gilda); Giuseppe di Stefano (Duke); Tito Gobbi (Rigoletto); Nicola Zaccaria (Sparafucile); Adriana Lazzarini (Maddalena); Plinio Clabassi (Monterone); Renato Ercolani (Borsa); Elvira Galassi (Countess Ceprano); Giuse Gerbino (Giovanna); William Dickie (Marullo); Carlo Forti (Count Ceprano); Vittorio Tatozzi (Usher); Luisa Mandelli (Page); with the Orchestra and Chorus of La Scala, Tullio Serafin, c. Released in Great Britain on Columbia 33 CX 1324–26 in Feb. 1956 and in the United States on Angel 3537 in Mar. 1956.
Sep. 29*	Berlin, Städtische Oper (La Scala Opera Company)	*Lucia di Lammermoor:* (Lucia); Giuseppe di Stefano (Edgardo); Rolando Panerai (Enrico); Nicola Zaccaria (Raimondo); Giuseppe Zampieri (Arturo); Luisa Villa (Alisa); Mario Carlin (Normanno); with the RIAS Orchestra, Herbert von Karajan, c. (La Scala production.)
Oct. 2	"	*Lucia di Lammermoor:* Same cast as Sep. 29 except Giuseppe di Stefano was replaced, after becoming indisposed, by Giuseppe Zampieri in the final scene.
Oct. 31	Chicago, Civic Opera House (Lyric Theatre of Chicago)	*I Puritani:* (Elvira); Giuseppe di Stefano (Arturo); Ettore Bastianini (Riccardo); Nicola Rossi-Lemeni (Giorgio); William Wilder-

		man (Gualtiero); Mariano Caruso (Bruno); Eunice Alberts (Enrichetta); Nicola Rescigno, c.
Nov. 2	"	*I Puritani:* Same cast as Oct. 31.
Nov. 5	"	*Il Trovatore:* (Leonora); Ebe Stignani (Azucena); Jussi Björling (Manrico); Ettore Bastianini (Count di Luna); William Wilderman (Ferrando); Eunice Alberts (Inez); Mariano Caruso (Ruiz); Jonas Vaznelis (Old Gypsy); Nicola Rescigno, c.
Nov. 8	"	*Il Trovatore:* Same cast as Nov. 5 except Claramae Turner (Azucena); Robert Weede (Count di Luna).
Nov. 11	"	*Madama Butterfly:* (Cio-Cio-San); Giuseppe di Stefano (Pinkerton); Eunice Alberts (Suzuki); Robert Weede (Sharpless); Mariano Caruso (Goro); Lloyd Harris (Yamadori); Kenneth Smith (The Bonze); Andrew Foldi (Imperial Commissioner); Miles Nekolny (Registrar); Marilu Adams (Kate Pinkerton); Nicola Rescigno, c. (Production directed by Hizi Koyke.)
Nov. 14	"	*Madama Butterfly:* Same cast as Nov. 11.
Nov. 17	"	*Madama Butterfly:* Same cast as Nov. 11.
Dec. 7*	Milan, Teatro alla Scala	*Norma:* (Norma); Mario del Monaco (Pollione); Giulietta Simionato (Adalgisa); Nicola Zaccaria (Oroveso); Gabriella Car-

		turan (Clotilde); Giuseppe Zampieri (Flavio); Antonino Votto, c.
Dec. 11	"	*Norma:* Same cast as Dec. 7.
Dec. 14	"	*Norma:* Same cast as Dec. 7.
Dec. 17	"	*Norma:* Same cast as Dec. 7.
Dec. 21	"	*Norma:* Same cast as Dec. 7.
Dec. 29	"	*Norma:* Same cast as Dec. 7 except Elena Nicolai (Adalgisa).

1956

Jan. 1	Milan, Teatro alla Scala	*Norma:* Same cast as Dec. 7.
Jan. 5	"	*Norma:* Same cast as Dec. 7.
Jan. 8	"	*Norma:* Same cast as Dec. 7 except Elena Nicolai (Adalgisa).
Jan. 19*	"	*La Traviata:* (Violetta); Gianni Raimondi (Alfredo); Ettore Bastianini (Germont); Silvana Zanolli (Flora); Arturo La Porta (Duphol); Silvio Maionica (Dr. Grenvil); Luisa Mandelli (Annina); Giuseppe Zampieri (Gastone); Dario Caselli (D'Obigny); Franco Ricciardi (Giuseppe); Carlo Forti (Messenger); Vittorio Tatozzi (Servant); Carlo Maria Giulini, c.
Jan. 23	"	*La Traviata:* Same cast as Jan. 19 except Aldo Protti (Germont).
Jan. 26	"	*La Traviata:* Same cast as Jan. 19.
Jan. 29	"	*La Traviata:* Same cast as Jan. 19.
Feb. 2	"	*La Traviata:* Same cast as Jan. 19.
Feb. 5	"	*La Traviata:* Same cast as Jan. 19.
Feb. 16*	"	*Il Barbiere di Siviglia:* (Rosina); Tito Gobbi (Figaro); Luigi Alva (Almaviva); Nicola Rossi-Lemeni (Don Basilio); Melchiorre Luise

		(Dr. Bartolo); Anna Maria Canali (Berta); Pierluigi Latinucci (Fiorello); Giuseppe Nessi (Official); Carlo Maria Giulini, c.
Feb. 18	"	*La Traviata:* Same cast as Jan. 19.
Feb. 21	"	*Il Barbiere di Siviglia:* Same cast as Feb. 16.
Feb. 26	"	*La Traviata:* Same cast as Jan. 19.
Mar. 3	"	*Il Barbiere di Siviglia:* Same cast as Feb. 16.
Mar. 6	"	*Il Barbiere di Siviglia:* Same cast as Feb. 16 except Nicola Monti (Almaviva); Carlo Badioli (Dr. Bartolo).
Mar. 9	"	*La Traviata:* Same cast as Jan. 19 except Carlo Tagliabue (Germont); Antonio Tonini, c.
Mar. 15	"	*Il Barbiere di Siviglia:* Same cast as Feb. 16 except Nicola Monti (Almaviva); Carlo Badioli (Dr. Bartolo).
Mar. 22*	Naples, Teatro San Carlo	*Lucia di Lammermoor:* (Lucia); Gianni Raimondi (Edgardo); Rolando Panerai (Enrico); Antonio Zerbini (Raimondo); Piero de Palma (Arturo); Anna Maria Borrelli (Alisa); Pietro Moccia (Normanno); Francesco Molinari-Pradelli, c.
Mar. 24	"	*Lucia di Lammermoor:* Same cast as Mar. 22.
Mar. 27	"	*Lucia di Lammermoor:* Same cast as Mar. 22.
Apr. 5	Milan, Teatro alla Scala	*La Traviata:* Same cast as Jan. 19 except Mariella Angioletti (Flora).
Apr. 14	"	*La Traviata:* Same cast as Jan. 19.

Apr. 18	"	*La Traviata:* Same cast as Jan. 19 except Anselmo Colzani (Germont).
Apr. 21	"	*La Traviata:* Same cast as Jan. 19.
Apr. 25	"	*La Traviata:* Same cast as Jan. 19.
Apr. 27	"	*La Traviata:* Same cast as Jan. 19.
Apr. 29	"	*La Traviata:* Same cast as Jan. 19 except Antonio Tonini, c.
May 6	"	*La Traviata:* Same cast as Jan. 19 except Antonio Tonini, c.
May 21*	"	*Fedora:* (Fedora); Franco Corelli (Loris); Silvana Zanolli (Olga); Anselmo Colzani (De Siriex); Enzo Cassata (Dimitri); Mariano Caruso (Désiré); Gino del Signore (Baron Rouvel); Paolo Montarsolo (Cyril); Michele Cazzato (Boroff); Eraldo Coda (Grech); Giuseppe Morresi (Lorek); Carlo Forti (Nicola); Franco Ricciardi (Sergio); Sergio Mazzola (Shepherd); Elio Cantamessa (Boleslao Lazinski); Gianandrea Gavazzeni, c.
May 23	"	*Fedora:* Same cast as May 21.
May 27	"	*Fedora:* Same cast as May 21.
May 30	"	*Fedora:* Same cast as May 21.
June 1	"	*Fedora:* Same cast as May 21.
June 3	"	*Fedora:* Same cast as May 21.
June 12	Vienna, Staatsoper (La Scala Opera Company)	*Lucia di Lammermoor:* (Lucia); Giuseppe di Stefano (Edgardo); Rolando Panerai (Enrico); Nicola Zaccaria (Raimondo); Giuseppe Zampieri (Arturo); Luisa Villa (Alisa); Renato Ercolani (Normanno); Herbert von Karajan, c. (La Scala production.)

June 14	"	*Lucia di Lammermoor:* Same cast as June 12.
June 16	"	*Lucia di Lammermoor:* Same cast as June 12.
Aug. 3– Aug. 9	Milan, Teatro alla Scala	Recording: *Il Trovatore:* (Leonora); Fedora Barbieri (Azucena); Giuseppe di Stefano (Manrico); Rolando Panerai (Count di Luna); Nicola Zaccaria (Ferrando); Luisa Villa (Inez); Renato Ercolani (Ruiz and Messenger); Giulio Mauri (Old Gypsy); with the Orchestra and Chorus of La Scala, Herbert von Karajan, c. Released in the United States on Angel 3554 in Mar. 1957 and in Great Britain on Columbia 33 CX 1483–85 in Nov. 1957.
Aug. 20– Aug. 25, Sep. 3– Sep. 4	"	Recording: *La Bohème:* (Mimì); Giuseppe di Stefano (Rodolfo); Rolando Panerai (Marcello); Anna Moffo (Musetta); Nicola Zaccaria (Colline); Manuel Spatafora (Schaunard); Carlo Badioli (Benoit and Alcindoro); Franco Ricciardi (Parpignol); Carlo Forti (Sergeant); with the Orchestra and Chorus of La Scala, Antonino Votto, c. Released in the United States on Angel 3560 in Sep. 1957 and in Great Britain on Columbia 33 CX 1464–65 in Mar. 1958.
Sep. 4– Sep. 12	"	Recording: *Un Ballo in Maschera:* (Amelia); Giuseppe di Stefano (Riccardo); Tito Gobbi (Renato); Fedora Barbieri (Ulrica);

		Eugenia Ratti (Oscar); Ezio Giordano (Silvano); Silvio Maionica (Samuel); Nicola Zaccaria (Tom); Renato Ercolani (A Judge and A Servant); with the Orchestra and Chorus of La Scala, Antonino Votto, c. Released in the United States on Angel 3557 in Apr. 1957 and in Great Britain on Columbia 33 CX 1472–74 in Oct. 1957; reissued in the United States on Seraphim IC-6087 in March 1974.
Sep. 27*	Milan, RAI Studios	Radio Broadcast: Concert: *La Vestale*—Tu che invoco; *Semiramide*—Bel raggio lusinghier; *Amleto* (*Hamlet*)—Ai vostri giuochi . . . Ed ora a voi canterò (Mad Scene); *I Puritani*—Vieni al tempio; with the Orchestra and Chorus of RAI, Milan, Alfredo Simonetto, c. (Recorded for broadcast. First broadcast on Dec. 8, 1956.)
Oct. 29	New York, Metropolitan Opera House	*Norma:* (Norma); Mario del Monaco (Pollione); Fedora Barbieri (Adalgisa); Cesare Siepi (Oroveso); Maria Leone (Clotilde); James McCracken (Flavio); Fausto Cleva, c.
Nov. 3	"	*Norma:* Same cast as Oct. 29.
Nov. 7	"	*Norma:* Same cast as Oct. 29.
Nov. 10	"	*Norma:* Same cast as Oct. 29.
Nov. 15	"	*Tosca:* (Tosca); Giuseppe Campora (Cavaradossi); George London (Scarpia); Clifford Harvuot

		(Angelotti); Fernando Corena (Sacristan); Alessio de Paolis (Spoletta); George Cehanovsky (Sciarrone); Louis Sgarro (Jailer); George Keith (Shepherd); Dimitri Mitropoulos, c.
Nov. 19	"	*Tosca:* Same cast as Nov. 15.
Nov. 22	"	*Norma:* Same cast as Oct. 29 except Kurt Baum (Pollione); Nicola Moscona (Oroveso); Helen Vanni (Clotilde).
Nov. 25*	New York, CBS Studio 53	Television Broadcast: Ed Sullivan Show: *Tosca*—Act II (from Tosca's words "Salvatelo!" to end of act with some omissions): (Tosca); George London (Scarpia); with orchestra, Dimitri Mitropoulos, c.
Nov. 27	Philadelphia, Academy of Music (Metropolitan Opera Company)	*Norma:* Same cast as Oct. 29 except Kurt Baum (Pollione); Nicola Moscona (Oroveso); Helen Vanni (Clotilde).
Dec. 3	New York, Metropolitan Opera House	*Lucia di Lammermoor:* (Lucia); Giuseppe Campora (Edgardo); Enzo Sordello (Enrico); Nicola Moscona (Raimondo); Paul Franke (Arturo); Thelma Votipka (Alisa); James McCracken (Normanno); Fausto Cleva, c.
Dec. 8*	"	*Lucia di Lammermoor:* Same cast as Dec. 3.
Dec. 14	"	*Lucia di Lammermoor:* Same cast as Dec. 3 except Frank Valentino (Enrico).
Dec. 17	Washington, D.C., Italian Embassy	Concert: *Norma*—Casta Diva; *Lucia di Lammermoor*—Regnava

		nel silenzio; *Il Trovatore*—D'amor sull'ali rosee; encore—a Puccini aria, possibly *Tosca*—Vissi d'arte; with piano, Theodore Schaefer, accompanist.
Dec. 19	New York, Metropolitan Opera House	*Lucia di Lammermoor:* Same cast as Dec. 3 except Richard Tucker (Edgardo); Frank Valentino (Enrico).

1957

Jan. 15	Chicago, Civic Opera House	Concert: *La Sonnambula*—Ah! non credea mirarti; *Dinorah*—Ombra leggiera; *Turandot*—In questa reggia; *Norma*—Casta Diva; *Il Trovatore*—D'amor sull'ali rosee; *Lucia di Lammermoor*—Il dolce suono (Mad Scene—Part I); with the Chicago Symphony Orchestra, Fausto Cleva, c.
Feb. 2	London, Royal Opera House, Covent Garden	*Norma:* (Norma); Giuseppe Vertecchi (Pollione); Ebe Stignani (Adalgisa); Nicola Zaccaria (Oroveso); Marie Collier (Clotilde); Dermot Troy (Flavio); John Pritchard, c.
Feb. 6	"	*Norma:* Same cast as Feb. 2.
Feb. 7–Feb. 14	London, Kingsway Hall	Recording: *Il Barbiere di Siviglia:* (Rosina); Tito Gobbi (Figaro); Luigi Alva (Almaviva); Nicola Zaccaria (Don Basilio); Fritz Ollendorf (Dr. Bartolo); Gabriella Carturan (Berta); Mario Carlin (Fiorello); with the Philharmonia Orchestra and Chorus, Alceo Galliera, c. Released in Great Britain on Co-

		lumbia 33 CX 1507–9 (mono) and SAX 2266–68 (stereo) in Feb. 1958 and in the United States on Angel 3559 (mono and stereo) in Apr. 1958.
Mar. 2*	Milan, Teatro alla Scala	*La Sonnambula:* (Amina); Nicola Monti (Elvino); Nicola Zaccaria (Rodolfo); Fiorenza Cossotto (Teresa); Eugenia Ratti (Lisa); Giuseppe Morresi (Alessio); Franco Ricciardi (Notary); Antonino Votto, c.
Mar. 3– Mar. 9	Milan, Basilica Santa Euphemia	Recording: *La Sonnambula:* (Amina); Nicola Monti (Elvino); Nicola Zaccaria (Rodolfo); Fiorenza Cossotto (Teresa); Eugenia Ratti (Lisa); Giuseppe Morresi (Alessio); Franco Ricciardi (Notary); with the Orchestra and Chorus of La Scala, Antonino Votto, c. Released in the United States on Angel 3568 and in Great Britain on Columbia 33 CX 1469–71, both in Oct. 1957.
Mar. 7	Milan, Teatro alla Scala	*La Sonnambula:* Same cast as Mar. 2.
Mar. 10	"	*La Sonnambula:* Same cast as Mar. 2.
Mar. 12	"	*La Sonnambula:* Same cast as Mar. 2.
Mar. 17	"	*La Sonnambula:* Same cast as Mar. 2.
Mar. 20	"	*La Sonnambula:* Same cast as Mar. 2 except Mario Spina (Elvino).
Apr. 14*	"	*Anna Bolena:* (Anna Bolena);

		Gianni Raimondi (Percy); Nicola Rossi-Lemeni (Enrico VIII); Giulietta Simionato (Giovanna Seymour); Plinio Clabassi (Rochefort); Luigi Rumbo (Hervey); Gabriella Carturan (Smeton); Gianandrea Gavazzeni, c. (New production directed by Luchino Visconti.)
Apr. 17	"	*Anna Bolena:* Same cast as Apr. 14.
Apr. 20	"	*Anna Bolena:* Same cast as Apr. 14.
Apr. 24	"	*Anna Bolena:* Same cast as Apr. 14.
Apr. 27	"	*Anna Bolena:* Same cast as Apr. 14.
Apr. 30	"	*Anna Bolena:* Same cast as Apr. 14.
May 5	"	*Anna Bolena:* Same cast as Apr. 14.
June 1*	"	*Ifigenia in Tauride:* (Ifigenia); Francesco Albanese (Pilade); Anselmo Colzani (Toante); Fiorenza Cossotto (Artemide); Dino Dondi (Oreste); Stefania Malagù and Eva Perotti (Priestesses); Edith Martelli (Greek Slave); Costantino Ego (Servant); Nino Sanzogno, c. (New production directed by Luchino Visconti.)
June 3	"	*Ifigenia in Tauride:* Same cast as June 1.
June 5	"	*Ifigenia in Tauride:* Same cast as June 1.
June 10	"	*Ifigenia in Tauride:* Same cast as June 1.

June 19	Zürich, Tonhalle	Concert: *La Traviata*—Ah, fors'è lui and Sempre libera; *Lucia di Lammermoor*—Il dolce suono . . . Spargi d'amaro pianto (Mad Scene); with the Winterthurer Stadtorchester, Rudolf Moralt, c.
June 26*	Rome, RAI Studios	Radio Broadcast: *Lucia di Lammermoor:* (Lucia); Eugenio Fernandi (Edgardo); Rolando Panerai (Enrico); Giuseppe Modesti (Raimondo); Dino Formichini (Arturo); Elvira Galassi (Alisa); Valiano Natali (Normanno); with the Orchestra and Chorus of RAI, Rome, Tullio Serafin, c.
July 4	Cologne, Grosses Haus (La Scala Opera Company)	*La Sonnambula:* (Amina); Nicola Monti (Elvino); Nicola Zaccaria (Rodolfo); Fiorenza Cossotto (Teresa); Mariella Angioletti (Lisa); Dino Mantovani (Alessio); Franco Ricciardi (Notary); Antonino Votto, c. (La Scala production.)
July 6	"	*La Sonnambula:* Same cast as July 4.
July 9–July 15	Milan, Teatro alla Scala	Recording: *Turandot:* (Turandot); Elisabeth Schwarzkopf (Liù); Eugenio Fernandi (Calaf); Nicola Zaccaria (Timur); Mario Borriello (Ping); Renato Ercolani (Pang); Piero de Palma (Pong); Giuseppe Nessi (Altoum); Giulio Mauri (Mandarin); with the Orchestra and Chorus of La Scala, Tullio Serafin, c. Released in the United States on Angel 3571 in Jan. 1958 and in

		Great Britain on Columbia 33 CX 1555–57 in Sep. 1958.
July 18– July 27	"	Recording: *Manon Lescaut:* (Manon); Giuseppe di Stefano (Des Grieux); Giulio Fioravanti (Lescaut); Franco Calabrese (Geronte); Dino Formichini (Edmondo); Carlo Forti (Innkeeper); Vito Tatone (Dancing Master); Fiorenza Cossotto (Musician); Giuseppe Morresi (Sergeant); Franco Ricciardi (Lamplighter); Franco Ventriglia (Captain); with the Orchestra and Chorus of La Scala, Tullio Serafin, c. Released in Great Britain on Columbia 33 CX 1583–85 in Dec. 1959 and in the United States on Angel 3564 in Feb. 1960.
Aug. 5*	Athens, Amphitheater of Herodes Atticus (Athens Festival)	Concert: *Il Trovatore*—D'amor sull'ali rosee; *La Forza del Destino*—Pace, pace, mio Dio; *Lucia di Lammermoor*—Regnava nel silenzio . . . Quando rapito in estasi; *Tristano e Isotta*—Morte de Isotta; *Hamlet*—À vos jeux, mes amis (Mad Scene); encore—second part of *Hamlet* Mad Scene; with the Athens Festival Orchestra, Antonino Votto, c.
Aug. 19	Edinburgh, King's Theatre (Edinburgh Festival—Piccola Scala Company)	*La Sonnambula:* (Amina); Nicola Monti (Elvino); Nicola Zaccaria (Rodolfo); Fiorenza Cossotto (Teresa); Edith Martelli (Lisa); Dino Mantovani (Alessio); Franco

		Ricciardi (Notary); with the Orchestra and Chorus of the Piccola Scala, Antonino Votto, c. (La Scala production.)
Aug. 21*	"	*La Sonnambula:* Same cast as Aug. 19.
Aug. 26*	"	*La Sonnambula:* Same cast as Aug. 19.
Aug. 29	"	*La Sonnambula:* Same cast as Aug. 19.
Sep.	Milan, Teatro alla Scala	Recording: *Medea:* (Medea); Mirto Picchi (Jason); Renata Scotto (Glauce); Giuseppe Modesti (Creon); Miriam Pirazzini (Neris); Lidia Marimpietri and Elvira Galassi (Maidservants); Alfredo Giacommotti (Captain of the Guard); with the Orchestra and Chorus of La Scala, Tullio Serafin, c. Released in the United States on Mercury OL-104 (mono) and SR-9000 (stereo) in June 1958 and in Great Britain on Columbia 33 CX 1618–20 (mono) and SAX 2290–92 (stereo) in Feb. 1959.
Nov. 21	Dallas, State Fair Music Hall	Concert: *Il Ratto dal Serraglio* (*Die Entführung aus dem Serail*)—Tutte le torture (Martern aller Arten); *I Puritani*—Qui la voce and Vien, diletto; *Macbeth*—Vieni! t'affretta!; *La Traviata*—Ah, fors'è lui and Sempre libera; *Anna Bolena*—Mad Scene; with the Dallas Symphony Orchestra, Nicola Rescigno, c.

Dec. 7*	Milan, Teatro alla Scala	*Un Ballo in Maschera:* (Amelia); Giuseppe di Stefano (Riccardo); Ettore Bastianini (Renato); Giulietta Simionato (Ulrica); Eugenia Ratti (Oscar); Giuseppe Morresi (Silvano); Antonio Cassinelli (Samuel); Marco Stefanoni (Tom); Angelo Mercuriali (Judge); Antonio Ricci (Servant); Gianandrea Gavazzeni, c.
Dec. 10	"	*Un Ballo in Maschera:* Same cast as Dec. 7.
Dec. 16	"	*Un Ballo in Maschera:* Same cast as Dec. 7.
Dec. 19	"	*Un Ballo in Maschera:* Same cast as Dec. 7.
Dec. 22	"	*Un Ballo in Maschera:* Same cast as Dec. 7 except Ettore Bastianini, after becoming indisposed, was replaced by Romano Roma in Act III.
Dec. 31*	Rome, RAI Studios	Television Appearance: *Norma*—Casta Diva, with orchestra.

1958

Jan. 2*	Rome, Teatro dell'Opera	*Norma:* (Norma); Franco Corelli (Pollione); Miriam Pirazzini (Adalgisa); Giuseppe Neri (Oroveso); Piero de Palma (Flavio); Gabriele Santini, c. (Performance canceled after Act I after Callas became indisposed.)
Jan. 22	Chicago, Civic Opera House	Concert: *Don Giovanni*—Non mi dir; *Macbeth*—Vieni! t'affretta!; *Il Barbiere di Siviglia*—Una voce poco fa; *Mefistofele*—L'altra

		notte; *Nabucco*—Anch'io dischiuso; *Hamlet*—À vos jeux, mes amis (Mad Scene); with the Chicago Symphony Orchestra, Nicola Rescigno, c.
Feb. 6	New York, Metropolitan Opera House	*La Traviata:* (Violetta); Daniele Barioni (Alfredo); Mario Zanasi (Germont); Helen Vanni (Flora); Calvin Marsh (Duphol); Louis Sgarro (Dr. Grenvil); Mildred Allen (Annina); Charles Anthony (Gastone); George Cehanovsky (D'Obigny); Robert Nagy (Giuseppe); Osie Hawkins (Gardener); Fausto Cleva, c.
Feb. 10	"	*La Traviata:* Same cast as Feb. 6 except Giuseppe Campora (Alfredo); Gabor Carelli (Gastone).
Feb. 13	"	*Lucia di Lammermoor:* (Lucia); Carlo Bergonzi (Edgardo); Mario Sereni (Enrico); Nicola Moscona (Raimondo); Charles Anthony (Arturo); Thelma Votipka (Alisa); Robert Nagy (Normanno); Fausto Cleva, c.
Feb. 20	"	*Lucia di Lammermoor:* Same cast as Feb. 13 except Norman Scott (Raimondo).
Feb. 25	"	*Lucia di Lammermoor:* Same cast as Feb. 13 except Eugenio Fernandi (Edgardo); Giorgio Tozzi (Raimondo).
Feb. 28	"	*Tosca:* (Tosca); Richard Tucker (Cavaradossi); Walter Cassel (Scarpia); Norman Scott (Angelotti); Lawrence Davidson (Sac-

		ristan); Alessio de Paolis (Spoletta); Osie Hawkins (Sciarrone); Ezio Flagello (Jailer); Peter Burke (Shepherd); Dimitri Mitropoulos, c.
Mar. 5	"	*Tosca:* Same cast as Feb. 28 except George London (Scarpia); Clifford Harvuot (Angelotti); Gerhard Pechner (Sacristan).
Mar. 24	Madrid, Cinema Monumental	Concert: *Norma*—Casta Diva; *Il Trovatore*—D'amor sull'ali rosee; *Mefistofele*—L'altra notte; *Hamlet*—À vos jeux, mes amis (Mad Scene); with the Orquesta de Camara, Giuseppe Morelli, c.
Mar. 27	Lisbon, Teatro Nacional de San Carlos	*La Traviata:* (Violetta); Alfredo Kraus (Alfredo); Mario Sereni (Germont); Laura Zannini (Flora); Alvaro Malta (Duphol); Alessandro Maddalena (Dr. Grenvil); Maria Cristina de Castro (Annina); Piero de Palma (Gastone); Vito Susca (D'Obigny); Manuel Leitão (Messenger); Franco Ghione, c.
Mar. 30	"	*La Traviata:* Same cast as Mar. 27.
Apr. 9	Milan, Teatro alla Scala	*Anna Bolena:* (Anna Bolena); Gianni Raimondi (Percy); Cesare Siepi (Enrico VIII); Giulietta Simionato (Giovanna Seymour); Silvio Maionica (Rochefort); Luigi Rumbo (Hervey); Gabriella Carturan (Smeton); Gianandrea Gavazzeni, c.
Apr. 13	"	*Anna Bolena:* Same cast as Apr. 9.

Apr. 16	"	*Anna Bolena:* Same cast as Apr. 9.
Apr. 19	"	*Anna Bolena:* Same cast as Apr. 9.
Apr. 23	"	*Anna Bolena:* Same cast as Apr. 9.
May 19	"	*Il Pirata:* (Imogene); Franco Corelli (Gualtiero); Ettore Bastianini (Ernesto); Luigi Rumbo (Itulbo); Plinio Clabassi (Goffredo); Angela Vercelli (Adele); Antonino Votto, c.
May 22	"	*Il Pirata:* Same cast as May 19.
May 25	"	*Il Pirata:* Same cast as May 19.
May 28	"	*Il Pirata:* Same cast as May 19.
May 31	"	*Il Pirata:* Same cast as May 19.
June 10	London, Royal Opera House, Covent Garden	Centenary Gala (Callas, Joan Sutherland, John Lanigan, Blanche Thebom, Jon Vickers, et al.): *I Puritani*—Qui la voce . . . Vien, diletto; with Forbes Robinson (Giorgio); John Shaw (Riccardo); John Pritchard, c.
June 17*	London, Chelsea Empire Theatre	Television Broadcast: Chelsea at Eight (Callas and others): *Tosca*—Vissi d'arte; *Il Barbiere di Siviglia*—Una voce poco fa; with orchestra, John Pritchard, c.
June 20*	London, Royal Opera House, Covent Garden	*La Traviata:* (Violetta); Cesare Valletti (Alfredo); Mario Zanasi (Germont); Marie Collier (Flora); Forbes Robinson (Duphol); David Kelly (Dr. Grenvil); Leah Roberts (Annina); Dermot Troy (Gastone); Ronald Lewis (D'Obigny); David Tree (Giuseppe); Keith Raggett (Messenger); Charles Morris (Servant); Nicola Rescigno, c.

Date	Place	Event
June 23	"	*La Traviata:* Same cast as June 20.
June 26	"	*La Traviata:* Same cast as June 20.
June 28	"	*La Traviata:* Same cast as June 20.
June 30	"	*La Traviata:* Same cast as June 20.
Sep. 19–Sep. 24	London, EMI Studio No. 1 and Kingsway Hall	Recording: Callas Portrays Verdi Heroines: *Macbeth*—Nel dì della vittoria . . . Vieni! t'affretta!; *Macbeth*—La luce langue; *Macbeth*—Una macchia (Sleepwalking Scene); *Nabucco*—Ben io t'invenni . . . Anch'io dischiuso; *Ernani*—Sorta è la notte . . . Ernani! Ernani, involami!; *Don Carlo*—Tu che le vanità; with the Philharmonia Orchestra, Nicola Rescigno, c. Released in Great Britain on Columbia 33 CX 1628 (mono) and SAX 2293 (stereo) in Mar. 1959 and in the United States on Angel 35763 (mono and stereo) in July 1959.
Sep. 24–Sep. 25	"	Recording: Mad Scenes: *Anna Bolena*—Piangete voi? . . . Al dolce guidami with Monica Sinclair (Smeton), John Lanigan (Percy), Joseph Rouleau (Rochefort); Duncan Robertson (Hervey) and chorus; *Hamlet*—À vos jeux . . . Partagez-vous mes fleurs . . . Et maintenant écoutez; *Il*

		Pirata—Oh! s'io potessi . . . Col sorriso d'innocenza; with the Philharmonia Orchestra, Nicola Rescigno, c. Released in Great Britain on Columbia 33 CX 1645 (mono) and SAX 2320 (stereo) in May 1959 and in the United States on Angel 35764 (mono and stereo) in Nov. 1959.
Sep. 23*	London, Chelsea Empire Theatre	Television Broadcast: Chelsea at Eight: *Norma*—Casta Diva; *Madama Butterfly*—Un bel dì; with orchestra, John Pritchard, c.
Oct. 11	Birmingham, Municipal Auditorium	Concert: *La Vestale*—Tu che invoco; *Macbeth*—Ambizioso spirto . . . Vieni! t'affretta!; *Il Barbiere di Siviglia*—Una voce poco fa; *Mefistofele*—L'altra notte; *La Bohème*—Musetta's Waltz; *Hamlet*—À vos jeux, mes amis (Mad Scene); with Symphony Orchestra, Nicola Rescigno, c.
Oct. 14	Atlanta, Municipal Auditorium	Concert: Same as Oct. 11.
Oct. 17	Montreal, Forum	Concert: Same as Oct. 11.
Oct. 21	Toronto, Maple Leaf Gardens	Concert: Same as Oct. 11.
Oct. 31	Dallas, State Fair Music Hall (Civic Opera Company)	*La Traviata:* (Violetta); Nicola Filacuridi (Alfredo); Giuseppe Taddei (Germont); Mary MacKenzie (Flora); Peter Bender (Duphol); Paolo Montarsolo (Dr. Grenvil); Judith Raskin (Annina); John Jenista (D'Obigny);

		Richard Krause (Gastone); Nicola Rescigno, c. (New production directed by Franco Zeffirelli.)
Nov. 2	"	*La Traviata:* Same cast as Oct. 31.
Nov. 6*	"	*Medea:* (Medea); Jon Vickers (Jason); Elizabeth Carron (Glauce); Nicola Zaccaria (Creon); Teresa Berganza (Neris); Judith Raskin and Mary MacKenzie (Handmaidens); Peter Bender (Captain of the Guard); Nicola Rescigno, c. (New production directed by Alexis Minotis.)
Nov. 8	"	*Medea:* Same cast as Nov. 6.
Nov. 15	Cleveland, Public Music House	Concert: Same as Oct. 11.
Nov. 18	Detroit, Masonic Auditorium	Concert: Same as Oct. 11.
Nov. 22	Washington, D.C., Constitution Hall	Concert: Same as Oct. 11.
Nov. 26	San Francisco, Civic Auditorium	Concert: Same as Oct. 11.
Nov. 29	Los Angeles, Shrine Auditorium	Concert: Same as Oct. 11.
Dec. 19*	Paris, Opéra	Concert: *Norma*—Casta Diva; *Il Trovatore*—D'amor sull'ali rosee; *Il Trovatore*—Miserere with Albert Lance (Manrico) and chorus; *Il Barbiere di Siviglia*—Una voce poco fa; *Tosca*—Act II with Albert Lance (Cavaradossi); Tito Gobbi (Scarpia); Louis Rialland (Spoletta); Jean-Pierre Hurteau (Sciarrone); Georges Sebastian, c.

1959

Jan. 11	St. Louis, Kiel Auditorium	Concert: Same as Oct. 11; with the St. Louis Symphony Orchestra.
Jan. 24	Philadelphia, Academy of Music	Concert (102d Anniversary of the Academy of Music—Callas and Van Cliburn); *Mefistofele*—L'altra notte; *Il Barbiere di Siviglia*—Una voce poco fa; *Hamlet*—À vos jeux, mes amis (Mad Scene); with the Philadelphia Orchestra, Eugene Ormandy, c.
Jan. 27*	New York, Carnegie Hall (American Opera Society)	*Il Pirata* (Concert version): (Imogene); Pier Miranda Ferraro (Gualtiero); Costantino Ego (Ernesto); Glade Peterson (Itulbo); Chester Watson (Goffredo); Regina Sarfaty (Adele); Nicola Rescigno, c.
Jan. 29	Washington, D.C., Constitution Hall (American Opera Society)	*Il Pirata:* Same cast as Jan. 27.
Mar. 16–Mar. 21	London, Kingsway Hall	Recording: *Lucia di Lammermoor:* (Lucia); Ferruccio Tagliavini (Edgardo); Piero Cappuccilli (Enrico); Bernard Ladysz (Raimondo); Leonard del Ferro (Arturo); Margreta Elkins (Alisa); Renzo Casellato (Normanno); with the Philharmonia Orchestra and Chorus, Tullio Serafin, c. Released in the United States on Angel 3601 (mono and stereo) in Dec. 1959 and in Great Britain on Columbia 33 CX 1723–24 (mono)

		and SAX 2316–17 (stereo) in July 1960.
May 2	Madrid, Zarzuela	Concert: *Don Giovanni*—Non mi dir; *Macbeth*—Nel dì della vittoria . . . Vieni! t'affretta!; *Semiramide*—Bel raggio lusinghier; *La Gioconda*—Suicidio!; *Il Pirata*—Final Scene; with the Orquesta Sinfonica de Madrid, Nicola Rescigno, c.
May 5	Barcelona, Gran Teatro del Liceo	Concert: *Don Carlo*—Tu che le vanità; *Mefistofele*—L'altra notte; *Il Barbiere di Siviglia*—Una voce poco fa; *Tosca*—Vissi d'arte; *La Bohème*—Musetta's Waltz; *Il Pirata*—Final Scene; with the Orquesta Sinfonica del Gran Teatro del Liceo, Nicola Rescigno, c.
May 15	Hamburg, Musikhalle	Concert: *La Vestale*—Tu che invoco; *Macbeth*—Nel dì della vittoria . . . Vieni! t'affretta!; *Il Barbiere di Siviglia*—Una voce poco fa; *Don Carlo*—Tu che le vanità; *Il Pirata*—Final Scene; with the Sinfonieorchester des Norddeutschen Rundfunks, Nicola Rescigno, c.
May 19*	Stuttgart, Liederhalle	Concert: Same as May 15 with the Südfunk Symphonieorchester.
May 21	Munich, Kongress-Saal, Deutschen Museum	Concert: Same as May 15 with the Bayerische Staatsorchester.
May 24	Wiesbaden, Kursaal	Concert: Same as May 15 with the Pfalz-Orchester.
June 17	London, Royal Opera House,	*Medea:* (Medea); Jon Vickers (Jason); Joan Carlyle (Glauce);

	Covent Garden	Nicola Zaccaria (Creon); Fiorenza Cossotto (Neris); Mary Wells and Elizabeth Rust (Handmaidens); David Allen (Captain of the Guard); Nicola Rescigno, c. (Dallas production.)
June 22	"	*Medea:* Same cast as June 17.
June 24	"	*Medea:* Same cast as June 17.
June 27	"	*Medea:* Same cast as June 17.
June 30*	"	*Medea:* Same cast as June 17.
July 11*	Amsterdam, Concertgebouw	Concert: *La Vestale*—Tu che invoco; *Ernani*—Ernani! Ernani, involami!; *Don Carlo*—Tu che le vanità; *Il Pirata*—Final Scene; with the Concertgebouw Orchestra, Nicola Rescigno, c.
July 14	Brussels, Théâtre de la Monnaie	Concert: Same as July 11 with the Orchestre du Théâtre de la Monnaie.
Sep. 5– Sep. 10	Milan, Teatro alla Scala	Recording: *La Gioconda:* (La Gioconda); Fiorenza Cossotto (Laura); Irene Companeez (La Cieca); Pier Miranda Ferraro (Enzo); Piero Cappuccilli (Barnaba); Ivo Vinco (Alvise); Leonardo Monreale (Zuane); Renato Ercolani (Isepo); Carlo Forti (Singer and Pilot); Bonaldo Giaiotti (Barnabite Monk); with the Orchestra and Chorus of La Scala, Antonino Votto, c. Released in the United States on Angel 3606 (mono and stereo) in Aug. 1960 and in Great Britain on Columbia 33 CX 1706–8 (mono) and SAX 2359–61 (stereo) in Oct. 1960; reissued in

		the United States on Seraphim SIC-6031 in Sep. 1968.
Sep. 17	Bilbao, Coliseo Albia	Concert: *Don Carlo*—Tu che le vanità; *Hamlet*—À vos jeux, mes amis (Mad Scene); *Ernani*—Ernani! Ernani, involami!; *Il Pirata*—Final Scene; with the Orquesta Sinfonica del Gran Teatro Liceo de Barcelona, Nicola Rescigno, c.
Sep. 23*	London, Royal Festival Hall	Concert: *Don Carlo*—Tu che le vanità; *Hamlet*—À vos jeux . . . Partagez-vous mes fleurs! . . . Et maintenant écoutez ma chanson! (Mad Scene); *Macbeth*—Una macchia è qui tuttora (Sleepwalking Scene); *Il Pirata*—Oh! s'io potessi . . . Col sorriso d'innocenza (Final Scene); with the London Symphony Orchestra, Nicola Rescigno, c.
Oct. 3*	London, Wood Green Theatre	Television Broadcast: Gala (with Tito Gobbi, José Iturbi, and Alicia Markova): *La Bohème*—Mi chiamano Mimì; *Mefistofele*—L'altra notte; with the Royal Philharmonic Orchestra, Sir Malcolm Sargent, c. (Taped for telecast. First televised on Oct. 7.)
Oct. 23	Berlin, Titania Palast	Concert: *Don Giovanni*—Non mi dir; *Ernani*—Ernani! Ernani, involami!; *Don Carlo*—Tu che le vanità; *Hamlet*—À vos jeux, mes amis (Mad Scene); with the Radio Symphonie Orchester, Nicola Rescigno, c.

Oct. 28	Kansas City, Midland Theater	Concert: *Don Giovanni*—Non mi dir; *Lucia di Lammermoor*—Regnava nel silenzio and Quando rapito in estasi; *Ernani*—Ernani! Ernani, involami!; *Il Pirata*—Final Scene; with Symphony Orchestra, Nicola Rescigno, c.
Nov. 6	Dallas, State Fair Music Hall (Civic Opera Company)	*Lucia di Lammermoor:* (Lucia); Gianni Raimondi (Edgardo); Ettore Bastianini (Enrico); Nicola Zaccaria (Raimondo); Glade Peterson (Arturo); Ruth Kobart (Alisa); Thomas Hageman (Normanno); Nicola Rescigno, c. (Covent Garden production directed by Franco Zeffirelli.)
Nov. 8	"	*Lucia di Lammermoor:* Same cast as Nov. 6.
Nov. 19	"	*Medea:* (Medea); Jon Vickers (Jason); Katherine Williams (Glauce); Nicola Zaccaria (Creon); Nan Merriman (Neris); Su Harmon and Margot Blum (Handmaidens); Spelios Constantino (Captain of the Guard); Nicola Rescigno, c.
Nov. 21	"	*Medea:* Same cast as Nov. 19.

1960

July	Watford, England, Town Hall	Recording: *Semiramide*—Bel raggio lusinghier; *Armida*—D'amore al dolce impero; *I Vespri Siciliani*—Arrigo! ah parli a un core; with the Philharmonia Orchestra, Antonio Tonini, c. (Unreleased EMI recordings.)

Aug. 24	Epidaurus, Ancient Greek Theater (Greek National Opera Company)	*Norma:* (Norma); Mirto Picchi (Pollione); Kiki Morfoniou (Adalgisa); Ferruccio Mazzoli (Oroveso); Emilie Koussi (Clotilde); Ar. Pandazinakos (Flavio); Tullio Serafin, c. (Production directed by Alexis Minotis.)
Aug. 28	"	*Norma:* Same cast as Aug. 24.
Sep. 5–Sep. 12	Milan, Teatro alla Scala	Recording: *Norma:* (Norma); Franco Corelli (Pollione); Christa Ludwig (Adalgisa); Nicola Zaccaria (Oroveso); Edda Vincenzi (Clotilde); Piero de Palma (Flavio); with the Orchestra and Chorus of La Scala, Tullio Serafin, c. Released in the United States on Angel 3615 (mono and stereo) in Oct. 1961 and in Great Britain on Columbia 33 CX 1766–68 (mono) and SAX 2412–14 (stereo) in Nov. 1961.
Dec. 7*	Milan, Teatro alla Scala	*Poliuto:* (Paolina); Franco Corelli (Poliuto); Ettore Bastianini (Severo); Nicola Zaccaria (Callistene); Rinaldo Pelizzoni (Felice); Piero de Palma (Nearco); Virgilio Carbonari and Giuseppe Morresi (Christians); Antonino Votto, c.
Dec. 10	"	*Poliuto:* Same cast as Dec. 7.
Dec. 14	"	*Poliuto:* Same cast as Dec. 7.
Dec. 18	"	*Poliuto:* Same cast as Dec. 7.
Dec. 21	"	*Poliuto:* Same cast as Dec. 7 except Antonio Tonini, c.

1961

Mar. 28–	Paris, Salle	Recording: Maria Callas Sings

Mar. 31, Apr. 4– Apr. 5	Wagram	Great Arias from French Operas: *Orphée et Eurydice*—J'ai perdu mon Eurydice; *Alceste*—Divinités du Styx; *Carmen*—L'amour est un oiseau rebelle (Habanera); *Carmen*—Près des remparts de Séville (Séguedille); *Samson et Dalila*—Printemps qui commence; *Samson et Dalila*—Amour! viens aider; *Roméo et Juliette*—Je veux vivre (Valse); *Mignon*—Je suis Titania (Polonaise); *Le Cid*—Pleurez, mes yeux; *Louise*—Depuis le jour; with the Orchestre National de la RTF, Georges Prêtre, c. Released in Great Britain on Columbia 33 CX 1771 (mono) and SAX 2410 (stereo) in Oct. 1961 and in the United States on Angel 35882 (mono and stereo) in Jan. 1962.
May 30*	London, St. James's Palace	Concert: *Norma*—Casta Diva; *Le Cid*—Pleurez, mes yeux; *Don Carlo*—Tu che le vanità; *Mefistofele*—L'altra notte; with piano, Sir Malcolm Sargent, accompanist.
Aug. 6	Epidaurus, Ancient Greek Theater (Greek National Opera Company)	*Medea:* (Medea); Jon Vickers (Jason); Soula Glantzi (Glauce); Giuseppe Modesti (Creon); Kiki Morfoniou (Neris); A. Dracopoulou and A. Maragaki (Handmaidens); G. Zakkas (Captain of the Guard); Nicola Rescigno, c. (Production directed by Alexis Minotis.)
Aug. 13	"	*Medea:* Same cast as Aug. 6.

Nov. 15	London, Kingsway Hall	Recording: *Il Pirata*—Sorgete, è in me dover . . . Lo sognai ferito . . . Sventurata anch'io deliro, with Alexander Young (Itulbo) and Monica Sinclair (Adele); with the Philharmonia Orchestra and Chorus, Antonio Tonini, c. Released in the United States on Angel 36852 and in Great Britain on HMV ASD 2791, both in March 1972 in the album "Maria Callas—By Request" along with arias from Feb./Apr. 1964 Paris recording sessions.
Nov.	"	Recording: *Lucrezia Borgia*—Com'è bello; *La Cenerentola*—Nacqui all'affanno; *Guglielmo Tell*—Selva opaca; *Anna Bolena*—Legger potessi in me!; *Semiramide*—Bel raggio lusinghier; with the Philharmonia Orchestra and Chorus, Antonio Tonini, c. (Unreleased EMI recordings.)
Dec. 11*	Milan, Teatro alla Scala	*Medea:* (Medea); Jon Vickers (Jason); Ivana Tosini (Glauce); Nicolai Ghiaurov (Creon); Giulietta Simionato (Neris); Edith Martelli and Maddalena Bonifaccio (Handmaidens); Alfredo Giacommotti (Captain of the Guard); Thomas Schippers, c. (New production directed by Alexis Minotis.)
Dec. 14	"	*Medea:* Same cast as Dec. 11 except Limbania Leoni (Second Handmaiden).

Dec. 20	"	*Medea:* Same cast as Dec. 11 except Bruna Rizzoli (Glauce).

1962

Feb. 27	London, Royal Festival Hall	Concert: *Oberon*—Ocean! Thou mighty monster; *Le Cid*—Pleurez, mes yeux; *La Cenerentola*—Nacqui all'affanno; *Macbeth*—La luce langue; *Don Carlo*—O don fatale; *Anna Bolena*—Mad Scene and Finale, Act II; with the Philharmonia Orchestra, Georges Prêtre, c.
Mar. 12	Munich, Kongress-Saal, Deutsches Museum	Concert: *Le Cid*—Pleurez, mes yeux; *Carmen*—L'amour est un oiseau rebelle (Habanera); *Carmen*—Près des remparts de Séville (Séguedille); *Ernani*—Sorta è la notte . . . Ernani! Ernani, involami!; *La Cenerentola*—Nacqui all'affanno; *Don Carlo*—O don fatale; with the Bayerisches Staatsorchester, Georges Prêtre, c.
Mar. 16*	Hamburg, Musikhalle	Concert: Same as Mar. 12 with the Sinfonieorchester des Norddeutschen Rundfunks.
Mar. 19	Essen, Städtischer Saalbau	Concert: Same as Mar. 12 with the Orchester der Stadt Essen.
Mar. 23	Bonn, Beethovenhalle	Concert: Same as Mar. 12 with the Niedersächsisches Symphonieorchester.
Apr.	London, Kingsway Hall	Recording: *La Cenerentola*—Nacqui all'affanno; *Oberon*—Ocean! Thou mighty monster; *Don Carlo*—O don fatale; with the Philharmonia Orchestra, Antonio Tonini,

		c. (Unreleased EMI recordings.)
May 19*	New York, Madison Square Garden	Forty-fourth Birthday Celebration of President Kennedy (Callas and others): *Carmen*—L'amour est un oiseau rebelle (Habanera); *Carmen*—Près des remparts de Séville (Séguedille); with piano, Charles Wilson, accompanist.
May 29	Milan, Teatro alla Scala	*Medea:* (Medea); Jon Vickers (Jason); Bruna Rizzoli (Glauce); Nicolai Ghiaurov (Creon); Giulietta Simionato (Neris); Jeda Valtriani and Maddalena Bonifaccio (Handmaidens); Alfredo Giacommotti (Captain of the Guard); Thomas Schippers, c.
June 3	"	*Medea:* Same cast as May 29.
Nov. 4*	London, Royal Opera House, Covent Garden	Television Broadcast: A Golden Hour from the Royal Opera House (with Giuseppe di Stefano, Mischa Elman, José Greco, etc.): *Don Carlo*—Tu che le vanità; *Carmen*—L'amour est un oiseau rebelle (Habanera); *Carmen*—Près des remparts de Séville (Séguedille); Georges Prêtre, c.

1963

May 3–May 8	Paris, Salle Wagram	Recording: Callas in Paris: *Iphigénie en Tauride*—O malheureuse Iphigénie!; *La Damnation de Faust* — D'amour l'ardente flamme; *Les Pêcheurs de Perles*—Me voilà seule . . . Comme autrefois; *Manon*—Je ne suis que faiblesse . . . Adieu, notre petite ta-

		ble; *Manon*—Suis-je gentille ainsi? . . . . Je marche sur tous les chemins; *Werther*—Werther! Qui m'aurait dit . . . Des cris joyeux (Air des lettres); *Faust*—Il était un Roi de Thulé . . . O Dieu! que de bijoux!; with the Orchestre de la Société des Concerts du Conservatoire, Georges Prêtre, c. Released in Great Britain on Columbia 33 CX 1858 (mono) and SAX 2503 (stereo) in Sept. 1963 and in the United States on Angel 36147 (mono and stereo) in Oct. 1963.
May 17*	Berlin, Deutsche Oper	Concert: *Semiramide*—Bel raggio lusinghier; *Norma*—Casta Diva . . . Ah! bello a me ritorna; *Nabucco*—Ben io t'invenni . . . Anch'io dischiuso un giorno; *La Bohème*—Quando m'en vo'; *Madama Butterfly*—Con onor muore . . . Tu? tu? piccolo Iddio!; with the Orchester der Deutschen Oper, Georges Prêtre, c.
May 20	Düsseldorf, Rheinhalle	Concert: Same as May 17 with the Niedersächsisches Symphonieorchester.
May 23*	Stuttgart, Liederhalle	Concert: Same as May 17 with the Südfunk Symphonieorchester.
May 31*	London, Royal Festival Hall	Concert: Same as May 17 plus encore *Gianni Schicchi*—O mio babbino caro; with the Philharmonia Orchestra.
June 5*	Paris, Théâtre des Champs-Élysées	Concert: *Semiramide*—Bel raggio; *La Cenerentola*—Nacqui all'af-

		fanno; *Manon*—Adieu, notre petite table; *Werther*—Air des lettres; *Nabucco*—Ben io t'invenni . . . Anch'io dischiuso un giorno; *La Bohème*—Quando m'en vo'; *Madama Butterfly*—Tu? tu? piccolo Iddio!; encore: *Gianni Schicchi*—O mio babbino caro; with the Orchestre Philharmonique de la RTF, Georges Prêtre, c.
June 9	Copenhagen, Falkoner Centret	Concert: Same as May 17 with the Danmarks Radiosymfoni Orkester.
Dec., Jan.	Paris, Salle Wagram	Recording: Maria Callas Sings Mozart, Beethoven, Weber Arias: Ah, perfido!; *Don Giovanni*—Or sai chi l'onore; *Le Nozze di Figaro*—Porgi amor; *Oberon*—Ocean! Thou mighty monster; *Don Giovanni*—Crudele? . . . Non mi dir; *Don Giovanni*—In quali eccessi . . . Mi tradì; with the Orchestre de la Société des Concerts du Conservatoire, Nicola Rescigno, c. Released in Great Britain on Columbia 33 CX 1900 (mono) and SAX 2540 (stereo) in Aug. 1964 and in the United States on Angel 36200 (mono and stereo) in Oct. 1964.
Dec., Feb.	Paris, Salle Wagram	Recording: Maria Callas Sings Verdi Arias: *Otello*—Mia madre aveva una povera ancella . . . Ave Maria, piena di grazie; *Aroldo*—Ciel, ch'io respiri! . . . Salvami, salvami; *Don Carlo*—O don fatale; *Aroldo*—O cielo! Dove son

		io; *Don Carlo*—Non pianger, mia compagna; with the Orchestre de la Société des Concerts du Conservatoire, Nicola Rescigno, c. Released in Great Britain on Columbia 33 CX 1910 (mono) and SAX 2550 (stereo) in Aug. 1964 and in the United States on Angel 36221 (mono and stereo) in Dec. 1964.
Dec., Feb., Apr.	Paris, Salle Wagram	Recording: Maria Callas Sings Arias by Rossini and Donizetti: *La Cenerentola*—Nacqui all'affanno; *Guglielmo Tell*—S'allontanano alfine . . . Selva opaca; *La Figlia del Reggimento*—Convien partir; *Semiramide*—Bel raggio lusinghier; *Lucrezia Borgia*—Tranquillo ei posa . . . Com'è bello; *L'Elisir d'Amore*—Prendi, per me sei libero; with the Orchestre de la Société des Concerts du Conservatoire, Nicola Rescigno, c. Released in Great Britain on Columbia 33 CX 1923 (mono) and SAX 2564 (stereo) in Mar. 1965 and in the United States on Angel 36239 (mono and stereo) in May 1965.

1964

Jan. 21*	London, Royal Opera House, Covent Garden	*Tosca:* (Tosca); Renato Cioni (Cavaradossi); Tito Gobbi (Scarpia); Victor Godfrey (Angelotti); Eric Garrett (Sacristan); Robert Bowman (Spoletta); Dennis

		Wicks (Sciarrone); Edgar Boniface (Jailer); David Sellar (Shepherd); Carlo Felice Cillario, c. (New production directed by Franco Zeffirelli.)
Jan. 24*	〃	*Tosca:* Same cast as Jan. 21.
Jan. 27	〃	*Tosca:* Same cast as Jan. 21.
Jan. 30	〃	*Tosca:* Same cast as Jan. 21.
Feb. 1	〃	*Tosca:* Same cast as Jan. 21.
Feb. 5	〃	*Tosca:* Same cast as Jan. 21.
Feb. 9*	〃	Television Broadcast: A Golden Hour from the Royal Opera House: *Tosca*—Act II: Same cast as Jan. 21.
Feb., Apr.	Paris, Salle Wagram	Recording: *Attila*—Liberamente or piangi . . . Oh! nel fuggente nuvolo; *I Vespri Siciliani*—Arrigo! ah parli a un core; *Un Ballo in Maschera*—Ecco l'orrido campo . . . Ma dall'arido stelo divulsa; *I Lombardi*—O madre dal cielo . . . Se vano è il pregare; *Aida*—Ritorna vincitor!; with the Orchestre de la Société des Concerts du Conservatoire, Nicola Rescigno, c. Released in the United States on Angel 36852 and in Great Britain on HMV ASD 2791, both in March 1972 in the album "Maria Callas—By Request" along with aria from Nov. 1961 London recording sessions.
Apr.	〃	Recording: *I Lombardi*—Salve Maria, di grazie il petto; *Un Ballo in Maschera*—Morrò, ma prima

		in grazia; *Il Trovatore*—Tacea la notte placida; *Il Trovatore*—D'amor sull'ali rosee; with the Orchestre de la Société des Concerts du Conservatoire, Nicola Rescigno, c. (Unreleased EMI recordings.)
May 22	Paris, Opéra	*Norma:* (Norma); Charles Craig (Pollione); Fiorenza Cossotto (Adalgisa); Ivo Vinco (Oroveso); Marie-Luce Bellary (Clotilde); Claude Calès (Flavio); Georges Prêtre, c.
May 25	"	*Norma:* Same cast as May 22.
May 31	"	*Norma:* Same cast as May 22.
June 6	"	*Norma:* Same cast as May 22 except Franco Corelli (Pollione).
June 10	"	*Norma:* Same cast as May 22 except Franco Corelli (Pollione).
June 14	"	*Norma:* Same cast as May 22.
June 19	"	*Norma:* Same cast as May 22.
June 24	"	*Norma:* Same cast as May 22.
June	Paris, Salle Wagram	Recording: *Aida*—Pur ti riveggo, with Franco Corelli and the Orchestre de la Société des Concerts du Conservatoire, Georges Prêtre, c. (Unreleased EMI recording.)
July 6–July 20	Paris, Salle Wagram	Recording: *Carmen:* (Carmen); Nicolai Gedda (Don José); Andréa Guiot (Micaëla); Robert Massard (Escamillo); Nadine Sautereau (Frasquita); Jane Berbié (Mercédès); Jean-Paul Vauquelin (Le Dancaïre); Jacques Pruvost and Maurice Maievski (Le Remendado); Claude Calès (Moralès); Jacques Mars (Zuniga);

		with the Choeurs René Duclos and the Orchestre du Théâtre National de l'Opéra, Georges Prêtre, c. Released in Great Britain on HMV (Angel) AN (mono) and SAN (stereo) 143–145 in Dec. 1964 and in the United States on Angel 3650 (mono and stereo) in Jan. 1965.
Dec. 3–Dec. 14	Paris, Salle Wagram	Recording: *Tosca:* (Tosca); Carlo Bergonzi (Cavaradossi); Tito Gobbi (Scarpia); Leonardo Monreale (Angelotti); Giorgio Tadeo (Sacristan); Renato Ercolani (Spoletta); Ugo Trama (Sciarrone); Leonardo Monreale (Jailer); David Sellar (Shepherd); with the Choeurs du Théâtre National de l'Opéra and the Orchestre de la Société des Concerts du Conservatoire, Georges Prêtre, c. Released in the United States on Angel 3655 (mono and stereo) in Apr. 1965 and in Great Britain on HMV (Angel) AN (mono) and SAN (stereo) 149–150 in July 1965.

1965

Feb. 19	Paris, Opéra	*Tosca:* (Tosca); Renato Cioni (Cavaradossi); Tito Gobbi (Scarpia); Robert Geay (Angelotti); Jean-Christophe Benoît (Sacristan); Louis Rialland (Spoletta);

		Roger Soyer (Sciarrone); Pierre Thau (Jailer); Jacqueline Broudeur (Shepherd); Georges Prêtre, c. (Covent Garden production.)
Feb. 22	"	*Tosca:* Same cast as Feb. 19.
Feb. 26	"	*Tosca:* Same cast as Feb. 19 except Janine Collard (Shepherd).
Mar. 1*	"	*Tosca:* Same cast as Feb. 19 except Jean-Pierre Hurteau (Angelotti); Nicola Rescigno, c.
Mar. 3*	"	*Tosca:* Same cast as Feb. 19 except Jean-Pierre Hurteau (Angelotti); Nicola Rescigno, c.
Mar. 5	"	*Tosca:* Same cast as Feb. 19 except Janine Collard (Shepherd); Nicola Rescigno, c.
Mar. 8	"	*Tosca:* Same cast as Feb. 19 except Janine Collard (Shepherd); Nicola Rescigno, c.
Mar. 10	"	*Tosca:* Same cast as Feb. 19 except Nicola Rescigno, c.
Mar. 13	"	*Tosca:* Same cast as Feb. 19 except Jean-Pierre Hurteau (Angelotti); Georges Daum (Jailer); Janine Collard (Shepherd); Nicola Rescigno, c.
Mar. 19*	New York, Metropolitan Opera House	*Tosca:* (Tosca); Franco Corelli (Cavaradossi); Tito Gobbi (Scarpia); Clifford Harvuot (Angelotti); Lawrence Davidson (Sacristan); Andea Velis (Spoletta); Russell Christopher (Sciarrone); Robert Goodloe (Jailer); Stuart Fischer (Shepherd); Fausto Cleva, c.

Mar. 25*	"	*Tosca:* Same cast as Mar. 19 except Richard Tucker (Cavaradossi).
May *	Paris, RTF Studios	Television Broadcast: Les Grands Interprètes: *Manon*—Adieu, notre petite table; *La Sonnambula*—Ah! non credea; *Gianni Schicchi*—O mio babbino caro; with the Orchestre National de l'ORTF, Georges Prêtre, c. (Taped for telecast. First televised on May 18. Duparc's L'invitation au voyage also taped at this time but was excluded from the telecast for lack of time.)
May 14*	Paris, Opéra	*Norma:* (Norma); Gianfranco Cecchele (Pollione); Giulietta Simionato (Adalgisa); Ivo Vinco (Oroveso); Marie-Luce Bellary (Clotilde); Claude Calès (Flavio); Georges Prêtre, c.
May 17*	"	*Norma:* Same cast as May 14.
May 21*	"	*Norma:* Same cast as May 14 except Fiorenza Cossotto (Adalgisa).
May 24	"	*Norma:* Same cast as May 14 except Fiorenza Cossotto (Adalgisa).
May 29*	"	*Norma:* Same cast as May 14 except Fiorenza Cossotto (Adalgisa). (Last act canceled after Callas became indisposed.)
July 5*	London, Royal Opera House, Covent Garden	*Tosca:* (Tosca); Renato Cioni (Cavaradossi); Tito Gobbi (Scarpia); Victor Godfrey (Angelotti); Eric Garrett (Sacristan); John Dobson (Spoletta); Dennis

July 5, 1965

Wicks (Sciarrone); Rhydderch Davies (Jailer); Richard Bedell (Shepherd); Georges Prêtre, c.

SUMMARY 1947–1965

The following table summarizes the performances of Maria Callas for the period 1947–1965. This table shows the number of performances each year and the total for all years for each opera, for concerts, and for other appearances. Recordings are omitted from the table. The opera totals include only complete stage performances, therefore the RAI opera broadcasts (*Parsifal, Norma,* and *Lucia di Lammermoor*) are omitted from the totals for these operas. Similarly omitted are the incomplete performances of *Norma* (Rome, 1958 and Paris, 1965). These particular performances are included in the categories "Operas (Radio)" and "Other Appearances." In the category of "Concerts" are included those performances in which Mme. Callas was the only soloist or in which her appearance was the major part of the program. The category "Other Appearances" contains performances in which Callas sang one or two arias in a much larger program (such as at the Covent Garden Centenary Concert or the Birthday Celebration for President John F. Kennedy at Madison Square Garden). Also in this category are those performances which do not fit readily into any of the other categories (such as the incomplete *Normas* and the telecasts of Act II of *Tosca*).

PERFORMANCES — 1947–1965

	1947	1948	1949	1950	1951	1952	1953	1954	1955	1956	1957	1958	1959	1960	1961	1962	1963	1964	1965	Total
Aida		7	1	13	4		8													33
Alceste								4												4
Andrea Chénier									6											6
Anna Bolena											7	5								12
Armida						3														3
Un Ballo in Maschera											5									5
Il Barbiere di Siviglia										5										5
Don Carlo								5												5
Fedora										6										6
La Forza del Destino		4						2												6
La Gioconda	5					5	3													13
Ifigenia in Tauride											4									4
Lucia di Lammermoor						3	11	14	2	10		3	2							45
Macbeth						5														5
Madama Butterfly									3											3
Medea							6	5	4			2	7		5	2				31
Mefistofele								3												3
Nabucco			3																	3
Norma		2	4	14	9	14	12	2	6	9	2			2				8	4	88
Orfeo ed Euridice					2															2
Parsifal			4																	4
Il Pirata												5	2							7
Poliuto														5						5
I Puritani			3		4	7			2											16
Il Ratto dal Serraglio						4														4
Rigoletto						2														2
San Giovanni Battista			1																	1
La Sonnambula									10		12									22
Tosca				5	1	2		3		2		2						6	12	33
La Traviata					15	9	5	2	4	17		11								63
Tristano e Isotta	1	6		5																12
Il Trovatore				3	3		12		2											20
Turandot		16	8																	24
Il Turco in Italia				4					5											9
I Vespri Siciliani					10	1														11
La Vestale								5												5
La Walkiria			6																	6
Concerts (Stage)			1		2					1	4	12	14		1	5	6			46
Concerts (Radio)			1	1	1	1		1		1										6
Operas (Radio)*				1					1		1									3
Other Appearances:																				
Stage					1							2				1			1	5
Radio & Television					1					1	1	2	1			1		1	1	9
TOTAL	6	35	32	46	53	56	57	46	45	52	36	44	26	7	6	9	6	15	18	595

* *Parsifal*, *Norma*, and *Lucia di Lammermoor*, respectively.

Part Three
1965 – 1974

The performance of *Tosca* at Covent Garden on July 5, 1965, marked Callas's last stage appearance for a number of years. During this period she became involved in such varied roles as film star, teacher, and director. These activities are listed below. It should be noted that the selections listed in the Master Classes are those sung by the students. These selections are shown here to indicate the wide range of operatic roles to which Callas could bring authoritative comment. In a number of instances Callas would illustrate her comments by singing a phrase or an extended portion of the aria. The pianist for most of the Juilliard classes was Eugene Kohn.

During the years after 1965 there were a number of reports that Callas would resume her career. These reports were not fulfilled, however, until October 1973, when she made her long-awaited return to the stage to begin a world-wide concert tour with Giuseppe di Stefano. All the selections sung in the concerts of this tour are listed below, including the solos by Mr. Di Stefano. Most readers familiar with opera will be able to distinguish from the title which of these selections were duets and which were solo arias sung by Callas or Di Stefano. To avoid any possible confusion, however, the following notations have been made after each selection: (D), (C), or (DiS) indicating, respectively, duet, solo by Callas, or solo by Di Stefano.

1969

Feb.–Mar.	Paris, Salle Wagram	Recording: *Il Corsaro*—Non so le tetre immagini (Romanza di Medora); *Il Corsaro*—Vola talor dal carcere; *I Lombardi*—Salve Maria, di grazie il petto; *I Vespri Siciliani*—Arrigo! ah parli a un core; *Attila*—Liberamente or piangi . . . Oh! nel fuggente nuvolo; with the Orchestre de la Société des Concerts du Conservatoire, Nicola Rescigno, c. (Unreleased EMI recordings.)
June–July	Goreme (near Ankara, Turkey); Aleppo (Syria); Grado, Pisa, and Rome (Italy)	Film: *Medea:* screenplay by Pier Paolo Pasolini after Euripides; directed by Pier Paolo Pasolini, produced by Franco Rossellini; Maria Callas (Medea); Giuseppe Gentile (Jason); Margareth Clementi (Glauce); Massimo Girotti (Creon); Laurent Terzieff (The Centaur); and others. World première—Rome, Jan. 9, 1970.

1971

Feb.	Philadelphia, Curtis Institute of Music	Master Class: Group session.
Feb.	"	Master Class: Arias from *Manon, Macbeth,* and *Pagliacci.*
Oct. 11	New York, Juilliard Theater (Juilliard School of Music)	Master Class: *Il Trovatore*—Il balen; *La Bohème*—Che gelida manina; *Norma*—Sgombra è la sacra selva; *I Capuleti e i Mon-*

tecchi—Oh! quante volte; *Lucia di Lammermoor*—Regnava nel silenzio.

Oct. 15 ″ Master Class: *Die Zauberflöte*—Ach, ich fühl's; *Il Trovatore*—D'amor sull'ali rosee; *La Forza del Destino*—O tu che in seno; *Turandot*—Signore, ascolta; *Norma*—Casta Diva; *La Traviata*—Ah, fors'è lui; *Pagliacci*—Ballatella.

Oct. 18 ″ Master Class: *Pagliacci*—Ballatella (resumed); *La Bohème*—Che gelida manina; *La Bohème*—Mi chiamano Mimì; *La Bohème*—Musetta's Waltz; *I Vespri Siciliani*—O tu Palermo; *I Puritani*—Qui la voce; *La Bohème*—Donde lieta uscì.

Oct. 21 ″ Master Class: *I Puritani*—Qui la voce; *Anna Bolena*—Piangete voi? (Final Scene); *Pagliacci*—Prologo; *La Sonnambula*—Care compagne . . . Come per me sereno.

Oct. 25 ″ Master Class: *Die Zauberflöte*—O zitt're nicht; *Don Carlo*—Ella giammai m'amò; *Carmen*—Je dis que rien (Micaëla's Aria); *Aida*—Judgment Scene.

Oct. 28 ″ Master Class: *Aida*—Judgment Scene (resumed); *Tosca*—Recondita armonia; *La Bohème*—Mi chiamano Mimì; *Don Carlo*—Tu che le vanità; *Ernani*—Ernani! Ernani, involami!

Nov. 1 ″ Master Class: *Werther*—Air des

		lettres; *Don Carlo*—Ella giammai m'amò (resumed from Oct. 25); *Manon Lescaut*—Sola, perduta, abbandonata; *Lucia di Lammermoor*—Tomb Scene; *Lucia di Lammermoor*—Mad Scene.
Nov. 4	"	Master Class: *Rigoletto*—Caro nome; *Pagliacci*—Prologo; *Mefistofele*—L'altra notte; *La Sonnambula*—Ah! non credea mirarti; *Pagliacci*—Vesti la giubba; *Così fan tutte*—Come scoglio.
Nov. 8	"	Master Class: *Adriana Lecouvreur*—O vagabonda stella d'Oriente; *L'Arlesiana*—Lamento di Federico; *I Puritani*—A te, o cara; *La Vestale*—Tu che invoco; *Guglielmo Tell*—Selva opaca.
Nov. 11	"	Master Class: *Guglielmo Tell*—Selva opaca (resumed); *I Puritani*—Qui la voce; *Lucia di Lammermoor*—Mad Scene; *Turandot*—Non piangere, Liù; *Il Barbiere di Siviglia*—Una voce poco fa.
Nov. 15	"	Master Class: *Lucia di Lammermoor*—Regnava nel silenzio; *Ernani*—Ernani! Ernani, involami!; *Faust*—Jewel Song; *I Puritani*—Qui la voce; *Mefistofele*—L'altra notte; *Medea*—De tuoi figli.
Nov. 19	"	Master Class: *Il Pirata*—Final Scene; *La Damnation de Faust*—D'amour l'ardente flamme; *Adriana Lecouvreur*—Io son l'umile ancella.

1972

Feb. 7	New York, Juilliard Theater (Juilliard School of Music)	Master Class: *La Bohème*—Mi chiamano Mimì; *La Bohème*—Sono andate?; *La Bohème*—Vecchia zimarra; *La Bohème*—O Mimì, tu più; *La Bohème*—Mimì-Marcello Scene, Act III.
Feb. 10	"	Master Class: *La Forza del Destino*—Madre, pietosa Vergine; *I Puritani*—Ah! per sempre; *Il Barbiere di Siviglia*—Una voce poco fa; *I Puritani*—A te, o cara; *Rigoletto*—Caro nome.
Feb. 13	"	Master Class: *Mefistofele*—L'altra notte; *Simon Boccanegra*—Il lacerato spirito; *La Battaglia di Legnano*—Quante volte come un dono; *La Sonnambula*—De' lieti auguri (Lisa's Aria); *La Forza del Destino*—Me, pellegrina ed orfana.
Feb. 17	"	Master Class: *Norma*—Va, crudele (Pollione-Adalgisa Duet); *Fidelio*—Abscheulicher!; *Otello*—Credo; *La Gioconda*—Stella del marinar; *La Forza del Destino*—O tu che in seno; *La Traviata*—Addio del passato.
Feb. 21	"	Master Class: *Don Pasquale*—Quel guardo il cavaliere . . . So anch'io la virtù magica; *Rigoletto*—Cortigiani; *Otello*—Piangea cantando (Willow Song); *Adriana Lecouvreur*—Io son l'umile ancella; *Ernani*—Ernani! Ernani, involami!
Feb. 24	"	Master Class: Ah, perfido!; *Na-*

		bucco—Tu sul labbro; *Madama Butterfly*—Che tua madre dovrà; *Don Carlo*—Nei giardin del bello (Veil Song); *Un Ballo in Maschera*—Eri tu.
Feb. 28	"	Master Class: Ah, perfido!; *La Traviata*—Di Provenza il mar; *Andrea Chénier*—Nemico della patria; *Roméo et Juliette*—Je veux vivre; *Manon Lescaut*—Guardate, pazzo son; *La Forza del Destino*—Pace, pace, mio Dio; *La Traviata*—Ah, fors'è lui.
Mar. 2	"	Master Class: *Rigoletto*—Gilda-Duke Scene, Act II; *La Vestale*—Tu che invoco; *Il Trovatore*—Stride la vampa . . . Condotta ell' era in ceppi; *Norma*—Casta Diva.
Mar. 9	"	Master Class: *Madama Butterfly*—Bimba dagli occhi (Love Duet); *Rigoletto*—Mio padre! . . . Tutte le feste; *Werther*—Pourquoi me réveiller; *La Forza del Destino*—Me, pellegrina ed orfana; *Madama Butterfly*—Addio, fiorito asil.
Mar. 14	"	Master Class: *Don Giovanni*—Non mi dir; *Cavalleria Rusticana*—Tu qui, Santuzza? (Santuzza-Turiddu Duet); *Un Ballo in Maschera*—Re dell'abisso.
Mar. 16	"	Master Class: *La Cenerentola*—Nacqui all'affanno . . . Non più mesta; *Lucia di Lammermoor*—Appressati, Lucia (Lucia-Enrico Duet); *La Forza del Destino*—Final Scene and Trio.

Nov. 30–Dec. 20	London, St. Giles's Church	Recording: Duets with Giuseppe di Stefano: *Don Carlo*—Io vengo a domandar; *La Forza del Destino*—Ah, per sempre, o mio bell' angiol; *Otello*—Già nella notte densa; *I Vespri Siciliani*—Quale, o prode, al tuo coraggio; *L'Elisir d'Amore*—Una parola, o Adina; *Aida*—Pur ti riveggo (incomplete); with the London Symphony Orchestra, Antonio de Almeida, c. (Unreleased Philips recordings.)

1973

Apr. 10	Turin, Teatro Regio	Directed (in collaboration with Giuseppe di Stefano) *I Vespri Siciliani:* cast included Raina Kabaivanska (Elena); Gianni Raimondi (Arrigo); Lucinio Montefusco (Monforte); Bonaldo Giaiotti (Procida); Fulvio Vernizzi, c. New production designed by Aligi Sassu. This performance marked the reopening of the Teatro Regio, rebuilt after being destroyed by fire in 1936.
May 20	Osaka, Japan, Festival Hall	Master Class (with Giuseppe di Stefano) for the winners of the Madama Butterfly Competition: *Manon Lescaut*—Donna non vidi mai; *Madama Butterfly*—Con onor muore; *Tosca*—E lucevan le stelle; *Madama Butterfly*—Addio, fiorito asil; *Madama Butterfly*—Bimba dagli occhi (Love Duet).

1973
European Concert Tour
(with Giuseppe di Stefano)

Oct. 25	Hamburg, Congress Centrum	Concert: *L'Elisir d 'Amore*—Una parola, o Adina (D); *Faust*—O silence! o bonheur! . . . O nuit d'amour! (D); *Carmen*—C'est toi? C'est moi! (D); *I Vespri Siciliani*—Quale, o prode, al tuo coraggio (D); *Cavalleria Rusticana*—Tu qui, Santuzza? (D); encores: *Fedora*—Amor ti vieta (DiS); *Gianni Schicchi*—O mio babbino caro (C); with piano, Ivor Newton, accompanist.
Oct. 29	Berlin, Philharmonie	Concert: *L'Elisir d'Amore*—Una parola, o Adina (D); *Faust*—O silence! o bonheur! . . . O nuit d'amour! (D); *Carmen*—C'est toi? C'est moi! (D); *La Forza del Destino*—Ah, per sempre, o mio bell' angiol (D); *Don Carlo*—Io vengo a domandar (D); *Cavalleria Rusticana*—Tu qui, Santuzza? (D); encores: *Fedora*—Amor ti vieta (DiS); *Gianni Schicchi*—O mio babbino caro (C); with piano, Ivor Newton, accompanist.
Nov. 2	Düsseldorf, Rheinhalle	Concert: *L'Elisir d'Amore*—Una parola, o Adina (D); *Faust*—O silence! o bonheur! . . . O nuit d'amour! (D); *Carmen*—C'est toi? C'est moi! (D); *La Forza del Destino*—Ah, per sempre, o mio bell' angiol (D); *Don Carlo*—Io vengo a domandar (D); *Cavalleria Rusticana*—Tu qui, Santuzza?

		(D); encores: *Le Roi d'Ys*—Vainement, ma bien-aimée (DiS); *Gianni Schicchi*—O mio babbino caro (C); with piano, Ivor Newton, accompanist.
Nov. 6	Munich, Kongress Saal, Deutsches Museum	Concert: *Don Carlo*—Io vengo a domandar (D); *Faust*—O silence! o bonheur! . . . O nuit d'amour! (D): *La Gioconda*—Suicidio! (C); *Carmen*—C'est toi? C'est moi! (D); *Cavalleria Rusticana*—Tu qui, Santuzza? (D); encores: *Le Roi d'Ys*—Vainement, ma bien-aimée (DiS); *Gianni Schicchi*—O mio babbino caro (C); with piano, Ivor Newton, accompanist.
Nov. 9	Frankfurt, Jahrhundert Halle Höchst	Concert: *Don Carlo*—Io vengo a domandar (D); *Faust*—O silence! o bonheur! . . . O nuit d'amour! (D): *La Gioconda*—Suicidio! (C); *Carmen*—C'est toi? C'est moi! (D); *Cavalleria Rusticana*—Tu qui, Santuzza? (D); encores: *Le Roi d'Ys*—Vainement, ma bien-aimée (DiS); *Gianni Schicchi*—O mio babbino caro (C); *L'Elisir d'Amore*—Una parola, o Adina (D); with piano, Ivor Newton, accompanist.
Nov. 12	Mannheim, Nationaltheater	Concert: *I Vespri Siciliani*—Quale, o prode, al tuo coraggio (D); *Don Carlo*—Io vengo a domandar (D); *Le Roi d'Ys*—Vainement, ma bien-aimée (DiS);

		La Gioconda—Suicidio! (C); *Carmen*—C'est toi? C'est moi! (D); *Cavalleria Rusticana*—Tu qui, Santuzza? (D); encores: *Gianni Schicchi*—O mio babbino caro (C); *L'Elisir d'Amore*—Una parola, o Adina (D); with piano, Ivor Newton, accompanist.
Nov. 20	Madrid, Palacio Nacional de Congresos y Exposiciones	Concert: *Don Carlo*—Io vengo a domandar (D); *Le Roi d'Ys*—Vainement, ma bien-aimée (DiS); *La Gioconda*—Suicidio! (C); *Carmen*—C'est toi? C'est moi! (D); *I Vespri Siciliani*—Quale, o prode, al tuo coraggio (D); Neapolitan Songs—Non t'amo più and Core 'ngrato (DiS); *Cavalleria Rusticana*—Voi lo sapete (C); *Cavalleria Rusticana*—Tu qui, Santuzza? (D); encore: *Gianni Schicchi*—O mio babbino caro (C); with piano, Robert Sutherland, accompanist.
Nov. 26	London, Royal Festival Hall	Concert: *Don Carlo*—Io vengo a domandar (D); *Le Roi d'Ys*—Vainement, ma bien-aimée (DiS); *La Gioconda*—Suicidio! (C); *Carmen*—C'est toi? C'est moi! (D); *I Vespri Siciliani*—Quale, o prode, al tuo coraggio (D); Neapolitan Songs—Non t'amo più and Marechiare (DiS); *Cavalleria Rusticana*—Voi lo sapete (C); *Cavalleria Rusticana*—Tu qui, Santuzza? (D); encore: *Gianni*

		Schicchi—O mio babbino caro (C); with piano, Ivor Newton, accompanist.
Dec. 2	London, Royal Festival Hall	Concert: *Don Carlo*—Io vengo a domandar (D); *La Gioconda*—Suicidio! (C); *Le Roi d'Ys*—Vainement, ma bien-aimée (DiS); *Carmen*—C'est toi? C'est moi! (D); *I Vespri Siciliani*—Quale, o prode, al tuo coraggio (D); *Carmen*—La fleur que tu m'avais jetée (DiS): *Cavalleria Rusticana*—Voi lo sapete (C); *Cavalleria Rusticana*—Tu qui, Santuzza? (D); with piano, Ivor Newton, accompanist.
Dec. 7	Paris, Théâtre des Champs-Élysées	Concert: *Don Carlo*—Io vengo a domandar (D); *Le Roi d'Ys*—Vainement, ma bien-aimée (DiS); *La Gioconda*—Suicidio! (C); *Carmen*—C'est toi? C'est moi! (D); *I Vespri Siciliani*—Quale, o prode, al tuo coraggio (D); *Carmen*—La fleur que tu m'avais jetée (DiS); *Cavalleria Rusticana*—Voi lo sapete (C); *Cavalleria Rusticana*—Tu qui, Santuzza? (D); encore: *Gianni Schicchi*—O mio babbino caro (C); with piano, Robert Sutherland, accompanist.
Dec. 11	Amsterdam, Concertgebouw	Concert: *Don Carlo*—Io vengo a domandar (D); *Le Roi d'Ys*—Vainement, ma bien-aimée (DiS); *La Gioconda*—Suicidio! (C); *Carmen*—C'est toi? C'est moi! (D); *I Vespri Siciliani*—Quale, o

		prode, al tuo coraggio (D); *Carmen*—La fleur que tu m'avais jetée (DiS); *Cavalleria Rusticana*—Voi lo sapete (C); *Cavalleria Rusticana*—Tu qui, Santuzza? (D); encore: *Gianni Schicchi*—O mio babbino caro (C); with piano, Robert Sutherland, accompanist.

1974

Jan. 20	Milan, Istituto Nazionale per lo Studio alla Cura dei Tumori	Private concert for patients of the Institute: *L'Elisir d'Amore*—Una parola, o Adina (D); *Cavalleria Rusticana*—Tu qui, Santuzza? (D); *La Bohème*—Che gelida manina (DiS); *Gianni Schicchi*—O mio babbino caro (C); with piano, Robert Sutherland, accompanist.
Jan. 23	Stuttgart, Liederhalle	Concert scheduled for this date was canceled because Mr. Di Stefano was indisposed. Callas sang *Gianni Schicchi*—O mio babbino caro, however, for the audience after the announcement that the concert would be canceled; with piano, Robert Sutherland, accompanist.

1974

American Concert Tour
(with Giuseppe di Stefano)
All concerts were accompanied at the piano by Robert Sutherland.

Feb. 11	Philadelphia, Academy of Music	Concert: *I Vespri Siciliani*—Quale, o prode, al tuo coraggio

		(D); *La Gioconda*—Suicidio! (C); *Carmen*—La fleur que tu m'avais jetée (DiS); *Carmen*—C'est toi? C'est moi! (D); *Don Carlo*—Io vengo a domandar (D); *Le Roi d'Ys*—Vainement, ma bien-aimée (DiS); *Cavalleria Rusticana*—Voi lo sapete (C); *Cavalleria Rusticana*—Tu qui, Santuzza? (D); encore: *Gianni Schicchi*—O mio babbino caro (C).
Feb. 21	Toronto, Massey Hall	Concert: *I Vespri Siciliani*—Quale, o prode, al tuo coraggio (D); *La Gioconda*—Suicidio! (C); *Carmen*—C'est toi? C'est moi! (D): *Don Carlo*—Io vengo a domandar (D); *Cavalleria Rusticana*—Voi lo sapete (C); *Cavalleria Rusticana*—Tu qui, Santuzza? (D); encores: *Gianni Schicchi*—O mio babbino caro (C); *Le Roi d'Ys*—Vainement, ma bien-aimée (DiS).
Feb. 24	Washington, D.C., Constitution Hall	Concert: *I Vespri Siciliani*—Quale, o prode, al tuo coraggio (D); *La Gioconda*—Suicidio! (C); *Carmen*—La fleur que tu m'avais jetée (DiS); *Don Carlo*—Io vengo a domandar (D); *L'Elisir d'Amore*—Una parola, o Adina (D); *Faust*—O silence! o bonheur! . . . O nuit d'amour! (D); *Carmen*—C'est toi? C'est moi! (D); *La Bohème*—Che gelida manina (DiS); *Cavalleria*

		Rusticana—Voi lo sapete (C); *Cavalleria Rusticana*—Tu qui, Santuzza? (D); encore: *Gianni Schicchi*—O mio babbino caro (C).
Feb. 27	Boston, Symphony Hall	Concert: *La Gioconda*—Suicidio!; *Tosca*—Vissi d'arte; *Cavalleria Rusticana*—Voi lo sapete; *Manon Lescaut*—Sola, perduta, abbandonata; *Don Carlo*—Tu che le vanità; encore: *Gianni Schicchi*—O mio babbino caro. (Mr. Di Stefano was indisposed, and his place on the program was taken by the pianist Vasso Devetzi, who played a Handel Chaconne, Schumann's Papillons, and Chopin's Andante Spianato and Grande Polonaise.)
Mar. 2	Chicago, Civic Opera House	Concert: *I Vespri Siciliani*—Quale, o prode, al tuo coraggio (D); *La Gioconda*—Suicidio! (C); *Le Roi d'Ys*—Vainement, ma bien-aimée (DiS); *Don Carlo*—Io vengo a domandar (D) (broken off partway through because Di Stefano was troubled by a cold); *Cavalleria Rusticana*—Voi lo sapete (C); *L'Elisir d'Amore*—Una parola, o Adina (D); *Tosca*—Vissi d'arte (C); *La Bohème*—Che gelida manina (DiS); *Cavalleria Rusticana*—Tu qui, Santuzza? (D); encores: *Gianni Schicchi*—O mio babbino caro (C); Neapolitan Songs—

		Non t'amo più and Core 'ngrato (DiS).
Mar. 5	New York, Carnegie Hall	Concert: *I Vespri Siciliani*—Quale, o prode, al tuo coraggio (D); *La Gioconda*—Suicidio! (C); *Le Roi d'Ys*—Vainement, ma bien-aimée (DiS); *Cavalleria Rusticana*—Voi lo sapete (C); *Cavalleria Rusticana*—Tu qui, Santuzza? (D); *Faust*—O silence! o bonheur! . . . O nuit d'amour! (D); *Manon Lescaut*—Sola, perduta, abbandonata (C); *Carmen*—La fleur que tu m'avais jetée (DiS); *Don Carlo*—Io vengo a domandar (D); encores: *Gianni Schicchi*—O mio babbino caro (C); *L'Elisir d'Amore*—Una parola, o Adina (D).
Mar. 9	Detroit, Masonic Auditorium	Concert: *La Gioconda*—Suicidio!; *Cavalleria Rusticana*—Voi lo sapete; *Manon Lescaut*—Sola, perduta, abbandonata; *Gianni Schicchi*—O mio babbino caro; *Don Carlo*—Tu che le vanità; *Tosca*—Vissi d'arte. (Mr. Di Stefano was indisposed, and his place on the program was taken by the pianist Ralph Votapek, who played pieces by Debussy, Brahms, Mozart, and Ravel.)
Mar. 12	Dallas, State Fair Music Hall	Concert: *La Gioconda*—Suicidio!; *Cavalleria Rusticana*—Voi lo sapete; *Manon Lescaut*—Sola, perduta, abbandonata; *Tosca*—Vissi d'arte; *Don Carlo*—Tu che le

		vanità; *Carmen*—L'amour est un oiseau rebelle (Habanera); encore: *Gianni Schicchi*—O mio babbino caro. (Mr. Di Stefano was indisposed, and his place on the program was taken by the pianist Earl Wild, who played pieces by Liszt, Chopin, Fauré, and D'Albert.)
Mar. 21	Miami Beach, Auditorium	Concert: *I Vespri Siciliani*—Quale, o prode, al tuo coraggio (D); *La Gioconda*—Suicidio! (C); *Le Roi d'Ys*—Vainement, ma bien-aimée (DiS); *Carmen*—L'amour est un oiseau rebelle (Habanera) (C); *Carmen*—C'est toi? C'est moi! (D); *Don Carlo*—Io vengo a domandar (D); *Cavalleria Rusticana*—Voi lo sapete (C); *Cavalleria Rusticana*—Tu qui, Santuzza? (D); encore: *Gianni Schicchi*—O mio babbino caro (C).
Apr. 4	Columbus, Ohio Theatre	Concert: *I Vespri Siciliani*—Quale, o prode, al tuo coraggio (D); *Le Roi d'Ys*—Vainement ma bien-aimée (DiS); *La Gioconda*—Suicidio! (C); *Carmen*—L'amour est un oiseau rebelle (Habanera) (C); *Carmen*—C'est toi? C'est moi! (D); Neapolitan Songs—Marechiare and L'ultima canzone (DiS); *Werther*—Air des lettres (C); *Cavalleria Rusticana*—Voi lo sapete (C); *Cavalleria Rusticana*—Tu qui, Santuzza?

		(D); encores: *La Bohème*—Che gelida manina (DiS); *Gianni Schicchi*—O mio babbino caro (C).
Apr. 9	Brookville, L.I., New York, C. W. Post Center Auditorium	Concert: *Don Carlo*—Io vengo a domandar (D); *La Gioconda*—Suicidio! (C); *La Bohème*—Che gelida manina (DiS); *Carmen*—L'amour est un oiseau rebelle (Habanera) (C); *Carmen*—C'est toi? C'est moi! (D); *Manon*—Adieu, notre petite table (C); *Werther*—Air des lettres (C); Neapolitan Songs—L'ultima canzone and Marechiare (DiS); *Cavalleria Rusticana*—Voi lo sapete (C); *Cavalleria Rusticana*—Tu qui, Santuzza? (D); encores: *L'Elisir d'Amore*—Una parola, o Adina (D); *Gianni Schicchi*—O mio babbino caro (C).
Apr. 15	New York, Carnegie Hall	Concert: *Don Carlo*—Io vengo a domandar (D); *Werther*—Air des lettres (C); *Carmen*—L'amour est un oiseau rebelle (Habanera) (C); *Carmen*—C'est toi? C'est moi! (D); *La Gioconda*—Suicidio! (C); Neapolitan Songs—L'ultima canzone and Marechiare (DiS); *Cavalleria Rusticana*—Voi lo sapete (C); *Cavalleria Rusticana*—Tu qui, Santuzza? (D); encore: *Manon*—Adieu, notre petite table (C).
Apr. 18	Cincinnati, Music Hall	Concert: *La Gioconda*—Suicidio! (C); *Le Roi d'Ys*—Vainement, ma bien-aimée (DiS); *Carmen*—

		L'amour est un oiseau rebelle (Habanera) (C); *Carmen*—C'est toi? C'est moi! (D); *Werther*—Air des lettres (C); Neapolitan Songs—Non t'amo più and Marechiare (DiS); *Cavalleria Rusticana*—Voi lo sapete (C); *Cavalleria Rusticana*—Tu qui, Santuzza? (D); encores: *L'Elisir d'Amore*—Una parola, o Adina (D); *Gianni Schicchi*—O mio babbino caro (C).
Apr. 24	Seattle, Opera House	Concert: *I Vespri Siciliani*—Quale, o prode, al tuo coraggio (D); *Don Carlo*—Io vengo a domandar (D); *Werther*—Air des lettres (C); *Carmen*—La fleur que tu m'avais jetée (DiS); *Carmen*—L'amour est un oiseau rebelle (Habanera) (C); *Carmen*—C'est toi? C'est moi! (D); Neapolitan Songs—Marechiare and Non t'amo più (DiS); *La Gioconda*—Suicidio! (C); *La Bohème*—Che gelida manina (DiS); *Cavalleria Rusticana*—Voi lo sapete (C); *Cavalleria Rusticana*—Tu qui, Santuzza? (D).
Apr. 27	Portland, Civic Auditorium	Concert: *I Vespri Siciliani*—Quale, o prode, al tuo coraggio (D); *Werther*—Air des lettres (C); *Le Roi d'Ys*—Vainement, ma bien-aimée (DiS); *Carmen*—L'amour est un oiseau rebelle (Habanera) (C); *Carmen*—C'est toi? C'est moi! (D); *La Gioconda*

		—Suicidio! (C); Sicilian Folk Songs—Abbalatti and Muttettu de lu Paliu (Ujè, Ujè) (DiS); *Cavalleria Rusticana*—Voi lo sapete (C); *Cavalleria Rusticana*—Tu qui, Santuzza? (D); encore: *L'Elisir d'Amore*—Una parola, o Adina (D).
May 1	Vancouver, Queen Elizabeth Theatre	Concert: *Werther*—Air des lettres (C); *Carmen*—L'amour est un oiseau rebelle (Habanera) (C); *Carmen*—C'est toi? C'est moi! (D); *La Gioconda*—Suicidio! (C); Sicilian Folk Songs—Abbalatti and Muttettu de lu Paliu (Ujè, Ujè) and Neapolitan Songs—Marechiare and L'ultima canzone (DiS); *Gianni Schicchi*—O mio babbino caro (C); *Cavalleria Rusticana*—Voi lo sapete (C); *Cavalleria Rusticana*—Tu qui, Santuzza? (D). (At the beginning of the program it was announced that Mr. Di Stefano was indisposed and that his place would be taken by the pianist Daniel Pollack. Partway through the concert Di Stefano felt well enough to make an appearance. Daniel Pollack remained on the program and played a selection of Chopin pieces: five Etudes, the F Major Ballade, the Polonaise in A Flat Major, and the Nocturne in C Sharp Major.)
May 5	Los Angeles, Shrine Auditorium	Concert: *I Vespri Siciliani*—Quale, o prode, al tuo coraggio

		(D); *Werther*—Air des lettres (C); *Le Roi d'Ys*—Vainement, ma bien-aimée (DiS); *Carmen*—L'amour est un oiseau rebelle (Habanera) (C); *Carmen*—C'est toi? C'est moi! (D); *Don Carlo*—Io vengo a domandar (D); *La Gioconda*—Suicidio! (C); Sicilian Folk Songs—Abbalatti and Muttettu de lu Paliu (Ujè, Ujè) (DiS); *Cavalleria Rusticana*—Voi lo sapete (C); *Cavalleria Rusticana*—Tu qui, Santuzza? (D); encores: *Gianni Schicchi*—O mio babbino caro (C); *L'Elisir d'Amore*—Una parola, o Adina (D).
May 9	San Francisco, War Memorial Opera House	Concert: *I Vespri Siciliani*—Quale, o prode, al tuo coraggio (D); *Werther*—Air des lettres (C); *Le Roi d'Ys*—Vainement, ma bien-aimée (DiS); *Carmen*—L'amour est un oiseau rebelle (Habanera) (C); *Carmen*—C'est toi? C'est moi! (D); *La Gioconda*—Suicidio! (C); Sicilian Folk Songs—Abbalatti and Muttettu de lu Paliu (Ujè, Ujè) and Neapolitan Song—L'ultima canzone (DiS); *Cavalleria Rusticana*—Voi lo sapete (C); *Cavalleria Rusticana*—Tu qui, Santuzza? (D); encore: *Gianni Schicchi*—O mio babbino caro (C).
May 13	Montreal, Salle Wilfrid Pelletier, Place des Arts	Concert: *I Vespri Siciliani*—Quale, o prode, al tuo coraggio (D); *Le Roi d'Ys*—Vaine-

ment, ma bien-aimée (DiS); *Werther*—Air des lettres (C); *Carmen*—L'amour est un oiseau rebelle (Habanera) (C); *Carmen*—La fleur que tu m'avais jetée (DiS); *Carmen*—C'est toi? C'est moi! (D); *La Gioconda*—Suicidio! (C); Sicilian Folk Songs—Abbalatti and Muttettu de lu Paliu (Ujè, Ujè) and Neapolitan Song—L'ultima canzone (DiS); *Cavalleria Rusticana*—Voi lo sapete (C); *Cavalleria Rusticana*—Tu qui, Santuzza? (D).

1974

Korean–Japanese Concert Tour
(with Giuseppe di Stefano)

The Callas–Di Stefano world tour continued in the fall of 1974 with nine concerts in the Far East. All the concerts were accompanied at the piano by Robert Sutherland. The tour began with two concerts in Korea on October 5 and 8 in Seoul (Auditorium of the University for Women), followed by seven concerts in Japan: October 12 and 19 Tokyo (NHK Hall), October 24 Fukuoka (Fukuoka Shimin Kaikan), October 27 Tokyo (Tokyo Bunka Kaikan), November 2 Osaka (Osaka Festival Hall), November 7 Hiroshima (Hiroshima Yubin Chokin Hall), and November 11 Sapporo (Hokkaido Koseinenkin Kaikan). The October 12 Tokyo program was typical of the programs on the tour, consisting of the following selections: *Vespri*—Duet; *Don Carlo*—Tu che le vanità; *Roi d'Ys*—Vainement; *Carmen*—Habanera; *Carmen*—Flower Song; *Gioconda*—Suicidio!; *Carmen*—Final Scene; *Don Çarlo*—Duet; Songs—L'ultima canzone and Marechiare; *Cavalleria*—Voi lo sapete; *Cavalleria*—Duet; encores *Gianni Schicchi*—O mio babbino caro and *L'Elisir*—Duet. In several subsequent concerts Mme. Callas substituted *Bohème*—Mi chiamano Mimì for the Suicidio. The second Tokyo concert was videotaped and selections were televised on October 27.

IV

Discography of Private Recordings Compiled by Henry Wisneski

RECORDINGS of Maria Callas in performance have appeared on eleven limited edition series to date: BJR (BJR and Robin Hood labels), EJS (white label "Golden Age of Opera" and UORC, Unique Opera Records Corporation, series), ERR label, FWR (red label series and Penzance Records), Gemma Records (published in Amsterdam), JLT ("Opera Viva" series published in Paris), Limited Edition Society (LES, LERWC, and LESWC labels), Morgan Records (published in Italy), MRF (red and silver label series), OPA ("Operatic Archives" blue and silver label series), and OPR ("Raritas" label, released in Germany). The number of discs in each set and release dates are listed after the series number in the discography.

BELLINI: *Norma.* (Norma); Ebe Stignani (Adalgisa); Mirto Picchi (Pollione); Giacomo Vaghi (Oroveso); Joan Sutherland (Clotilde); Vittorio Gui, c. Covent Garden, Nov. 18, 1952. MRF-11 (3) [2/68]

———(BJR) OMY-200 (3) [3/68]

BELLINI: *Norma.* (Norma); Ebe Stignani (Adalgisa); Mario del Monaco (Pollione); Giuseppe Modesti (Oroveso); Tullio Serafin, c. Orchestra and chorus of Radio Italiana, Rome. Foro Italico, Rome, June 29, 1955. JLT-6 (3) [12/71]

BELLINI: *Norma.* (Norma); Giulietta Simionato (Adalgisa); Mario del Monaco (Pollione); Nicola Zaccaria (Oroveso); Antonino Votto, c. La Scala, Dec. 7, 1955. LERWC-103 (3) [7/74]

BELLINI: *Il Pirata.* (Imogene); Piero Miranda Ferraro (Gualtiero); Chester Watson (Goffredo); Regina Sarfaty (Adele); Nicola Rescigno, c. American Opera Society, Carnegie Hall, Jan. 27, 1959. FWR-641 (2) [1/65]

———MRF-51 (2) [8/70]

BELLINI: *I Puritani.* (Elvira); Giuseppe di Stefano (Arturo); Piero Campolonghi (Riccardo); Roberto Silva (Giorgio); Guido Picco, c. Palacio de Bellas Artes, Mexico City, May 29, 1952.
Side 6, band 2: ROSSINI: *Armida,* "D'amore al dolce impero," radio concert of Dec. 27, 1954, San Remo, Alfredo Simonetto, c. MRF-28 (3) [6/69]

———(EJS) Unique Opera Records Corporation UORC-191 (2) [2/74]

BELLINI: *La Sonnambula.* (Amina); Cesare Valletti (Elvino); Giuseppe Modesti (Rodolfo); Eugenia Ratti (Lisa); Leonard Bernstein, c. La Scala, March 5, 1955. Raritas OPR-3 (3) [1/73] Pressed in France, released in Germany.

———ERR-108 (3) [1/74]

CHERUBINI: *Medea.* (Medea); Teresa Berganza (Neris); Jon Vickers (Jason); Nicola Zaccaria (Creon); Nicola Rescigno, c. Dallas Civic Opera Co., Nov. 6, 1958. FWR-647 (2) [1/65]

———(FWR) Penzance Records PR-41 [1/73] Remastered edition.

CHERUBINI: *Medea.* (Medea); Fiorenza Cossotto (Neris); Jon Vickers (Jason); Nicola Zaccaria (Creon); Nicola Rescigno, c. Covent Garden, June 30, 1959. BJR-105 (2) [1/69]. Opening scene with Glauce omitted.

CHERUBINI: *Medea.* (Medea); Fedora Barbieri (Neris); Gino Penno (Jason); Giuseppe Modesti (Creon); Leonard Bernstein, c. La Scala, Dec. 10, 1953. Morgan Records (3) [4/72]

———(EJS) Unique Opera Records Corporation UORC-138 (2) [12/72]

———BJR-129 (3) [4/73]

DONIZETTI: *Anna Bolena.* (Anna Bolena); Giulietta Simionato (Giovanna Seymour); Nicola Rossi-Lemeni (Enrico VIII); Gianni Raimondi (Riccardo Percy); Gianandrea Gavazzeni, c. La Scala, April 14, 1957.

Side 5b: BELLINI: *Norma,* "Casta Diva" and "Ah! bello a me ritorna" from the 1949 Cetra 12″ 78-rpm CB 20482.

Side 6: VERDI: *Aida,* Act III complete. (Aida); Kurt Baum (Radames); Jess Walters (Amonasro); Giulietta Simionato (Amneris); John Barbirolli, c. Covent Garden, June 4, 1953. FWR-646 (3) [1/65]

———FWR-646 (3) [6/69] Remastered; with selections from Callas's rehearsal in Dallas, Nov. 20, 1957, on *Side 5b:* VERDI: *La Traviata,* "È strano" through "Sempre libera"; *Side 5c:* BELLINI: *I Puritani,* "Qui la voce" and "Vien, diletto"; *Side 6: Anna Bolena,* Final Scene, beginning "Piangete voi? Donde tal pianto?"

———BJR-109 (3) [9/69]

———MRF-42 (3) [12/69] The set contains additional music, most of which was not in the Scala production: the Overture (Lamberto Gardelli, c., Glyndebourne, Aug. 4, 1968); Smeton's "Chi pensierosa e tacita" and "È sgombro il loco . . . Addio, beltade" (Janet Baker, American Opera Society, Nov. 15, 1966); Percy's aria "Vivi tu" (Mario Solis, piano acc., New York, Oct. 19, 1969).

DONIZETTI: *Lucia di Lammermoor.* (Lucia); Giuseppe di Stefano (Edgardo); Piero Campolonghi (Enrico); Guido Picco, c. Palacio de Bellas Artes, Mexico City, June 10, 1952.

Side 4b: VERDI: *La Traviata,* "È strano" to end of Act I and "Addio del passato." Maria Callas, Cesare Valletti (Alfredo); Oliviero de Fabritiis, c. Mexico City, July 17, 1951. FWR-650 (2) [10/65]

DONIZETTI: *Lucia di Lammermoor.* (Lucia); Giuseppe di Stefano (Edgardo); Rolando Panerai (Enrico); Nicola Zaccaria (Raimondo); Herbert von Karajan, c. RIAS Orchestra, Städtische Oper, Berlin, Sept. 29, 1955. Limited Edition Society LERWC-101 (3) [11/73]

DONIZETTI: *Poliuto.* (Paolina); Franco Corelli (Poliuto); Ettore

Bastianini (Severo); Nicola Zaccaria (Callistene); Antonino Votto, c. La Scala, Dec. 7, 1960. FWR-644 (2) [1/65]

———FWR-644 (2) [3/69] Remastered edition with new material on *side 4:* an unpublished EMI recording of BELLINI: *La Sonnambula,* "Care compagne . . . Come per me sereno," Milan, June 1955, Tullio Serafin, c.

———BJR-106 (2) [3/69]

———BJR-106 (2) [4/71] Remastered edition.

———MRF-31 (2) [6/69]

GIORDANO: *Andrea Chénier.* (Maddalena di Coigny); Mario del Monaco (Andrea Chénier); Aldo Protti (Carlo Gérard); Lucia Danieli (Madelon); Antonino Votto, c. La Scala, Jan. 8, 1955. OPA-1010/1011 (2) [3/71]

GLUCK: *Alceste* (selections, sung in Italian translation). (Alceste); Renato Gavarini (Admeto); Paolo Silveri (High Priest); Carlo Maria Giulini, c.

Side 4: "Divinités du Styx," "Ou suis-je? . . . Eh! pourrai-je vivre sans toi," "Ah! malgré moi," "Grands dieux, soutenez mon courage!" to the beginning of the final trio. La Scala, April 4, 1954. *Sides 1–3;* GLUCK: *Iphigénie en Tauride.* Montserrat Caballé, Jean Cox, Paul Schoeffler; Antonio de Almeida, c. Lisbon, Feb. 3, 1961. Penzance Records PR-27 (2) [1/72]

GLUCK: *Iphigénie en Tauride* (in Italian translation). (Ifigenia); Fiorenza Cossotto (Artemide); Francesco Albanese (Pilade); Anselmo Colzani (Toante); Nino Sanzogno, c. La Scala, June 1, 1957. FWR-649 (2) [9/65]

———MRF-63 (2) [12/70]

PUCCINI: *Tosca* (highlights). (Tosca); Gianni Poggi (Cavaradossi); Paolo Silveri (Scarpia); Antonino Votto, c. Act I from Tosca's entrance, "Mario! Mario!" through her first exit, "Ma falle gli occhi neri!" Act III, Tosca's entrance to the end of the opera. Act I "Te Deum." Act II, from "Floria!" "Amore . . ." to "Muori!" Teatro Municipal, Rio de Janeiro, Sept. 24, 1951. Penzance Records PR-11 (1) [3/72]

PUCCINI: *Tosca.* (Tosca); Mario Filippeschi (Cavaradossi); Robert Weede (Scarpia); Umberto Mugnai, c. Palacio de Bellas Artes, Mexico City, June 8, 1950. UORC-184 (2) [1/74]

ROSSINI: *Armida.* (Armida); Francesco Albanese (Rinaldo); Mario Filippeschi (Gernando and Ubaldo); Gianni Raimondi (Carlo); Tullio Serafin, c. Teatro Comunale, Florence, April 26, 1952. FWR-657 [2/68]. The last-act Rinaldo-Carlo duet through the Rinaldo-Armida duet lacking.

SPONTINI: *La Vestale.* (Giulia); Franco Corelli (Licinio); Ebe Stignani (High Priestess); Nicola Rossi-Lemeni (Pontifex Maximus); Antonino Votto, c. La Scala, Dec. 7, 1954. UORC-217 (2) [9/74]

VERDI: *Aida.* (Aida); Oralia Domínguez (Amneris); Mario del Monaco (Radames); Giuseppe Taddei (Amonasro); Oliviero de Fabritiis, c. Palacio de Bellas Artes, Mexico City, July 3, 1951. BJR-104 (3) [8/68]

———MRF-21 (3) [8/68]

VERDI: *Aida.* (Aida); Giulietta Simionato (Amneris); Kurt Baum (Radames); Robert Weede (Amonasro); Guido Picco, c. Palacio de Bellas Artes, Mexico City, May 30, 1950. UORC-200 (2) [5/74]

VERDI: *Un Ballo in Maschera.* (Amelia); Giuseppe di Stefano (Riccardo); Ettore Bastianini (Renato); Giulietta Simionato (Ulrica); Eugenia Ratti (Oscar); Gianandrea Gavazzeni, c. La Scala, Dec. 7, 1957.

Side 6:

MASSENET: *Le Cid,* "Pleurez, mes yeux"

BIZET: *Carmen,* "Habanera" and "Séguedille"

VERDI: *Don Carlo,* "O don fatale"

[Hamburg concert, March 16, 1962, Georges Prêtre, c.]

ROSSINI: *Semiramide,* "Bel raggio lusinghier"

PUCCINI: *Madama Butterfly,* "Tu? tu? piccolo Iddio!"

PUCCINI: *La Bohème,* "Quando me'n vo'"

[Berlin concert, May 17, 1963, Georges Prêtre, c.]

MRF-83 (3) [6/72]

———BJR-127 (3) [6/72]

VERDI: *Macbeth.* (Lady Macbeth); Enzo Mascherini (Macbeth); Gino Penno (Macduff); Italo Tajo (Banco); Victor de Sabata, c. La Scala, Dec. 7, 1952.

Side 6:

VERDI: *Macbeth,* "Vieni! t'affretta!" [two versions: the first from a radio concert of Feb. 18, 1952, Oliviero de Fabritiis, c.; the second from the Dallas rehearsal of Nov. 20, 1957, Nicola Rescigno, c.]

MOZART: *Die Entführung aus dem Serail,* "Martern aller Arten" [sung in Italian, Dallas rehearsal, Nov. 20, 1957]

FWR-655 (3) [8/66]

———Opera Viva JLT-3 (3) [10/69]

———BJR-117 (3) [11/69]

———MRF-61 (3) [12/69]

VERDI: *Nabucco.* (Abigaille); Gino Bechi (Nabucco); Luciano

Neroni (Zaccaria); Amalia Pini (Fenena); Vittorio Gui, c. Teatro San Carlo, Naples, Dec. 20, 1949. ERR-114 (3) [8/74]

———FWR-653 (1) [7/66]. Highlights containing all of Abigaille's music.

———(FWR) Penzance Records PR-3 (1) [5/70]. Remastered. The previous edition begins at the top of page 40 in the Ricordi vocal score; this edition begins with Abigaille's entrance, page 42.

VERDI: *Rigoletto.* (Gilda); Giuseppe di Stefano (Duke); Piero Campolonghi (Rigoletto); Ignacio Ruffino (Sparafucile); Umberto Mugnai, c. Palacio de Bellas Artes, Mexico City, June 17, 1952. BJR-101 (2) [12/67]. Orchestral prelude omitted.

VERDI: *La Traviata.* (Violetta); Cesare Valletti (Alfredo); Mario Zanasi (Germont); Marie Collier (Flora); Nicola Rescigno, c. Covent Garden, June 20, 1958. FWR-652 (2) [3/66]

———LESWC-102 (2) [3/74]

VERDI: *La Traviata.* (Violetta); Giuseppe di Stefano (Alfredo); Ettore Bastianini (Germont); Silvana Zanolli (Flora); Carlo Maria Giulini, c. La Scala, May 28, 1955. MRF-87(2) [8/72]

VERDI: *La Traviata.* (Violetta); Giuseppe di Stefano (Alfredo); Piero Campolonghi (Germont); Umberto Mugnai, c. Palacio de Bellas Artes, Mexico City, June 3, 1952. UORC-181 (2) [11/73]

———BJR-130 (3) [9/74]. *Side 6:* VERDI: *La Traviata.* "Libiamo," "Un dì felice," "Ah, fors'è lui" and "Sempre libera," "Addio del passato." (Violetta); Cesare Valletti (Alfredo); Oliviero de Fabritiis, c. Palacio de Bellas Artes, July 17, 1951.

VERDI: *Il Trovatore.* (Leonora); Cloe Elmo (Azucena); Giacomo Lauri-Volpi (Manrico); Paolo Silveri (Di Luna); Tullio Serafin, c. Teatro San Carlo, Naples, Jan. 27, 1951. FWR-654 (2) [7/66]

VERDI: *Il Trovatore* (highlights). (Leonora); Giulietta Simionato (Azucena); Kurt Baum (Manrico); Leonard Warren (Di Luna); Guido Picco, c. Palacio de Bellas Artes, Mexico City, June 20, 1950. BJR-102 (1) [6/68]

———FWR-651 (1) [5/68]. Selections from the above performance. *Side 2, bands 3–6:* "Tacea la notte," Act I trio finale, Act IV Leonora-Di Luna duet, Act IV finale. Palacio de Bellas Artes, June 27, 1950, same cast as June 20, except Ivan Petroff (Di Luna).

VERDI: *Il Trovatore.* (Leonora); Ebe Stignani (Azucena); Gino Penno (Manrico); Carlo Tagliabue (Di Luna); Antonino Votto, c. La Scala, Feb. 23, 1953. MRF-78 (2) [11/71]

———(BJR) Robin Hood RHR-5001 (3) [5/72]. *Side 5, band 2;*

side 6: VERDI: *Aida,* Act III. (Aida); Kurt Baum (Radames); Jess Walters (Amonasro); Giulietta Simionato (Amneris); John Barbirolli, c. Covent Garden, June 10, 1953.

VERDI: *I Vespri Siciliani.* (Elena); Boris Christoff (Giovanni); Enzo Mascherini (Guido); Giorgio Bardi-Kokolios (Arrigo); Erich Kleiber, c. Teatro Comunale, Florence, May 26, 1951. FWR-645 (3) [1/65]

———(FWR) Penzance PR-6 [5/70]. Remastered and divided into bands by arias and scenes.

———MRF-46 (3) [3/70]

WAGNER: *Parsifal* (in Italian). (Kundry); Africo Baldelli (Parsifal); Boris Christoff (Gurnemanz); Rolando Panerai (Amfortas); Giuseppe Modesti (Klingsor); Vittorio Gui, c. Orchestra and chorus of Radio Italiana, Rome, Nov. 20–21, 1950. FWR-648 (4) [1/65]

——(FWR) Penzance PR-10 (1) [6/70]. Act II complete.

Recitals and Interviews

EJS-360 (1) [3/66]

"Golden Age of Opera" Potpourri no. 19.

ROSSINI: *Armida,* "D'amore al dolce impero," radio concert, Dec. 27, 1954, San Remo, Alfredo Simonetto, c.

FWR-656 (1) [11/66]

PUCCINI: *Madama Butterfly,* "Un bel dì" sung by Nina Foresti on the Major Bowes Amateur Hour broadcast of April 7, 1935. (Callas has stated that she did not appear as Nina Foresti on the Major Bowes Amateur Hour.)

ROSSINI: *Armida,* Act I Quartet, with Callas, Gianni Raimondi, Alessandro Ziliani, and Mario Frosini, Florence, April 26, 1952, Tullio Serafin, c.

VERDI: *Aida,* Act II finale, Mexico City, May 30, 1950, Guido Picco, c.

VERDI: *Aida,* "Ritorna vincitor!" and Act II finale, Mexico City, July 3, 1951, Oliviero de Fabritiis, c.

BELLINI: *La Sonnambula,* "Ah! non credea mirarti" and "Ah! non giunge," from an unpublished EMI recording, Milan, June 1955, Tullio Serafin, c.

BELLINI: *I Puritani,* "Qui la voce" and "Vien, diletto," Dallas rehearsal, Nov. 20, 1957, Nicola Rescigno, c.

BJR-103 (1) [6/68]

"Maria Callas in Amsterdam"

SPONTINI: *La Vestale,* "Tu che invoco"

VERDI: *Ernani,* "Sorta è la notte . . . Ernani, involami!"
VERDI: *Don Carlo,* "Tu che le vanità"
BELLINI: *Il Pirata,* Final Scene
Amsterdam, Concertgebouw Orchestra, July 11, 1959, Nicola Rescigno, c.

Opera Viva JLT-1 (1) [1/70]
MOZART: *Die Entführung aus dem Serail,* "Martern aller Arten" (in Italian), radio concert, Dec. 27, 1954, San Remo, Alfredo Simonetto, c.
SPONTINI: *La Vestale,* "Tu che invoco," pre-recorded for broadcast Sept. 27, 1956, Milan, Alfredo Simonetto, c.
ROSSINI: *Semiramide,* "Bel raggio lusinghier," broadcast concert recorded Sept. 27, 1956.
MEYERBEER: *Dinorah,* "Ombra leggiera," broadcast concert of Dec. 27, 1954.
THOMAS: *Hamlet,* "Mad Scene" (in Italian), pre-recorded Sept. 27, 1956.
VERDI: *Macbeth,* "Vieni! t'affretta!" broadcast concert of Feb. 18, 1952, Rome, Oliviero de Fabritiis, c.
VERDI: *Macbeth,* "Brindisi" from the Scala performance of Dec. 7, 1952, Victor de Sabata, c.

———Gemma Records WK-1001 (1) [11/72]. A dubbing of the Opera Viva recital, published in Amsterdam.

FWR-646 (1) [3/70]
"Maria Callas in arias from *La Traviata, I Puritani, Anna Bolena*"
Sides 5/6 of the second edition of the FWR *Anna Bolena,* released separately as a recital.

(FWR) Penzance PR-5 (1) [5/70]
"Small World"
A four-way conversation from the television program "Small World," broadcast Jan. 4 and Jan. 11, 1959, with Maria Callas from Milan, Sir Thomas Beecham from Nice, Victor Borge from Connecticut, and Edward R. Murrow from New York City.

Opera Viva JLT-4 (1) [12/70]
ROSSINI: *Semiramide,* "Bel raggio lusinghier"
ROSSINI: *La Cenerentola,* "Nacqui all'affanno . . . Non più mesta"
MASSENET: *Werther,* "Air des lettres"
MASSENET: *Manon,* "Adieu, notre petite table"
VERDI: *Nabucco,* "Ben io t'invenni"
PUCCINI: *La Bohème,* "Quando me'n vo' "

PUCCINI: *Madama Butterfly,* "Tu? tu? piccolo Iddio!"
PUCCINI: *Gianni Schicchi,* "O mio babbino caro"
Concert given at the Théâtre des Champs-Élysées, Paris, June 5, 1963, Orchestra des Concerts du Conservatoire, Georges Prêtre, c.

Gemma Records 30.006 (1) [11/72]

MOZART: *Die Entführung aus dem Serail,* "Martern aller Arten" (in Italian), San Remo, broadcast concert of Dec. 27, 1954, Alfredo Simonetto, c. [Other singers on the recital include Flagstad, Caballé, Tauber, Ponselle, and Fischer-Dieskau.]

(FWR) Penzance PR-15 (1) [12/72]

BELLINI: *La Sonnambula,* "Come per me serena," "Ah! non credea mirarti," and "Ah! non giunge," from an unpublished EMI recording, Milan, June 1955, Tullio Serafin, c.
VERDI: *Macbeth,* "Vieni! t'affretta!" Dallas rehearsal, Nov. 20, 1957, Nicola Rescigno, c.
MOZART: *Die Entführung aus dem Serail,* "Martern aller Arten" (in Italian), Dallas rehearsal.
From the concert given at St. James's Palace, London, May 30, 1961, Sir Malcolm Sargent, piano:
VERDI: *Don Carlo,* "Tu che le vanità" [final line, "Ah, il pianto mio reca a' piè del Signor," lacking]
MASSENET: *Le Cid,* "Pleurez, mes yeux"
BOÏTO: *Mefistofele,* "L'altra notte"

Limited Edition Society LES-100 (1) [6/73]

"The Callas Legacy"
Interview, Berlin, Oct. 1959 [one minute]
DONIZETTI: *Lucia di Lammermoor,* "Mad Scene," Berlin, Sept. 29, 1955, Herbert von Karajan, c.
ROSSINI: *Il Barbiere di Siviglia,* "Dunque io son" and "Contro un cor," from the Scala performance of Feb. 16, 1956, Carlo Maria Giulini, c.
BELLINI: *La Sonnambula,* Act I conclusion, beginning with the Count's line "Che veggio? Saria forse il notturno fantasma," Edinburgh, Aug. 21, 1957, Antonino Votto, c.
BELLINI: *La Sonnambula,* "Ah! non giunge," from the Scala performance of March 5, 1955, Leonard Bernstein, c.
DELIBES: *Lakmé,* "Bell Song," Rome, broadcast concert of Feb. 18, 1952, Oliviero de Fabritiis, c.

UORC-196 (1) [3/74]

VERDI: *Don Carlo,* "Io vengo a domandar" (Callas and Di Stefano)
LALO: *Le Roi d'Ys,* "Vainement ma bien-aimée" (Di Stefano)

BIZET: *Carmen,* "C'est toi? C'est moi!" (Callas and Di Stefano)
PONCHIELLI: *La Gioconda,* "Suicidio!" (Callas)
MASCAGNI: *Cavalleria Rusticana,* "Voi lo sapete" (Callas)
MASCAGNI: *Cavalleria Rusticana,* "Tu qui, Santuzza?" (Callas and Di Stefano)
PUCCINI: *Gianni Schicchi,* "O mio babbino caro" (Callas)
From the concert given at Royal Festival Hall, London, Nov. 26, 1973, Ivor Newton, piano.

SELECTED BIBLIOGRAPHY

Books

Bing, Rudolf. *5000 Nights at the Opera.* Garden City, N.Y.: Doubleday & Company, Inc., 1972.

Braddon, Russell. *Joan Sutherland.* New York: St. Martin's Press, 1962.

Cafarakis, Christian, and Harvey, Jacques. *The Fabulous Onassis.* Translated from the French by John Minahan. New York: William Morrow & Company, 1972.

Callas, Evangelia. *My Daughter—Maria Callas.* As told to Lawrence G. Blochman. New York: Fleet Publishing Corporation, 1960; London: Leslie Frewin Publishers, 1967 (with additional chapter by Blochman).

Cederna, Camilla. *Chi è Maria Callas?* Milano: Longanesi & C., 1968.

Davis, Ronald L. *Opera in Chicago.* New York: Appleton-Century-Crofts, 1966.

Eggers, Heino. *Giuseppe di Stefano.* Berlin: Rembrandt-Verlag GmbH., 1967.

Galatopoulos, Stelios. *Callas: La Divina.* Elmsford, N.Y.: London House & Maxwell, 1970.

Gara, Eugenio. *Die grossen Interpreten: Maria Callas.* Frankfurt/Main: Wilhelm Limpert-Verlag, 1959.

Gavoty, Bernard. *Vingt grands interprètes.* Lausanne: Éditions Rencontre, 1966.

Herzfeld, Friedrich. *La Callas.* 2d ed., rev. Berlin: Rembrandt-Verlag GmbH., 1962.

Jellinek, George. *Callas: Portrait of a Prima Donna.* New York: Ziff-Davis Publishing Company, 1960.

Lauri-Volpi, Giacomo. *Voci parallele.* Milano: Aldo Garzanti, 1955.

Merlin, Olivier. *Le Bel Canto.* Paris: René Julliard, 1961.

Picchetti, Maria Teresa, and Teglia, Marta. *El Arte de Maria Callas como Metalenguaje.* Buenos Aires: Editorial Bocarte, 1969.

Riemens, Leo. *Maria Callas.* Utrecht: A. W. Bruna & Zoon's Uitgevers-Mij. N.V., 1960.

Rosenthal, Harold D. *Great Singers of Today.* London: J. Calder & Boyars, Ltd., 1966.

Seroff, Victor. *Renata Tebaldi.* New York: Appleton-Century-Crofts, 1961.

—Selected Bibliography—

Callas Interviews, Conversations, and Autobiographical Articles

Askew, Rual. "Firing doesn't worry Callas." *Dallas Morning News,* November 8, 1958.

Barry, Naomi. "Maria Callas: 'The singer is nothing but the servant of genius.'" *International Herald Tribune,* June 30, 1971.

Buckley, Jack. "An ancient woman" [Medea]. *Opera News,* December 13, 1969, pp. 8–13.

Callas, Maria. "I am not guilty of all those Callas scandals." *Life,* April 20, 1959, pp. 118–34.

———. "Per la prima volta Maria Meneghini Callas si confida al pubblico." As told to Anita Pensotti. *Oggi* [Milano], January 10, 17, 24, 31; February 7, 1957.

Cassidy, Claudia. "On the aisle." *Chicago Tribune,* November 21, 1954.

Clerc, Michel. "La Callas: 'J'ai décidé d'être douce.'" *Paris-Match,* June 15, 1963, pp. 98–101.

Cuccio, Angela. "Callas on Callas." *Women's Wear Daily,* November 23, 1970.

Dettmer, Roger. "A legendary soprano discusses temperament." *New York Herald Tribune,* November 7, 1954.

Downes, Edward. Taped conversation. WQXR broadcast, December 30, 1967, and January 13, 1968.

Dragadze, Peter. "The controversy over a 'tiger who became a lamb.'" *Life,* October 30, 1964, pp. 62–69.

Fleetwood, Harry. Taped conversation. WNBC broadcast, March 13 and 27, 1958; rebroadcast, WNCN, February 14 and 17, 1974.

Frost, David. Videotaped conversation. WNEW telecast, December 10, 1970. Excerpts published in the *New York Post,* December 12, 1970.

Gambetti, Giacomo. *Medea: Un Film di Pier Paolo Pasolini,* pp. 13–24. Milano: Aldo Garzanti, 1970.

Gruen, John. "I am a very normal human being." *The New York Times,* October 31, 1971.

Harris, Kenneth. [Interview] *Observer Review* [London], February 8 and 15, 1970. Also published in *Kenneth Harris Talking to Maria Callas* [and others], pp. 1–17, London: George Weidenfeld & Nicolson, Ltd., 1971.

Klemesrud, Judy. "Maria Callas speaks her mind on fashions and friendship." *The New York Times,* November 30, 1970.

Maguire, Jan. "Callas, Serafin, and the art of bel canto." *Saturday Review,* March 30, 1968, pp. 47–49.

Murrow, Edward R. "Small World." Videotaped conversation with Maria Callas, Sir Thomas Beecham, and Victor Borge. CBS telecast, January 4 and 11, 1959. Excerpts published in *Musical America,* January 15, 1959, p. 15.

"Processo alla Callas." *The New Yorker,* April 24, 1971, pp. 31–33.

Prouse, Derek. "Maria Callas speaks." *Sunday Times* [London], March 19, 26; April 2, 1961.

Ross, Norman. Conversation taped in New York and broadcast in Chicago on November 17, 1957.

Saal, Hubert. "Callas on the record." *Newsweek,* February 15, 1971, pp. 90–91.

Sablosky, Irving. "Callas assures us: 'I love it here.'" *Chicago Daily News,* November 7, 1955.

Senior, Evan. "A star to sing Norma." *Music and Musicians,* November 1952, p. 4.

Tedesco, Dino. "Tavola rotonda a Palazzo Madama." *Gazzetta del Popolo* [Torino], April 12, 1973. Excerpts from a discussion with Maria Callas, Giuseppe di Stefano, and Fulvio Vernizzi.

Wallace, Mike. Videotaped conversation. CBS telecast, February 3, 1974. Excerpts published in the *New York Post,* February 9, 1974.

Walters, Barbara. Videotaped conversation. NBC telecast, April 15, 1974.

General Index

THEATERS and opera houses appear under their official names. Operas are listed by title. Proper names containing de, von, and related forms have been alphabetized according to the personal preference of, or accumulated tradition concerning, the individual. For example: Mario del Monaco under Del Monaco, Mario; Herbert von Karajan under Karajan, Herbert von. Page numbers in italics refer to photographs.

—Index—

—*Index*—

THIS index is by performance dates rather than by page number to enable the reader to determine the specific appearances of each artist listed in Parts Two and Three of the performance annals. The voice range or other description of the artist is indicated in parentheses following the artist's name. The following abbreviations are used: (s) soprano; (ms) mezzo-soprano; (t) tenor; (bar) baritone; (bs) bass; (c) conductor; (acc) piano accompanist; (dir) director; (p) piano soloist.

Dates are shown in numeric form in the sequence month/day/year. Dates are those of the artist's first appearance in each separate series of performances. In the case of recordings only the month and year are shown. Each date is followed by the name of the opera or indication of other type of performance. Operas are shown by the most important word of the work's title. Abbreviations used for other types of performances are RAI for radio broadcast, TV for telecast, and rec. for recording. The figure following the name of the opera indicates the number of appearances of the artist in each series of performances.

Adams, Marilu (ms) 11/11/55 (*Butterfly* 3)
Albanese, Francesco (t) 1/14/51 (*Traviata* 3); 4/26/52 (*Armida* 3); 1/8/53 (*Traviata* 2); 1/15/53 (*Traviata* 3); 9/53 (*Traviata* rec.); 1/22/55 (*Medea* 4); 6/1/57 (*Ifigenia* 4)
Albertini, Albert (bar) 9/53 (*Traviata* rec.)
Alberts, Eunice (ms) 10/31/55 (*Puritani* 2); 11/5/55 (*Trovatore* 2); 11/11/55 (*Butterfly* 3)
Algorta, Giorgio (bs) 3/14/53 (*Lucia* 2)
Allen, David (bar) 6/17/59 (*Medea* 5)
Allen, Mildred (s) 2/6/58 (*Traviata* 2)
Alonso, Francisco (bs) 6/8/50 (*Tosca* 2); 7/17/51 (*Traviata* 4); 6/17/52 (*Rigoletto* 2); 6/28/52 (*Tosca* 2)
Alva, Luigi (t) 2/16/56 (*Barbiere* 3); 2/57 (*Barbiere* rec.)
Amadini, Maria (ms) 1/8/49 (*Walkiria* 4); 9/52 (*Gioconda* rec.); 12/10/53 (*Medea* 2); 7/15/54 (*Mefistofele* 3); 1/8/55 (*Chénier* 6)
Amodei, Giovanni (t) 2/28/51 (*Aida* 1)
Andreassi, Maria (s) 5/7/53 (*Medea* 3); 3/2/54 (*Medea* 3)
Anelli, Anna Maria (ms) 1/19/52 (*Norma* 8)
Angelini, Giuseppina (ms) 1/14/51 (*Traviata* 3)
Angioletti, Mariella (s) 4/5/56 (*Traviata* 1); 7/4/57 (*Sonnambula* 2)
Anthony, Charles (t) 2/6/58 (*Traviata* 1); 2/13/58 (*Lucia* 3)
Ariè, Raffaele (bs) 1/25/53 (*Lucia* 4); 2/53 (*Lucia* rec.); 4/21/53 (*Lucia* 2)
Arizmendi, Helena (s) 5/20/49 (*Turandot* 4)
Asciak, Paul (t) 11/8/52 (*Norma* 5); 6/15/53 (*Norma* 4)
Assandri, Virginio (t) 11/8/54 (*Traviata* 2); 11/15/54 (*Lucia* 2)
Assante, Gianni (t) 2/12/49 (*Turandot* 4)
Avolanti, Gianni (t) 2/12/49 (*Turandot* 4); 1/27/51 (*Trovatore* 3)
Azzolini, Rodolfo (bar) 9/24/50 (*Tosca* 1)

Baccaloni, Salvatore (bs) 4/2/52 (*Ratto* 4)
Badiali, Vladimiro (t) 1/8/53 (*Traviata* 2)
Badioli, Carlo (bs) 3/6/56 (*Barbiere* 2); 8/56 (*Bohème* rec.)
Baldelli, Africo (t) 11/20/50 (*Parsifal* RAI)
Ballinari, Sandra (s) 4/12/54 (*Don Carlo* 5)
Baracchi, Aristide (bar) 8/2/47 (*Gioconda* 5); 10/20/51 (*Traviata* 2); 12/26/52 (*Gioconda* 6)
Barbesi, Attilio (bs) 12/30/47 (*Tristano* 4); 1/29/48 (*Turandot* 5); 7/27/48 (*Turandot* 4); 7/19/52 (*Gioconda* 2); 8/2/52 (*Traviata* 4); 12/7/52 (*Macbeth* 5); 12/26/52 (*Gioconda* 6); 8/15/53 (*Trovatore* 1)
Barbieri, Fedora (ms) 12/30/47 (*Tristano* 4); 11/30/48 (*Norma* 2); 6/17/49 (*Norma* 4); 7/2/49 (*Aida* 1); 4/12/50 (*Aida* 3); 9/7/51 (*Norma* 1); 9/52 (*Gioconda* rec.); 4/9/53 (*Norma* 4); 5/7/53 (*Medea* 3); 12/10/53 (*Medea* 5); 1/22/55 (*Medea* 4); 8/55 (*Aida* rec.); 8/56 (*Trovatore* rec.); 9/56 (*Ballo* rec.); 10/29/56 (*Norma* 6)
Barbirolli, Sir John (c) 6/4/53 (*Aida* 3)
Barioni, Daniele (t) 2/6/58 (*Traviata* 1)
Baronti, Duilio (bs) 2/2/50 (*Aida* 2)
Bartoletti, Bruno (acc) 6/11/51 (concert)
Basile, Arturo (c) 11/49 (rec.)
Bastianini, Ettore (bar) 1/25/53 (*Lucia* 4); 2/13/54 (*Lucia* 3); 5/28/55 (*Traviata* 4); 10/31/55 (*Puritani* 2); 11/5/55 (*Trovatore* 1); 1/19/56 (*Traviata* 14); 12/7/57 (*Ballo* 5); 5/19/58 (*Pirata* 5); 11/6/59 (*Lucia* 2); 12/7/60 (*Poliuto* 5)
Baum, Kurt (t) 5/23/50 (*Norma* 2); 5/30/50 (*Aida* 2); 6/20/50 (*Trovatore* 3); 6/4/53 (*Aida* 3); 11/22/56 (*Norma* 2)
Bechi, Gino (bar) 12/20/49 (*Nabucco* 3)
Bedell, Richard (boy soprano) 7/5/65 (*Tosca* 1)
Begali, Ottorino (t) 12/30/47 (*Tristano* 4); 7/15/54 (*Mefistofele* 3)
Beirer, Hans (t) 2/26/49 (*Parsifal* 4)
Bellary, Marie-Luce (ms) 5/22/64 (*Norma* 8); 5/14/65 (*Norma* 5)
Bellezza, Vincenzo (c) 10/2/50 (*Aida* 1)
Bender, Peter (bar) 10/31/58 (*Traviata* 2); 11/6/58 (*Medea* 2)
Benetti, Norma (s) 10/20/51 (*Traviata* 2)
Benoît, Jean-Christophe (bs) 2/19/65 (*Tosca* 9)
Benzi, Armando (t) 9/52 (*Gioconda* rec.)
Berbié, Jane (ms) 7/64 (*Carmen* rec.)
Berdini, Amedeo (t) 9/18/49 (*Battista* 1)
Berganza, Teresa (ms) 11/6/58 (*Medea* 2)
Bergonzi, Carlo (t) 2/13/58 (*Lucia* 2); 12/64 (*Tosca* rec.)
Bernardi, Nerio (speaking role) 4/2/52 (*Ratto* 4)

—Index—